Choosing in Groups

This book is an introduction to the logic and analytics of group choice. To understand how political institutions work, it is important to isolate what citizens – as individuals and as members of society – actually want. This book develops a means of "representing" the preferences of citizens so that institutions can be studied more carefully. This is the first book to integrate the classical problem of constitutions with modern spatial theory, connecting Aristotle and Montesquieu with Kenneth Arrow and James Buchanan.

MICHAEL C. MUNGER is a professor of political science and economics and the director of the Philosophy, Politics, and Economics (PPE) program at Duke University. He formerly served as a staff economist at the U.S. Federal Trade Commission. He has published four books and has contributed to the *American Journal of Political Science*, the *American Political Science Review*, the *Journal of Law and Economics*, and the *Journal of Politics*. He was North American editor of *Public Choice* from 2006 to 2010 and is a past president of the Public Choice Society. He currently coedits *The Independent Review*. Munger has won three teaching awards at Duke, and he gave the 2012 Toby Davis Lecture at George Mason University.

KEVIN M. MUNGER is a PhD student in New York University's Department of Politics, focusing on comparative political economy. Munger spent a year as an investigator at La Universidad del Desarrollo (UDD) in Santiago, Chile. He holds a degree in mathematics and economics from the University of North Carolina at Chapel Hill.

Choosing in Groups

Analytical Politics Revisited

MICHAEL C. MUNGER
Department of Political Science, Duke University

with

KEVIN M. MUNGER
Department of Politics, New York University

CAMBRIDGE
UNIVERSITY PRESS

CAMBRIDGE
UNIVERSITY PRESS

University Printing House, Cambridge CB2 8BS, United Kingdom

One Liberty Plaza, 20th Floor, New York, NY 10006, USA

477 Williamstown Road, Port Melbourne, VIC 3207, Australia

314-321, 3rd Floor, Plot 3, Splendor Forum, Jasola District Centre, New Delhi - 110025, India

79 Anson Road, #06-04/06, Singapore 079906

Cambridge University Press is part of the University of Cambridge.

It furthers the University's mission by disseminating knowledge in the pursuit of education, learning and research at the highest international levels of excellence.

www.cambridge.org
Information on this title: www.cambridge.org/9781107699625

© Michael C. Munger and Kevin M. Munger 2015

First published 2015

A catalogue record for this publication is available from the British Library

Library of Congress Cataloging in Publication data
Munger, Michael C.
Choosing in groups : analytical politics revisited / Michael C. Munger, Department of Political Science, Duke University, with Kevin M. Munger, Department of Political Science, New York University
    pages   cm
ISBN 978-1-107-07003-5 (Hardback) – ISBN 978-1-107-69962-5 (Paperback)
1. Social choice.   2. Group identity.   3. Voting.   4. Political participation.
I. Munger, Kevin M.   II. Title.
HB846.8.M855 2014
302′.13–dc23   2014021005

ISBN 978-1-107-07003-5 Hardback
ISBN 978-1-107-69962-5 Paperback

To Melvin J. Hinich (1939–2010)
You knew all the smalls, but you were drawn to the big.
Partner, mentor, and friend.

I remember standing at the polls one day, when the anger of the political contest gave a certain grimness to the faces of the independent electors, and a good man at my side looking on the people, remarked, "I am satisfied that the largest part of these men, on either side, mean to vote right." I suppose, considerate observers looking at the masses of men, in their blameless and in their equivocal actions, will assent, that in spite of selfishness and frivolity, the general purpose in the great number of persons is fidelity. The reason why any one refuses his assent to your opinion, or his aid to your benevolent design, is in you: he refuses to accept you as a bringer of truth, because, though you think you have it, he feels that you have it not. You have not given him the authentic sign.

Ralph Waldo Emerson, "New England Reformers," 1844

Contents

Figures

Tables

Preface

In 1997, Melvin Hinich and I coauthored a book, also published by Cambridge University Press, called *Analytical Politics*. It subsequently was translated into Chinese, Japanese, Korean, and Spanish. The book used spatial theory to bridge the gap between philosophical and mathematical treatments of politics.

We started to think about a second edition in the late 2000s. I had been a department chair at Duke University for ten years, and I wanted to get back to academic work. After Mel and I had a series of phone conversations, we planned to revise the first edition along the lines that Jeffrey Banks had suggested in an insightful review in the *Journal of Economic Literature*.

On Sunday, September 5, 2010, we talked on the phone. Mel was excited about the example we were planning to use to introduce the new book: the problem of group choice Meriwether Lewis and William Clark faced during their 1805 Corps of Discovery expedition. We hung up pledging to talk again later in the week.

But that never happened. On the morning of Monday, September 6, Melvin fell down the stairs in his home in Austin, Texas. He did not survive the fall.

After that, I put the book aside for more than a year. Mel had participated, over more than three decades, in the creation of many of the spatial models discussed in the 1997 book, and his sense of scientific advances in modeling was invaluable. I couldn't do it without him.

That is why I resolved to write a quite different book, one that in some ways would be less than I could have achieved with Mel, but that at least started from the preliminary plans we had made. I enlisted a new collaborator, my older son Kevin Munger of New York University, to update and expand the topics covered. He also is responsible for Chapter 9, and he did most of the work on the problems at the end of the chapters.

I hope Melvin would have been proud of the result. Though he was not able to participate in the writing of the final version, his intellectual fingerprints are on every page. Three of the chapters – 5, 6, and 9 – are adaptations of similar material in the 1997 book, though they are substantially reorganized and updated.

The book is new, however, because the motivation and organization are completely different. In large measure, this is because I tried to respond to Jeff Banks's suggestions. The problem of "choosing in groups" starts several steps earlier in terms of conceptual framework, considering the problem of why voluntary associations exist and how they are constituted. Given the debt owed, it is a shame that Jeff Banks, like Mel, is no longer with us to see the result.

I offer thanks to the many who have made comments and suggestions. The problem with listing people is that we are sure to forget some, and that omission is unintentional. But I want especially to thank John Aldrich, Jonny Anomaly, Geoffrey Brennan, Scott de Marchi, Ricardo Guzman, and Georg Vanberg for their suggestions and criticisms. My teaching assistants, Darren Beattie, Cindy Cheng, Matthew Cole, Clyde Ray, and Guadalupe Rojo, made it possible for me to get some work done while teaching three classes in fall 2013.

Zach Weiner created a remarkably apropos cartoon for *Saturday Morning Breakfast Cereal* and was kind enough to let us use it here. He also made some pointedly useful comments on an earlier draft of the manuscript. William Keech read much of the manuscript and made dozens of useful suggestions. He would still prefer that there were fewer long quotes, I'm sure. Elizabeth Jenke was ruthless about pointing out portions of an early version that made little sense. Carla St. John did a lot of very tedious but important work scanning material from sources and older versions. Laura Satterfield carefully fixed structure and reference formats. Kathrin DePue did a great job of copyediting and fixing infelicities in several chapters, making the manuscript much more coherent. George de Stefano went through the tedious job of preparing the manuscript with final copyediting. Dr. Nitin Gupta made it possible for me to see well enough to finish, though my retina went from aloof to completely detached. And thanks to my dear spouse Donna Gingerella for being uncharacteristically patient. As for my son Brian, I will have more time for baseball now. I can't see well enough to pitch anymore, and besides, you hit too hard. I'll shag those long flies in the outfield, after they hit the ground.

MCM
Durham, NC

I

BASICS

I

The Analysis of Politics

That argument ... maintained by many who assume to be authorities, was ... that the opinions of some men are to be regarded, and of other men not to be regarded. Now you, Crito, are a disinterested person who are not going to die tomorrow.... Tell me, then, whether I am right in saying that some opinions, and the opinions of some men only, are to be valued, and other opinions, and the opinions of other men, are not to be valued. I ask you whether I was right in maintaining this? (Socrates, in Plato's *Crito*)

CHOOSING IN GROUPS: POLITICS AS CONSTITUTED COOPERATIVE ACTION

Ambrose Bierce claimed, in *The Devil's Dictionary*, that politics is the "strife of interests masquerading as a contest of principles ... the conduct of public affairs for private advantage." At its crudest, politics may seem like nothing more than the use of power and authority to direct social relations. Franz de Waal, in *Chimpanzee Politics*, defined politics as "social manipulation to secure and maintain influential positions," and then pointed out that "politics involves every one of us ... in our family, at school, at work, and in meetings" (p. 208).

But there must be something more to politics, more merit to the idea that groups can choose well, *as* a group and *for* the group. Not as a state, or government, necessarily, but as a socially constituted group, because "politics" is really just choosing and acting in groups. It is a mistake to think that choosing in groups is zero sum, so that for every winner there is a loser. Long ago, the Greek philosopher Aristotle (Book III, part 9) claimed that we should understand politics not (only) as a means of choosing, but as a path to social connectedness. Politics is the set of social relations by which societies *become* good and people achieve fulfillment.

Aristotle's teacher, Plato, had a clear idea of politics as a kind of mutually beneficial exchange. In *The Republic*, Plato describes it this way:

A State, I said, arises, as I conceive, out of the needs of mankind; no one is self-sufficing, but all of us have many wants. Can any other origin of a State be imagined?

There can be no other.

Then, as we have many wants, and many persons are needed to supply them, one takes a helper for one purpose and another for another; and when these partners and helpers are gathered together in one habitation the body of inhabitants is termed a State.... And they exchange with one another, and one gives, and another receives, under the idea that the exchange will be for their good. (*Republic*, Book II)

This "exchange," however, is something more than an atomistic economic division of labor. The groupness of the arrangement, or the rules for fostering cooperation, are essential parts of what politics means, and how groups con-nect. The Greeks did not see man's political sense as a base or animal instinct. Our capacities for cooperation and the daily practice of *intentional* – not just instinctual – social interaction are what set us apart from the animals. Politics makes us human, even though groups sometimes act like animals.[1]

In modern societies, the link between a monolithic "state" and "groups" is much weaker, though the need to connect in groups and the division of labor collective action can provide is stronger than ever.[2] People choose in groups all the time, sometimes all sitting in the same room and sometimes facing a computer screen or smart phone and choosing as part of a group that exists only on some social media platform. However, the way that groups are formed, choose rules, and decide things is a very general problem, and an important one. Thus, "politics" will be taken to mean people choosing in groups according to rules they have agreed on in advance, with the understanding that everyone accepts the result if the rules are followed. Moreover, the reason that people form groups – as scholars from Emile Durkheim to James Buchanan have recognized – is to share the advantages from increasing returns that cooperation and specialization create.

This tension between selfishness and teamwork, between calculation and community, is what makes analytical political theory so much fun. When we work out an explanation for what we see, we often also conceive of what should be. Our focus in both realms, the commonly seen and the ideal, is a product of people choosing in groups for their mutual benefit. The claims we focus on for most of the book are those that we can write down in models. Nevertheless, the choices and groups that these models help us understand are very real.

A GROUP, CHOOSING

On November 24, 1805, Lewis and Clark's Corps of Discovery was in a rough spot. Forty-five men had traveled up the Missouri River, crossed the continental divide, and canoed down the Columbia River to the Pacific Ocean. Along the way, they had picked up Sacagawea – a Shoshone woman whom they had used as a translator and guide – along with her French trapper husband and their infant son, bringing the band to forty-eight souls.

Their arrival at the Pacific had completed their outbound mission (spelling in this and following nineteenth-century entries is as in original, from the journal entries[3]):

The river Missouri, & the Indians inhabiting it, are not as well known as is rendered desireable by their connection ... with us.... An intelligent officer with ten or twelve chosen men ... might explore the whole ... to the Western Ocean. (Confidential letter from Thomas Jefferson to the U.S. Congress, January 18, 1803)

To explore the Missouri River and such principal stream of it as by its course and communication with the waters of the Pacific Ocean, whether the Columbia, Oregon, Colorado or any other river that may offer the most direct and practicable water communication across this continent for the purpose of commerce. (Official Letter of Commission from President Thomas Jefferson, June 20, 1803)

Now the Corps had to get home. First, they somehow had to survive the winter. They were nearly out of supplies and trade goods, and terrible storms battered them relentlessly.

Nine days earlier, William Clark had written in his journal:

...from [November] 5th in the morng. untill the 16th is eleven days rain, and the most disagreeable time I have experienced confined in a tempiest coast wet, where I can neither git out to hunt, return to a better situation, or proceed on: in this situation we have been for Six days past.

Later, on November 22, Clark wrote:

a little before Day light the wind which was from the S S. E. blew with Such violence that we were almost overwhelmned with water blown from the river, this Storm did not Sease at day but blew with nearly equal violence throughout the whole day accompaned with rain. O! how horriable is the day waves brakeing with great violence against the Shore throwing the Water into our Camp &c. all wet and Confind to our Shelters,....

Socrates called Crito "a disinterested person who is not going to die tomorrow." In Plato's story, Socrates himself had to decide whether to leave in the night or stay and commit suicide by drinking hemlock. So Socrates saw himself as "interested," in the sense that he had a stake in the choice. Socrates appealed to Crito as "disinterested" because his views were more objective, and therefore less likely to be colored by having a stake in the outcome.

The Corps was in the position of Socrates, not Crito. Everyone shivering in that rude shelter was "interested." They were exhausted, held a weak defensive position, lacked supplies, and found themselves uncomfortably close to hostile native tribes.[4] A wrong choice would bring catastrophe.

According to the records from the expedition, on November 24 they considered three options.[5] Here is a summary of each of those options:[6]

Option A. Remain at the hastily constructed Station Camp on the north side of the Columbia, in what is now Washington, near the confluence of Seal Creek (now the Washougal River) and the Columbia. Station Camp was near the coast, so the Corps might make contact with a ship if one anchored. Further, there were plenty of fish, and lots of salt to cure them.

Option B. Explore the south side of the Columbia, in what is now Oregon, and build winter quarters there. There were reports (though no one knew for sure) that far more elk could be found on the south side, and there were deer to be taken one day's travel east. The Indian tribes (Clatsops) on the south side were reportedly friendly and might offer better rates for the Corps' few remaining trade goods. The Chinooks of the northern side were sharp and aggressive traders.[7]

Option C. Go back upriver as far as possible, to the Celilo falls of the Columbia, to reduce the length of the return trip. Although the weather would be colder inland, they could escape the savage storms and constant rains of the coast. The Corps also hoped that there would be fewer Indians and more game on the land further east, as everyone was most heartily sick of fish.[8]

Someone in the shelter might have described the scene this way: A group of more than forty people must choose between three very different alternatives.[9] Everyone knew the stakes were high, since crossing the continent would count for little if they could not survive the winter. Jefferson had concluded his official letter by requiring that Lewis should "repair yourself with your papers to the seat of government." Jefferson expected samples, records, and maps. To succeed, the Corps had to return.

The structure of command in the Corps, until that point, had been military and hierarchical. The two captains, Meriwether Lewis and William Clark, had given orders. The men had carried out those orders or suffered martial discipline. Dissent or neglect of duty was punished harshly: At least six members of the Corps had been whipped, receiving twenty-five or more lashes each. One of these (Alexander Willard) received 100 lashes on his bare back – for sleeping on duty – in four sets of twenty-five lashes to spare his life.[10]

But there was something different about the choice of where to spend the winter. They all agreed on the goal of the decision: to survive the winter and return home. There was no question of shirking, or deceit, because a wrong choice meant failure and death for everyone. In addition, there was no interconnected set of military strategies, no implementation of a complex plan. The problem was simple: choose from among three clearly defined locations the one that made survival most likely.

It is impossible to tell, looking back only at the notes in the journals, what the reasoning behind taking a vote may have been.[11] Nevertheless, there are two important reasons people choosing in groups often use some kind of voting mechanism: *information* and *legitimacy*.

INFORMATION: THE WISDOM OF CROWDS

The remarkable thing is that Lewis and Clark seem to have perceived that the unified command/military discipline model of decision-making was an obstacle to making the best choice in this situation. We cannot know exactly why, because they didn't say, but they may have called for a vote to get better information.

The leaders, Lewis and Clark, had the right to make a choice and see it carried out, but instead they tried to combine each individual judgment into the best collective wisdom they could uncover. Rather than focus on "the opinions of some men, and some men only," as Socrates had counseled, the captains took account of the opinion of each member of the company. Facing death, they wanted every scrap of information and every considered judgment available to them.

Collecting information by aggregating judgments can make the group smarter than any of its members. This recognition, that voting processes may be useful for collecting information, is ancient. As Aristotle put it: "It is possible that the many, no one of whom taken singly is a sound man, may yet, taken all together, be better than the few, not individually but collectively..." (*Politics*, Book I, Chapter 11).

In a famous example, statistician Francis Galton (1907) wrote of a fair in England where the statistical power of many independent guesses created an accurate estimation of an unknown quantity. What Galton saw was a contest to guess the weight of a large ox. The mean of the 800 guesses registered for the ox's weight was within one-half of one percentage point of the true weight. Perhaps more interestingly, the mean of the 800 guesses was closer than *any* of the individual guesses. Therefore, though "no one taken singly is a sound man," the combined wisdom of the group may be profound. Galton (1907: 51; emphasis added) recognized the (possible) implication for voting: "This result is, I think, more creditable to the trust-worthiness of a *democratic judgment* than might have been expected."

A more contemporary example of what Surowiecki (2004) called "wisdom of crowds" is the game show *Who Wants to Be a Millionaire?* Of the three lifelines (eliminate two alternatives, call a friend, ask the crowd) the best was "ask the crowd."[12] But the live audience had waited in line for hours to watch in person, from a distance, a show that each of them could have seen more easily on television. Very few of them are likely "sound" as Aristotle might define that term. Nevertheless, as a group, the average of their response is nearly always correct.

LEGITIMACY: OWNERSHIP AND MORALE

The two captains wanted everyone in the company to feel ownership in the choice the group made. The way to accomplish this is to give everyone a voice, both in making arguments and in registering their views publicly. Significant participation in the process of choice ensured that each member of the Corps kept a stake in what the group chose. The Corps was already a cohesive unit, but the decision to take a vote cemented the reciprocal trust between the leaders and the rank-and-file members.

The vote on November 24 allowed the members of the Corps to go on record in support of the alternative they preferred. It would have been easy, had the captains just imposed the choice, to have grumbling later: "I never wanted to stay here; I knew this wasn't going to work!" Having a vote, with compulsory "turnout," meant that human nature created a set of advocates for the choice. People who publicly support a choice have a stake in defending it. Even if things go badly, the group chose it, and now everyone is in this together.

THE CHOICE

In taking the vote, the captains were not shirking. They were obliged – as military leaders – to make the final decision, and to take responsibility for it. Earlier, when there had been a disagreement over which tributary fork was the "real" Missouri, the two captains had imposed their view on the men, who "disagreed to a man."[13] But this time, in Oregon, Lewis and Clark asked for data. They sought a systematic representation of the opinions of all thirty people present that night.[14]

At least two people, Captain William Clark and Sergeant Patrick Gass, recorded the event in journals Clark gave a full listing of each of the thirty opinions, or "votes." However, the record is confused. It appears that the Shoshone woman, Sakagawea, said only that she hoped the selection location had "plenty of wappato."[15] York, Clark's male slave, was asked his view, and voted for C, going back up the Columbia as far as possible before choosing a winter encampment. It is worth noting that the views of an Indian woman and a slave were recorded in the journal as data for the captains to ponder.

Clark recorded the vote totals in one way, but then lists in his journal the individual votes in a way that yields a different total, as shown in Table 1.1.[16]

The second account appears in the journal of Sergeant Gass[17], who wrote:

We took a vote of the men as to the location for our winter quarters. Some are for investigating the other side of the Columbia for a suitable site – while others prefer a camp upriver near the falls, or at least up the river where it is less rainy. Sacagawea is in favor of a place where there are plenty of wappato. The vote resulted: 5 for the falls, 12 for the Seal [Washougal] River, and 12 for across the Columbia. Therefore Capt. Lewis

TABLE 1.1. *Three Versions of the Vote Totals on November 24, 1805*

	Clark's Account	Clark's Journal	Gass's Account
Option A: Station Camp	10	9	12
Option B: Fort Clatsop	12	13	12
Option C: Upriver	6	6	5

and another man will cross to the other side to see if good hunting is there, for we cannot depend on the natives for food. We prefer to be near the harbor in the event a ship will come this winter. The advantage of procuring goods from a vessel would off-set living on poor deer and elk higher up the river.

Putting this report into our format for alternatives in the third column of Table 1.1, we see that Gass has a slightly different result for the vote totals. Gass also recorded one more vote than Clark did, but it is quite possible that someone expressed a clearer preference than Clark perceived during the raucous meeting.

In any event, alternative "B" – favored by no more than 43 percent of the voters in all accounts, well short of a majority – was selected. Fort Clatsop was built on the south bank of the Columbia, near what is now Astoria, Oregon. Elk were plentiful, the storms really were less fierce, and in the spring of 1806, the Corps began the trip home. They arrived back in St. Louis on September 23, 1806.

A SHORT CONJECTURAL HISTORY

Since they survived, and returned, they appear to have made a good choice. Nevertheless, one wonders. The votes were recorded, and the issue decided, in a way that political scientists call "first past the post" (or plurality rule). That is, everyone announces exactly one vote for their first preference, and then the votes are tallied. The alternative that receives the most votes is selected.

For the sake of example, suppose we had more information about the views of the people in that room. This information is entirely conjectural, but it is plausible enough, since we are certain about the first preferences. If a person could not get his or her first choice, then that person would certainly have a preference about the next-best thing to do.

Consider Table 1.2, which follows Clark's account. There are three groups: the ten people who preferred Station Camp (alternative A), the twelve who preferred Fort Clatsop (B), and the six who preferred to go back Up River (C). Thus, the groups' first preferences ("Best") and relative sizes are historically accurate, using the report that gives the most decisive advantage to the selection

TABLE 1.2. *A Conjecture about Secondary Preferences*

	Station Campers (10)	Fort C-ers (12)	Up River (6)
Best	A	B	C
Middle	*C*	*C*	*A*
Worst	*B*	*A*	*B*

of Fort Clatsop, choice B. Everything above the dark line is "true," or as true as can be deduced from the historical record.

The conjectural information appears in italics, to differentiate it from what is above the dark line. With this additional information about preferences, we can try a different decision procedure. Consider a comparison between just two alternatives, A and B. Obviously, those who thought A was the best alternative would vote for A, so that is ten votes. But what if those who wanted to go back up river also preferred A to B, in terms of the next-best alternative? If that were true, then that would be six more votes for A. In other words, in a pairwise vote, A would receive sixteen votes and B would receive only twelve. Choosing B actually ignores the judgment of the majority, if preferences looked like this.

What about B versus C? Again, those who liked C best would vote for it, yielding six votes. But what if those who preferred Station Camp also would have preferred going up river to Fort Clatsop (preferred C to B, in our formulation)? Then again, the result would be sixteen opposed to B, now favoring C. B receives only the twelve votes from its proponents, and again a majority opposes B.

Finally, what of the other comparison, A versus C? In our example, if those who preferred Fort Clatsop had not had this option, their second preference would have been going back up river. But that would mean that eighteen people favored C, and only ten favored A. If we combine these results, we find something disturbing. First, if our conjectures were correct, then B was arguably the *least preferred* choice. A majority thought A was better than B, and a (different) majority thought C was better than B.

Second, a strong argument can be made for Up River, alternative C. C beats both A and B in pairwise simple majority votes. This may seem strange, because only six people had C as their first choice. The problem with plurality or first past the post votes is that these rules ignore the ranking of secondary alternatives. Both those who preferred Station Camp (A) and those who preferred going back Up River (C) considered B (in our example) to be the worst choice.

Further, those who preferred Station Camp and those who preferred Fort Clatsop both considered Up River (C) the second best choice. So, though they disagreed about the best choice, they agreed on the second choice. Since the third group considered C to be the best alternative, a group might reasonably choose C. After all, unlike A and especially unlike B, no one thought C was the worst choice.

However, there was no way for anyone to find this out, because the Corps used simple plurality rule. They held the vote to collect information, but there was no way that this information would be revealed, given the decision rule the Corps selected.

IF YOU CHOOSE NOT TO DECIDE, YOU STILL HAVE MADE A CHOICE

The story of the choice by the Corps of Discovery is gripping, and revelatory. But it is not unique. In situations with high stakes, possibly dire consequences, and limited information, people fall back on some form of choosing in groups. If they fail to choose as a group, then they lose the benefits of cooperation, with catastrophic consequences.

This book presents models that help us understand how people choose in groups. We will often go into some deep abstractions. However, when we do, try to remember Lewis and Clark's Corps of Discovery voting in a freezing rainstorm on the bank of the Columbia River. We are stuck with the need to choose in groups; the information and ownership imperatives are too important. The problem is that the rules – not the preferences – may determine the outcome in any given situation. Thus, deciding to choose in groups is just the first step. *Then the group has to decide how to decide.* The problem of choosing in groups is fundamentally a kind of exchange, or cooperation. It is not a market exchange, however. Choosing in groups is logically prior to what we usually think of as market exchange. As James Buchanan (1999:50) put it:

basic 'political exchange,' the conceptual contract under which the constitutional order is itself established, must precede any meaningful economic interaction. Orderly trade in private goods and services can take place only within a defined legal structure that establishes individuals' rights of ownership and control of resources, that enforces private contracts, and that places limits on the exercise of governmental powers...Even within a well-defined and functioning legal order, 'political exchange' necessarily involves *all* members of the relevant community rather than the two trading partners that characterize economic exchange. (p. 50; emphasis original.)

Buchanan had a "state of nature" theory about politics, meaning that before the existence of a constituted group there are only individuals. His metaphor for the state of nature is Robinson Crusoe, on Thursday (that is, the day before Friday). Crusoe faces all of the standard economic problems, in terms of optimizing his use of resources and looking for efficient solutions. But there is no exchange, no social interaction, in the system.

Then Friday shows up. The first thing that happens is *not* exchange. There first has to be an agreement, perhaps an implicit agreement, that the two men not kill each other, at least not today, not now. That is the "political exchange," the decision to choose as a group, and for Buchanan it is logically prior to markets or economic exchange. The conceptual contract – the small-c "constitution" under which the men don't kill each other – comes first. The collection of individuals has to *become a group*, before it can choose *as a group*.

Choosing in groups is justified by the fact the people acting in a group are more effective, and more prosperous, than are people acting alone. Groups can be coercive, to be sure. However, in principle, at least the coercion can be voluntary, because all the members of the group consented to it. The essence of liberty, for the individual, is the ability to enter into a binding contract. However, "binding" means that if I violate the terms of the agreement I am punished. Still, I am punished with my consent, because I voluntarily signed the contract in the first place. Choosing in groups is different, in the sense that the contract is among many people rather than just two. But the ability to enter into a binding contract with a group of people is no less necessary for human thriving than the simplest bilateral contract. In fact, choosing in groups may be even more important, and more fundamental.

MATHEMATICAL MODELS OF A FUNDAMENTAL HUMAN IMPULSE

Yes, we have to divide up our time like that, between our politics and our equations. But to me our equations are far more important, for politics are only a matter of present concern. A mathematical equation stands forever. (Albert Einstein).[18]

This book uses equations to describe politics, exploring both sides of the tension Einstein highlighted. Newspaper articles about "present concerns" rarely analyze the issues we will focus on here. However, we will argue that no one can understand our politics fully without the deeper and timeless insights that have been developed in our equations.

Mathematical truths about politics – constituted groups of people choosing – are not just interesting because they are true. Being able to "prove" a proposition does establish its truth – one kind of truth – at a fundamental level, of course. But the more profound thing about mathematical truths is that they have *always been true*. All that has happened when we prove something using math is that we have recognized an eternal truth. It was there, shaping the world and the logic of political choice all along. Lewis and Clark "knew," on some level, why voting was a good way of choosing in groups, but they did not understand the importance of procedures. It was true that procedures matter, but they did not know it. The surprising thing is that mathematical models are directly relevant for real groups making real choices – our politics and our equations may not differ as much as Einstein supposed.

WHY USE MODELS?

Models are internally consistent bodies of theory that describe some elements of a phenomenon. We need not state models in the form of equations – precise wording with clear definitions is fine – but we will frequently use equations. This process of abstraction helps simulate a reality simpler than the real world of politics. Mathematical models focus on the logical consistency or internal validity of arguments. Our equations will focus on human *behavior* based on *preferences* aggregated and refracted through alternative *institutions*. Institutions are the name we give to many different norms, rules, constraints, and other factors that affect choosing in groups.[19]

Given a set of premises, we can characterize the *logical* or deductive truth of a conclusion in one of five ways:

- Conclusion is *true* – follows logically from the premises
- Conclusion is *not true* – cannot be deduced from the premises
- Conclusion is *false* – ruled out by the premises
- Conclusion is *specifically contingent* – may or may not follow from the premises, depending on the values of some intervening variables that can be identified and defined precisely
- Conclusion is *vaguely contingent* – may or may not follow from the premises, depending on poorly defined or unknown factors that the author ignores or is unaware of

One objection to analytic reasoning is that the simplifying assumptions in models are too abstract or unrealistic. But simplifying assumptions make analysis manageable and help us focus on the key components of a phenomenon. When we identify the assumptions, we can debate them. In much of political theory and philosophy, conclusions turn out on scrutiny to be vaguely contingent, because not even the author can list the cases and conditions on which the conclusion rests.

Therefore, what many see as a flaw in formal political theories is actually their chief virtue: Assumptions must be identified. This allows incremental changes and improvements by tinkering with this assumption or that definition. Precise consequences can be deduced because of the new assumption. Models can be falsified, refined, and corrected in ways that are simply impossible for vaguely contingent theories.

Analytical political theory sometimes starts with a counterfactual: *What would we observe if people were fully informed, thought strategically, and anticipated the future actions of others?* To the extent that the predictions of a model based on that premise are not borne out, we learn something useful about the process. Empirical examination can tell us whether – or more likely, when – people make strategic calculations.

Mathematical formats have a drawback, however, and we should acknowledge it. The practical or ethical value of the argument is nearly irrelevant to the formal truth or falsity of the propositions within the logic of a model. Mathematical statements that are true are correctly deduced, given the premises from which they are derived. False mathematical statements are those that do not follow from the premises. We need not invoke empirical referents because we know all we need to know about the truth or falsity of the claims within the logical framework of the model.

Whether these correctly deduced models *are of any value in describing the political world* is a different question. Mathematical models are long on precision, but for that reason they can be short on realism. Mathematical formulations may be deployed inappropriately, and the representation the analyst has chosen may fail to capture any useful part of the reality of politics. The math is eternally true, but the correspondence between the equation and group choice may be entirely contingent.

Still, it is precisely the dramatic abstraction from a complex reality that gives models their *potential* value. The problem is matching up the mathematical version with statements that have measurable, empirical meaning. The empirical versions of formal models generally focus on three kinds of variables:

(1) The *independent* variables – often denoted as "X" – which themselves are exogenous, or outside the model, but cause other variables to change

(2) The *dependent* variable – often denoted as "Y" – which is dependent on, or "caused" by the independent variables

(3) The *intervening* variables – often denoted as "W" or "V" – which mediate the effects of the independent variables on the dependent variable

Writing down the relationship among such variables in functional form, we see that the value of X, given the conditioning values of W and V, results in – that is, *causes* – a value for Y:

$$Y = f(X \mid W, V) \tag{1.1}$$

where f is a function, and "|" means "given."

The most empirically useful kinds of theoretical statements are those that make predictions that are specifically, contingently true. For example:

$$X \text{ implies } Y \text{ [if] } W \text{ is true [only if] } V \text{ is not true} \tag{1.2}$$

In words, we expect Y to happen if X is true, *provided* that W is also true, *unless* V is true. These specific contingencies can be tested, either using laboratory experiments or techniques of statistical elaboration such as ANOVA or regression analysis on random samples of voters or citizens. If the contingent claim is falsified, then we know something important is left out of the theory. In the example above, suppose we observe that W is true, V is not true, and yet X being true does not cause Y to happen. The theory is disconfirmed; something was left out. Having something left out is not a crippling problem. All theories "leave out" lots of things that we see in the real world. That is the nature of theory. However, if a specific contingency is falsified, we know that something important is missing, and the theory is wrong even on its own abstract terms.

We cannot falsify vaguely contingent statements, because we cannot nail down the specific prediction being made. Such statements often cannot be tested. For example, "High turnout is good for democracy." There are at least two problems with this statement:

- In an idealized democracy where all politicians do exactly what voters want, everyone who went to the polls would be indifferent. All the parties would be the same. That sounds like "rule by the people." But turnout would be negligible! Therefore, democracy can be good without high turnout.
- On the other hand, if voters choose not to acquire much information about alternatives and elections are determined primarily on vague platforms and bellicose promises, high turnout might be a sign of dysfunction. Jason Brennan (2011) has gone so far as to argue that citizens who have not paid attention have a moral duty *not* to vote. Therefore, democracy can be bad with high turnout.

The problem is not that the statement "High turnout is good for democracy" is false (or true). The problem is that we are not sure what the statement means, because it fails to identify the assumptions, or specific contingencies, on which its truth rests.

If claims are specifically contingent, we are more likely to be able to design dispositive tests. As Granger (1999) and de Marchi (2005) note, a dispositive test must do more than reject non-association. A dispositive test must contrast the specific predictions of one model with (different) specific predictions of the universe of alternative models. So dispositive tests are only possible in cases where the predictions are *specific* enough to state precisely and *different* enough that alternative models really are alternatives.

Vaguely contingent statements are not useful as alternative theories. Everything depends on everything else, and things are defined in different ways, or not really defined at all. Such conceptions can certainly be interesting, viewed as literature, because ambiguity enriches literature. But the desire by some theorists to insist that precise definitions are not just impossible, but dangerous, is a *cul de sac,* the skeptic's play. There is no way to test a theory whose central claim is that all coherent theories are false by definition.[20]

APPEAL TO AUTHORITY

Another kind of theory, which we do not take up in this book, at least not intentionally, rests on appeals to authority. For authority claims, the value of a statement depends not on an evaluation of the argument, but on the self-evident merit of whoever said it. To support our argument against appeals to authority, we appeal to two authorities. First, Thomas Hobbes:

By this it appears how necessary it is for any man that aspires to true knowledge to examine the definitions of former authors; and either to correct them, where they are negligently set down, or to make them himself. For the errors of definitions multiply themselves, according as the reckoning proceeds, and lead men into absurdities, which at last they see, but cannot avoid, without reckoning anew from the beginning; in which lies the foundation of their error...For words are wise men's counters; they do but reckon by them: but they are the money of fools, that value them by the authority of an Aristotle, a Cicero, or a Thomas, or any other doctor whatsoever, if but a man. (Hobbes, *Leviathan*, Chapter IV, "Of Speech.")

Hobbes is advocating reasoning from principles, rather than relying on his archenemies the "Schoole-men and pusled philosophers." He thought they made up new words, "yet their meaning not explained by Definition; whereof there have been aboundance coyned."[21] The "Schoole-men" cited views of authorities (such as Aristotle, Cicero, Thomas Aquinas) as foundational truth claims that needed no further defense.

But in analytical political theory, *everything* can be questioned. No conclusion is sacrosanct; no view expressed by a previous authority must be accepted at face value. If something is true, it can be proved, at least within the deductive framework created by granting a set of premises and assumptions.[22] One can even substitute alternative assumptions, impeaching the claim to universality of any theoretical perspective.

Second, consider this argument, made by René Descartes:

For my own part, I should doubtless have [believed in received authority], had I received instruction from but one master, or had I never known the diversities of opinion that from time immemorial have prevailed among men of the greatest learning. But I had become aware, even so early as during my college life, that no opinion, however absurd and incredible, can be imagined, which has not been maintained by some one of the philosophers. (Descartes, *Discourse on Method*, Chapter 2).

In short, it does not matter what [Great Person] said; we want to know if [Great Person] was correct. That takes a deductive argument, not a bibliographic reference.

NORMATIVE STATEMENTS, POSITIVE STATEMENTS, AND TRUE STATEMENTS

Most theories take as their primary focus either the *normative* (the "ought") or the *positive* (the "is"). In fact, some key problems spring from this positive/normative dichotomy. The division seems convenient and even natural. However, pure positivism is probably impossible and nearly useless if it does exist. At a minimum, positive results are contingent on the acceptance of several unspoken normative premises. James Buchanan, in his portion of the appendix to *The Calculus of Consent* (1962), said of this distinction that it:

has separated the moral philosopher on the one hand from the scientist on the other, but the dichotomy so achieved is too simple in relation to the problems that arise in political theory and philosophy.

A given set of rules describes a social organization, a political order. In discussing this order, we may draw a useful, indeed an essential, line between positive and normative theory. A positive science of politics should analyze the operation of an existing, or a postulated, set of rules for collective decision-making quite independently of the efficacy of this set in furthering or in promoting certain "social goals." A normative theory of politics by contrast should array the alternative sets of rules in accordance with their predicted efficiency in producing certain ends or goals, which, if possible, should be quite explicit. Normative theory must be erected upon and must draw its strength from the propositions of positive science, but it is only when this extension of normative theory is made that "reform" in existing institutions can be expected to emerge from specialized scholarship...We seek to learn how the world works in order to make it work "better," to "improve" things... (p. 307)

There are two mistakes often made in relating the positive (the "is") to the normative (the "ought"). A useful political analysis must avoid both the *moralistic fallacy* ("ought" implies "is") and the *naturalistic fallacy* ("is" implies "ought"). We will discuss each of these in turn.

"OUGHT" DOES NOT IMPLY "IS", THOUGH "OUGHT" ASSUMES "IS"

Normative political theory focuses on justice and morality in the political world. It is not clear, though, that mental conceptions of justice and morality can be exported intact from the philosophical imagination into the real political world of political engineering.[23] Hobbes' *Leviathan* conjured an entirely new and paradoxical justification for monarchy in the sovereignty of the individual. Still, Hobbes was on firm ground empirically because the monarchy he advocated on normative grounds could be exported to a recognizable real-world political institution.

Other political theorists, those who focus solely on the "ought," may fail to achieve their goal of transforming real politics because there exists no set of empirical institutions consistent with those goals. An artist could not build a beautiful bridge, unless that artist also understood the nuts and bolts of engineering. One cannot do practical normative theory without understanding the formal properties of choosing in groups: Normative theorists must show that the ideal political scheme is possible.[24]

"IS" DOES NOT IMPLY "OUGHT"

David Hume had perhaps the first clear statement of this problem.[25] G.E. Moore (1903) expanded the claim into what he called the "naturalistic fallacy." Moore argued that it is question-begging to found claims of virtue on empirical or "natural" observations (such as "more evolved" or "more pleasant"). There may be no *telos* that wills change in nature or society, and so attributing purpose to entities in the natural world is at best misleading. Therefore, survival does not imply goodness; just as in the previous section, we saw that goodness does not imply existence. It is not clear that cockroaches are better, or more virtuous, or more anything – except alive – than the beautiful but extinct Madeiran butterfly.

In Plato's *Republic* (written forty years after Athens' collapse as a democracy), Thrasymachus claims that "justice is nothing other than the interest of the stronger." If one nation is *stronger*, then in some sense its institutions and rules must be *better*. In 1956, Nikita Khrushchev beat his shoe on a podium and bellowed that Russia would "bury" the west. Russia was stronger, in Khrushchev's view. That meant that Russia's political and economic institutions must be morally better. Realist doctrines of international relations often focus solely on the competing interests of nations, leaving to domestic policy the question of whether these self-interested choices are morally defensible.[26]

There is another variant of the "is implies ought" doctrine that usually goes unquestioned. This is the "will of the majority" fallacy. Imagine that there are two factions with different views on a policy question. The question might be abortion, or prohibition of alcohol, or even enslavement of the minority. In a pure democracy, we might resort to the "justice is the will of the stronger" solution; the numerically larger faction gets to define morality and justice.

But this is an outrageous example of "is implies ought." Who expects to find rectitude in the multitude? The "will of the majority" is just what most people happen to think. The will of the majority and the morally justified choice could coincide, of course; morality and majority are not necessarily antagonistic. However, there may be a tension between majorities want and "what is right." The problem of survival we discussed earlier brings this difficulty into even sharper relief: Machiavelli (1952) thought that the "Prince" would be obliged to behave immorally, to preserve his nation.[27] In short, majorities may not be moral, and survival may actually *require* immorality. What is a group to do?

THE ANALYSIS OF POLITICS

The word *analysis* comes from the Greek analusis (ἀνάλυσις): dissolving, or loosening, a complex whole into parts. The sense of the word is close to untying a knot, or straightening a tangle. Analysis helps us understand the relations of the parts, as well as the nature of the whole. Without an analytical approach, "politics" is very hard to comprehend, especially if we want to know more than "What will happen tomorrow?" It may be possible to forecast results from opinion polls taken a day before the election, but forecasting issues or elections six months off is difficult.

One might say theories of politics are not very good if their predictions are so uncertain. It is, though, more accurate to focus on the peculiar difficulty of the problem: Political phenomena are wonderfully complex, and there are many connected moving parts. The analysis of politics using models "loosens" this complexity into more manageable (but still very interesting) components.

A DISTINCTION: JUDGMENTS VS. PREFERENCES

The problem faced by Lewis and Clark was a judgment. Judgment disputes are disagreements over means, when everyone agrees on ends. Preferences are different. Preference disputes are disagreements over ends.[28]

For Lewis and Clark, there was plausibly a "fact of the matter" in the debate over where to establish a winter camp.[29] Milton Friedman (1953; emphasis added) rather controversially presented the distinction between judgments and preferences this way:

[D]ifferences about economic policy among disinterested citizens derive predominantly from different predictions about the economic consequences of taking action – *differences that in principle can be eliminated by [logic and discussion]* – rather than from *fundamental differences in basic values*, differences about which men can ultimately only fight.

Nevertheless, sometimes groups do talk about values; sometimes people change their minds. Moreover, sometimes people fight about the distributional consequences of policy, even if they otherwise share values. It is useful to try to make the distinction based not on how fixed our views are, but on the origins of the views themselves.

1. *Preference disputes: Disagreement over ends, or values*: When people have different goals, or different ideological convictions, they will probably favor different means. Therefore, even if political choices are means, rather than ends in themselves, agreement through discussion may be hard to come by. So, if I like chocolate and you like vanilla, we can't agree (without fighting) on what ice cream is best. Talking about tastes won't help much, because at best I can persuade you that I really do like chocolate better. Values are different from simple tastes, however. It may be possible to reason about value, to make arguments that others find persuasive, or discuss the sources of disagreement.[30] Regardless, evidence is not generally very important in these discussions.

2. *Judgment disputes: Disagreements over judgments, or means*: Members of a group also disagree if they all have the same goal but not perfect information about the consequences of particular choices. This was the position of the Corps of Discovery: They wanted to find shelter, to hunt and gather food, and to be safe from attack. But they disagreed about which choice leads to this outcome. Consequently, their problem was to discover the collective wisdom of the group, not merely to add up their *preferences*.[31] For judgment disputes, deliberation and debate can be very helpful. Understanding the reasons you believe as you do, and ensuring that all of us have the same information, can improve the quality of decisions.

ON METHOD

The central approach of this book is public choice theory. There are many theories and approaches to understanding groups and political choices, and public choice has no claim of exclusivity, or even primacy. Nevertheless, it has shown value in explaining some actions, some choices, some times.

Public choice makes an assumption about purpose, a static behavioral claim, a dynamic behavioral claim, and adds a proviso.[32]

Assumption: Public choice rests on "the homely but important observation that politicians are, after all, no different than the rest of us."[33] Likewise, consumers do not become omniscient when they cross the threshold into the voting booth. It's quite true, of course, that consumers have limited information about their choices in the grocery or on the car sales lot. But the limitations on political information faced by *voters* may be even worse. If corporate CEOs are sometimes greedy or shortsighted, they do not become benevolent or wise when they enter public office.

Static Behavioral Claim: There are substantial mutual gains to cooperation and political "exchange." This exchange is different from the literal exchange of goods and services in private markets. In many circumstances, some form of collective action results in enormous net gains to everyone involved. Individuals form a collective, with the power to punish members who violate agreements to which those members gave their consent. The problem for the group is to avoid coercion without consent, but to reliably punish violations of consented agreements.

Dynamic Behavioral Claim: If the same group interacts repeatedly over time, then consistent obedience to rules can create the fulfilled expectation of future adherence to agreements. Once people "follow the rules," the transactions costs of monitoring and policing norm obedience fall dramatically. The group chooses rules that benefit all, but over time, each member benefits further when a norm of obeying the rules is internalized.

Proviso: One of James Buchanan's favorite metaphors for understanding scientific models was "windows," a description he attributed to Friedrich Nietzsche.[34] This metaphor is an apt description of the humility with which one should approach a task as monumental as the description of people choosing in groups. There are many different windows, and views of the world. The world will look different from each window, with different light, a different perspective, a different depth of field, and differences in angle. Each window has some claim to validity, to "truth," because it is a view of the world. No one window – including public choice theory – can claim exclusive rights to truth. The theories we talk about in the following chapters are universal, and there are other valid approaches to these problems.

On the other hand, there is a world – one world, an objective world – outside our windows. The views through different windows are of something objective, of something that exists. Some views may turn out, on examination, to be of more value than others in particular applications.

SUMMARY AND OUTLINE

It is worth taking a moment to summarize the main argument of the book, before we go any further. We offer a summary, and then an outline, to ensure that the thread of the argument is clear, rather than simply presenting a road map. We hope to make it clear just why we want the reader to travel this road.

Summary

People often must choose in groups. Individuals have preferences, but there are many decision contexts (public goods, collective action, externalities) that require group or public choice, using centralized non-market institutions. In these settings, individuals are better off, and often much better off, choosing in groups than going it alone. Politics is the practical process of group choice. Analytical politics is the study of choosing in groups.

Constituting a group comes before individual choices, though not before individual preferences and goals. Individuals have preferences and goals in a "state of nature," but they are not able to act to achieve those goals very well, if at all. Before Robinson Crusoe and Friday could exchange things, they had to "exchange" a credible promise not to kill each other. Politics is, or can be, thought of as a kind of exchange process that makes all participants better off. Consequently, people choose – in groups – the rules, memberships, and scope of control of that group. This "choice," however, is a social choice, and no individual can legitimately command or coerce others to participate or to agree to particular rules. Consensus and contract can only be obtained voluntarily, through persuasion or bargaining.

Once the group is constituted, it may appear that the chiefs, leaders, or shamans of the group exert coercive force on members. But the fact of coercive action may not be involuntary, if the members of the group gave their consent. Voluntary consent to contracts is the very essence of individual freedom; without it, people cannot cooperate very well. Suppose A has a car, but doesn't know much about cars. If A offers expert mechanic B something valuable to fix A's car, both people are better off, possibly much better off, if the exchange is enforceable. That means that if B accepts the money but then makes no effort to fix the car, A can use coercion to enforce the contract.

In a constituted group, consent scales up, and the "exchange" is still voluntary. The nature of the exchange requires non-market institutions, but the essential justification – mutually beneficial cooperative action – is preserved in constituted groups. If 50 people all agree to drain a swamp or build a road, and 49 contribute while one person refuses to contribute as agreed, the 49 can use coercion to enforce the contract. The key difference between coercion and "voluntary coercion" is whether the person(s) being coerced gave their consent at the constitutional stage. If a person agreed to the rules, and the rules are followed, then that person cannot reject the outcome, even if she disagrees with it. The "rule of law" requires consent to the process, the strict observance of the process, and the acceptance of outcomes of that process.

Notice that there is no claim here that the constituted group is a "state," in the traditional sense. A wide variety of constitutions, contracts, or arrangements are consistent with "politics as exchange." The essential differences from standard economic analysis are that (a) the horizon of cooperation required extends beyond just a buyer and a seller; (b) the institutions of choice require the selection of one from among several alternatives, but once that choice is made then all members of the group must accept the same outcome, because the choice cannot be divided or tailored to individuals; and (c) the institutions for effecting and enforcing the exchange are collective, rather than being based on private property rights. Just like in a two-person contract with private goods, however, coercion in the event of contract breach is justified if – but only if – all parties who are targets of coercion consented in advance to be coerced, by agreeing to the terms of the contract.

Analytical politics provides a lens for examining how people choose in groups. There are other lenses, other "windows," through which scholars can examine choosing in groups, and these other perspectives all have value. But as we look at the world through different windows, it is useful to remember that there is a world, an actual context in which groups of people try to achieve their individual and collective ends. Theories of group choice that ignore the practical problems of preference aggregation, disagreement, and resource constraints are views of the world through distorted windows.

Analysis requires a "loosening," or disentangling, of many interwoven threads of politics. One key aspect of analytical politics is a means of representing individual preferences so that groups and constitutions can be evaluated. The traditional mechanism for "representing" preferences is the utility function, developed in economics. But there are two problems with simply using economic-style utility functions in analytical politics. First, the nature of the "goods" at stake choosing by groups is often "public," rather than private, in the sense that public goods are non-rival and non-excludable. It turns out that there are no easily adapted economic utility functions that can be used to represent preferences for an economy that also has public goods.

Second, the very notion of a utility function is unnecessarily cumbersome and restrictive for many collective choice applications. In many group choice settings a more general, fundamental approach – weak orderings – is more flexible and more easily understood. So weak orderings are developed first in this book, as a means of presenting preferences directly rather than representing preferences using a restrictive utility function.

On the other hand, there are many settings where the portability and tractability of a utility function is convenient. For this purpose, we develop the "spatial model," a utility function based on distance. The intuition is simple: citizens choose the alternative that is "closest" to their most-preferred alternative, or ideal point. Several elaborations of this intuition are presented, including differences in importance, or "salience," for different issues, so that the trade-offs between distance along different dimensions can be compared. We also consider the problem of nonseparability, allowing for the preferences of the citizen on one or more dimensions to be contingent on the expected level provided of a different dimension of policy.

After the basic approach is described, some extensions and applications are considered. These include the limits on what can be said about collective choice, and the limits of the analogy likening group "exchange" to private exchange, the problem of uncertainty, and the problem of political participation. In these sections, we try to place signposts guiding the reader to the important advances that have been made in the field of analytical politics while highlighting the areas where we know less than we need to know.

Outline

The following chapter takes up the problem of "constituting" the group. A collection of people is not necessarily a group. Groups have ways of choosing that may be based on traditions, habits, informal norms, or formal written rules. Some groups might constitute themselves intentionally, but others perceive themselves as groups because of a shared historical or cultural experience. Constitutions may rest on agreements (negotiated) or identities (arising and evolving from particular events, real or imagined, in the past).

Chapter 3 presents the basic analytics of group choice, by defining preference and giving examples of how preferences might be aggregated. We take it as axiomatic that only individuals have preferences; groups do not "have a preference" unless there is unanimity. Even then, it is not clear that everyone in the group has the same reasons to prefer one alternative, even if they all agree on the best alternative. The most we can say is that the group chooses, or uses, decision rules, and the decision rule aggregates preferences into an outcome, or choice from the set of alternatives.

Chapter 4 presents the more advanced analytics of group choice, using formal methods. It also defines the idea of a "public good" more formally and gives a justification for the idea of "equilibrium" in taxation and expenditures. Chapter 4 also elaborates the idea that democratic procedures may not lead reliably to a determinate outcome.

We then start a new section introducing "spatial theory," or the idea that a particular utility function may help us to represent preferences, and thereby to understand political competition. Chapter 5 presents the simple one-dimensional model, and introduces the median voter theorem. Chapter 6 generalizes the spatial model to multiple dimensions, and extends preference representation to account for salience and nonseparability.

The third section returns to the problem of indeterminacy but generalizes it beyond the problem of majority rule to any collection of people trying to choose as a group. As Chapter 7 points out, even if preferences are "rational," aggregation procedures may not lead to determinate outcomes, at least if the decision rule obeys a plausible set of (apparently) harmless normative conditions. This is the celebrated Arrow Impossibility result, and represents a limit to the effectiveness of choosing in groups. The problem is not purely a political one, however, because Arrow himself conceived of the problem as a difficulty in welfare economics. The problem is more general than "just" politics, or markets. Arrow's social choice problem is a challenge to any group of people, using any aggregation mechanism.

Chapters 8 and 9 present topics on group choice, focusing on uncertainty and collective action, respectively. Uncertainty and information are the keys to understanding the importance and effects of a variety of political institutions. In addition, the collective action problem may be the central difficulty in political action, explaining why some groups succeed and others fail.

Some of the notation and techniques we will introduce will seem intimidating to a newcomer and may seem like a strange way of thinking about politics for someone used to concentrating on debates, television ads, and specific policy issues. But the reason for developing this approach is it explains a prior step: Why are those debates, those ads, and those specific policy issues important in the first place?

TERMS

  Analysis
  Appeal to authority
  Assumptions
  Behavior
  Constitution
  Contingent
  Judgments
  Legitimacy
  Models
  Normative
  Politics
  Positive
  Preferences
  Variables: Dependent, Independent, Intervening
  Voting mechanism
  Wisdom of Crowds

PROBLEMS FOR CHAPTER I

1.1 The following is a passage from Rousseau's *Social Contract*. Pick out the premises or assumptions, and the conclusions. Are the assumptions realistic, or do they seem implausible? Are the conclusions true, false, or contingent?

The general will is always right and tends to the public advantage; but it does not follow that the deliberations of the people are always equally correct. Our will is always for our own good, but we do not always see what that is; the people is never corrupted, but it is often deceived, and on such occasions only does it seem to will what is bad.

There is often a great deal of difference between the will of all and the general will. The latter considers only the common interest, while the former considers private interest, and is no more than a sum of particular wills. But take away from these same wills the pluses and minuses that cancel one another, and the general will remains as the sum of the differences.

1.2 Suppose you have a theory that asserts that older people are more likely to vote. You investigate this empirically, and find out that it is not true: overall, older people are about as likely to vote as anyone else is. Nevertheless, you notice something: Older people who graduated from college are more likely to vote than any other group of citizens. In this "model," what is the independent or causal variable, what is the dependent variable, and what is the intervening variable?

1.3 Suppose there were three people trying to decide where to spend the winter, and their choices are as follows: (A) Build cabins right where we are; (B) Climb the mountains and look for a cave to stay in; (C) Walk to the south, hoping the weather will be warmer, and then build cabins. Now, suppose Person 1 prefers option A. Person 2 prefers option B. Person 3 prefers option C. What additional information would you want to know to help them decide what they should do?

2

Becoming a Group: The Constitution

> There is but one law which, from its nature, needs unanimous consent. This is the social compact; for civil association is the most voluntary of all acts.. . . Apart from this primitive contract, the vote of the majority always binds all the rest. This follows from the contract itself. But it is asked how a man can be both free and forced to conform to wills that are not his own. How are the opponents at once free and subject to laws they have not agreed to?
>
> I retort that the question is wrongly put. The citizen gives his consent to all the laws, including those which are passed in spite of his opposition, and even those which punish him when he dares to break any of them. Rousseau, Book IV, Chapter 2, "Voting"

Three broad subjects interest political theorists: *axiology*, or the knowledge of ethics and "the good;" *ontology*, the knowledge of being and existence; and *epistemology*, the knowledge of knowledge and knowing.[1] We want to know, for example: What is the good society? What are the types or categories of human societies? How do we assess empirical evidence to understand the effects of real policies on that society?

The study of voting and collective choice most often has been conceived as a problem in epistemology. That is, given that we – the members of a group – all want something, how do we know if a particular voting system can lead us to it? If the "right thing to do" is *known to exist*, the problem is making sure that voting processes can help *discover* it.

Recent scholarship has undermined this perspective, perhaps fatally. Imagine there are two alternatives; call them "A" and "B." It is possible to define the parts of the following statement quite precisely:

I like A better than B

Presented with alternatives A and B, the chooser believes that she derives higher satisfaction from A. The chooser believes, subjectively and based on the information at hand, that A is preferable.

Likewise, we can carefully define what it means to say:

You like B better than A

Again, presented with two alternatives, the chooser believes you like B better. Now, imagine there is a third person involved, and we can say

She likes A better than B

Again, it is possible to be quite specific about what this means, because the nature of the comparison and the (subjective) definition of "like" are clear. But what if we put the three individuals together into a group? Since two like A better than B and one likes B better than A, can we reach any conclusion about the group?

Premise: I like A better than B
Premise: You like B better than A
Premise: She likes A better than B

Conclusion: As a Group, We like A better than B

Since the group disagrees, it must be true that there is some additional premise at work in the group, something not required for any individual. For a group, there needs to be some *decision rule*, some means of aggregating or adding up preferences of individuals. All of the members of the group, unanimously, must give their consent to the decision rule, though they may ultimately disagree about the *outcome* reached by applying the decision rule to actual alternatives.

The problem is that we are trying to infer what the group wants by asking each of the group's members, one at a time, what he or she wants. Can you do that? You could fail by choosing a bad voting procedure or distributing illegible or confusing ballots, but in that case, you simply failed to discover an objective hidden fact: The group is assumed to have a preference, and our job as political scientists is to discover what that preference is.

The real problem is deeper. It is not logically possible to construct a group preference using as data the individual preferences expressed by members of the group. In fact, it is by no means clear that it is even possible for groups to exhibit "preference," and there is no particular reason we should expect groups to have preferences. Even if the group is unanimous, the concept of preference does not apply to groups, as organic entities.[2] Group preference fails as a matter of ontology. It is a category mistake, like asking, "What color is seven?"

We, however, could sensibly make the following kinds of statements:

(1) Two members of the group like A better, and one member likes B better.
(2) Since the group *unanimously* agreed beforehand to accept the outcome of majority rule, A is selected because of the application of the decision rule, "majorities choose."

The goal is to start with the *individual* chooser, and justify the (entirely different) notion of a *group* choice the individual is obliged to accept, even if she disagrees with it. A number of scholars have addressed the problem, and we will discuss it at much greater length in later chapters. All we are trying to do at this point is clarify the distinction made by Runciman and Sen (1965), who recognize the problem of adding up preferences when people have private and public motives:

> Our interpretation, by contrast, does not require us to impute to each person more than a single set of orderings. On our view, each person has (as in Rousseau) a single and consistent aim. The conflict between the will of all and the general will arises not because the individual must be required to change his preference orderings, but because of the difference between the outcome of individual strategy and of enforced collusion. (p. 557).

The approach suggested by the recognition that single citizens may fail to act in the interests of the group, even when "enforced collusion" would ensure a better final outcome for the single citizen, is "methodological individualism." Methodological individualism has many sources, and many critics.[3] We use it because it allows us to capture the conflict between what individuals do on their own, and what they want from consenting to join a group.

This notion of consented and constituted group choice need not apply only to states. Consider a law firm, a partnership. The partners in the law firm formed their contract of partnership as a means of increasing their profits, by capturing gains from cooperation and division of labor. One partner might specialize in torts, another in tax litigation, another in criminal law, and so on. All the partners share staff, access to reference materials, and office space. They are obliged to write the decision-making rules for the group, ranging from hiring new partners to choices about staff to salary matters. Each member recognizes that he or she may disagree with some of the choices the group will make, but group membership is better than private practice. If a particular member finds that the partnership contract does not serve him or her, there are provisions for exit. Exit is not costless, however, and there may be substantial penalties and costs associated with leaving the group. It is plausible that associate attorneys want to become partners, even though that means that they will be part of a constituted group and subject to coercion if they violate the rules or expenses if they try to exit.

More generally, people do not just join groups because they like company. Groups are the context in which people choose, and act. Human beings cannot do without groups, and social scientists must account for them. In politics, this problem is especially acute, because while individuals may *choose*, groups *do*. Group choices are generally unitary: A road has one speed limit, a city has one budget for public works, and a nation has one defense budget. This brings the problem of *constitutions* into sharp focus.

If individuals have preferences, but groups act, and if they make one choice binding on all individuals using a consented decision process, then the way the group is constituted is fundamental.[4]

CONSTITUTING COLLECTIVE CHOICE

When a group constitutes itself, it forms an association through an agreement or contract. The contract is inherently "political," because it requires individuals to choose as a group, and then to accept the results, even if they disagree with it. The constitution must specify the rules on how to choose, who can enter the group, how members can leave the group, and how the rules can be changed. In this sense, most groups are political, regardless of whether they are institutions of the state or voluntary private associations. As Max Weber (1921) put it:

What is a 'political' association from the sociological point of view? What is a 'state'? Sociologically, the state cannot be defined in terms of its ends. There is scarcely any task that some political association has not taken in hand, and there is no task that one could say has always been exclusive and peculiar to those associations which are designated as political ones: today the state, or historically, those associations which have been the predecessors of the modern state. Ultimately, one can define the modern state sociologically only in terms of the specific means peculiar to it, as to every political association – namely, the use of physical force...

[A] state is a human community that (successfully) claims the monopoly of the legitimate use of physical force within a given territory. Note that 'territory' is one of the characteristics of the state. Specifically, at the present time, the right to use physical force is ascribed to other institutions or to individuals only to the extent to which the state permits it. The state is considered the sole source of the 'right' to use violence. Hence, 'politics' for us means striving to share power or striving to influence the distribution of power, either among states or among groups within a state. (pp. 396–7)

Weber summarized the core issue: Citizens who have constituted a group and consented to be subject to the use of force are, in some important sense, exercising their freedom.

Though there are countless examples of groups constituting themselves, one of the most striking comes from the Old Testament. It is the story of Samuel, the last Judge of Israel. Perhaps the most interesting thing about the story is the justifications offered for the creation of a constituted group, in this case a state with a monarch. According to the text of I Samuel[5], this is what happened.

When Samuel became old, he made his sons judges over Israel.

The name of his firstborn son was Joel, and the name of his second, Abijah; they were judges in Beer-sheba.

Yet his sons did not follow in his ways, but turned aside after gain; they took bribes and perverted justice.

Then all the elders of Israel gathered together and came to Samuel at Ramah,

and said to him, 'You are old and your sons do not follow in your ways;
   appoint for us, then, a king to govern us, like other nations.'
But the thing displeased Samuel when they said, 'Give us a king to govern
   us.' Samuel prayed to the Lord,
and the Lord said to Samuel, 'Listen to the voice of the people in all that they
   say to you; for they have not rejected you, but they have rejected me from
   being king over them.
Just as they have done to me, from the day I brought them up out of Egypt to
   this day, forsaking me and serving other gods, so also they are doing to
   you.
Now then, listen to their voice; only – you shall solemnly warn them, and
   show them the ways of the king who shall reign over them.'
So Samuel reported all the words of the Lord to the people who were asking
   him for a king.
He said, 'These will be the ways of the king who will reign over you: he will
   take your sons and appoint them to his chariots and to be his horsemen,
   and to run before his chariots;
and he will appoint for himself commanders of thousands and commanders
   of fifties, and some to plough his ground and to reap his harvest, and to
   make his implements of war and the equipment of his chariots.
He will take your daughters to be perfumers and cooks and bakers.
He will take the best of your fields and vineyards and olive orchards and give
   them to his courtiers.
He will take one-tenth of your grain and of your vineyards and give it to his
   officers and his courtiers.
He will take your male and female slaves, and the best of your cattle and
   donkeys, and put them to his work.
He will take one-tenth of your flocks, and you shall be his slaves.
And in that day you will cry out because of your king, whom you have
   chosen for yourselves; but the Lord will not answer you in that day.'
But the people refused to listen to the voice of Samuel; they said, 'No! but we
   are determined to have a king over us,
so that we also may be like other nations, and that our king may govern us
   and go out before us and fight our battles.'
When Samuel had heard all the words of the people, he repeated them in the
   ears of the Lord.
The Lord said to Samuel, 'Listen to their voice and set a king over them.'
Samuel then said to the people of Israel, 'Each of you return home.'

This is a story of political "constitution." The Hebrew people constituted
themselves as a political entity, with a king, not a tribe organized around a
set of (more or less) shared religious beliefs and in which judges settled disputes
by interpreting scripture. Montesquieu (1752, Bk I, chapter 1), referring to just
this passage in I Samuel, said,

[Man] might every instant forget his Creator; God has therefore reminded him of his duty by the laws of religion. Such a being is liable every moment to forget himself; philosophy has provided against this by the laws of morality. Formed to live in society, he might forget his fellow-creatures; legislators have therefore by political and civil laws confined him to his duty.

There are three sets of "laws" by this reasoning: religion, morality, and statutes. When we think of government, in modern terms, we are likely to focus on statutes alone. Nevertheless, how a society is constituted is likely to depend heavily on religion and morality as interpreted by judges and scholars. It is hardly surprising that in a traditional theocratic society the "will" of the people, which is really just the preference of most members of the group, carried little weight; the "law" was traditional or scriptural. As Montesquieu points out, the need for people living together in society brings laws, and the preferences of groups, to the forefront–but not until the group has been constituted as a nation, a city-state, or a tribe.

How does "constitution" take place? At this point, political theorists use an artifice, conjuring a time before the constitution. This conjectural creation myth goes by several names, including "state of nature" or "original position," and it turns out to be very useful in conceiving the constitutive moment.

COERCION AND THE CONSTITUTIONAL MOMENT

Thomas Hobbes called the unconstituted group the "state of nature."[6] John Rawls (1971) called it the "original position," when rules and institutions were to be decided behind a "veil of ignorance" ensuring that only principles of justice influence the reason of the citizens. If citizens constituted themselves without knowing their position in the resulting society, the resulting rules would be just, because it would be "fair" in the sense that universal principles, not self-interest, would be the origin of the rules. This is the argument for "rule of law" that Socrates used to put off Crito.

Buchanan and Tullock (1962) imagine a constitutional "moment" when a group of individuals confront the problem of deciding how to decide. They impose two conditions, or qualifications, on the decision process. First, the choice must be *unanimous.*[7] This is a means of solving the infinite regress problem (how to decide, how to decide how to decide, etc.). Unanimity protects each individual, ensuring that no minority, no matter how small, is subjected to involuntary coercion. Second, the choice must be *disinterested,* or made without complete knowledge of the rules' effects on the chooser's welfare, much like the Rawlsian "original position."

Unanimity answers the question raised by Rousseau, in the quotation used to begin this chapter. How can a person be both free and yet bound by wills not his own? Because he consented. Anyone who voluntarily signs a contract expects to benefit.[8] However, he would benefit even more if he could cheat while other parties perform as promised. Since this is true for each potential signer, monitoring and enforcement are required, and it is in the interest of all the signers to ensure that the contract is enforced. The "state" might be one way of enforcing contracts, but there are other mechanisms of enforcement – posting a bond or hiring a private arbitrator – that need not entail a formal state apparatus. What is necessary for people to be able to make free choices for mutual benefit is the ability to sign binding contracts. And binding contracts require a threat of enforcement if the contract is breached. [9] As Hobbes said, "Covenants, without the Sword, are but Words, and of no strength to secure a man at all."

But is the *ex post* enforcement – force and forfeiture of property – coercive or voluntarily imposed? If I agreed to be bound, am I bound by wills not my own? There are two states of play, one before the signing of the contract and one after. Oliver Williamson (1979) claims contractual relations undergo a "fundamental transformation." Before a contract is signed, there is no coercion in the negotiation process. Each party can exit without harm. But after the contract is signed, exit from the agreement may be expensive and reneging on the contract triggers punishment. If threats are made in the pre-contract stage, that would be coercion.

The contract would never have been signed unless the there was an *ex ante* expectation that *ex post* sanctions would be threatened and imposed. All parties to the contract are being coerced voluntarily, as a means of committing to the terms of the contract, which we assume they want to do. As the quote beginning this chapter shows, Rousseau focused on this problem of reconciling freedom and coercion.[10] Coercion is justified in three steps:

(1) Citizens agree unanimously to the rules specified in the original contract. Each consents to laws passed under these *rules*, even if one does not like the *outcomes*.
(2) This unanimity requirement applies only to those who voluntarily join the contract. I need not agree. Then I must exit the group, because membership (and the consequent enjoyment of the benefits of membership) implies consent.[11]
(3) The transcendent truth embodied in the constitution is the "general will," or the self-interest of the collective, rightly understood. It would be irrational for me to want something different from that which I *should* want; if I disagree with the general will, I am mistaken or evil.[12]

Exactly 200 years later, almost to the day, Buchanan and Tullock (1962) argued that the third step is unnecessary: A voluntary contract gets the group everything it needs. There is still the problem that "membership implies consent," because it is easy to imagine that a citizen in a state may have no real options to leave.[13] This is a problem with no good solution. Any group must balance the externality of involuntarily including someone against the costs of negotiating unanimity. Buchanan and Tullock argue that true unanimous consent rule is very expensive in terms of transactions costs, because it encourages strategizing and efforts at hold-up.

If I contract for coercion, if I voluntarily agree to have someone else punish me for violating my promise, the resulting use of force is no longer coercion, at least not in the usual sense. In Homer's *Odyssey*, Odysseus "contracted" with his men to bind him to the mast, so that he could resist the songs of the seductive Sirens.[14] The solution shows the power of enforceable contracts: Odysseus has to find a way to *order* his men to *ignore his orders*. The ropes literally bind Odysseus to do what he wants himself to want to do, rather than what he knows he will want to do later when the song of the Sirens attracts him. Odysseus must be able to enter voluntarily into this contract to be coerced, or he would not have been truly free.

However, if you were on a passing ship, you would see Odysseus struggling with the ropes and begging to be set free. The crew (apparently) disobeys his command and busily binds him even tighter. Clearly, Odysseus wants to escape, but he is being held against his will. Should you try to help? Whom would you help? Odysseus, who involuntarily now wants to be set free? Or would you help the men trying to carry out the orders Odysseus gave back when he controlled his will, before the call of the Sirens robbed him of the power to make choices? Whose "will" would you validate if you intervene?

If a constitution is an agreement, and people become members by consenting to the contract, then the members of that group agree to be coerced because they expect to be better off as a cooperating group than they were as non-cooperating individuals. Binding Odysseus to the mast and then binding him even more tightly when he changes his mind (as he knew he would when he gave the orders to prevent his escape) is not coercion in the usual sense. This means that agreeing to suffer coercion at the hands of a group is potentially better for each individual in the group, compared to collections of individuals who cannot enforce agreements. The ability to enter into agreements, and to agree now to be punished later if the agreement is violated, is the essence of the constitution of groups.

Thomas Hobbes tried to use this logic to take an additional step, justifying not just a contract but also a state, ruled by a monarch or sovereign:

...that a man be willing, when others are so too, as far forth as for peace and defence of himself he shall think it necessary, to lay down this right to all things; and be contented with so much liberty against other men as he would allow other men against himself. For as long as every man holdeth this right, of doing anything he liketh; so long are all men in the condition of war. But if other men will not lay down their right, as well as he, then there is no reason for anyone to divest himself of his...

For he that performs first has no assurance the other will perform after; because the bonds of words are too weak to bridle men's ambition, avarice, anger, and other Passions, without the fear of some coercive Power. ... But in a civil estate, where there is a Power set up to constrain those that would otherwise violate their faith, that fear is no more reasonable; and for that cause, he which by the Covenant is to perform first, is obliged so to do (Chapter 14).

Hobbes was quite correct that the ability to sign binding contracts is necessary for human survival and group flourishing. However, all he really established was to justify some kind of governance, which would improve the welfare of citizens over an anarchic state of nature. He does not say how the group would select *among* all the many kinds of governance structures, some private and some involving direct state action, that might be constituted? Hobbes showed that almost *any* viable constituted group is better than his "state of nature."[15] For a given group, however, the Hobbesian argument can provide no guidance about *which* constitution to select.

The pure contractarian answer extends the Hobbesian idea, but remains agnostic about what a particular collection of individuals would, or should, choose. The "best" agreement is whatever the parties to the particular exchange situation choose to agree on, knowing everything they know about local conditions and their own needs. The individuals constituting the group will use their moral intuitions in choosing the rules, and the rules become norms that guide moral intuitions.[16] To be free, the group has to be free to choose its contract, and then be free to enforce that contract. Maybe there is a state, maybe there is not. All that is necessary for politics to be important is that there is a group, and an enforceable contract.

After the group is constituted, of course, many people will look for ways to cheat, just as Odysseus did (and knew he would). After the agreement, people will try to escape the punishment they promised to accept. If they are caught, they will protest that the punishment is against their will, because they would prefer that everyone else be bound by the promise but that they, individually, can escape. However, the consent, the *unanimous* consent, to the original contract means that the coercion was agreed to voluntarily. One way of understanding constitutions is that they, in some circumstances, allow groups to solve collective action problems that otherwise would prevent the capture of substantial gains from cooperation.[17]

Of course, if I did not agree to the contract, even if I am the only one who did not agree, then the coercion is not voluntary because I did not consent. This is why the qualification of unanimity, even if it is hypothetical, is central to constitutive arguments.[18] If I consent, I am not bound by wills not my own, and I am still free.

As we mentioned at the start of this section, there is a second requirement for a constitution to be valid: impartiality. Like the "veil of ignorance" of Rawls (1971), it amounts to requiring that decisions about rules be made in ignorance of particular consequences. The description of this ignorance given by Buchanan and Tullock looks like this:

Agreement seems more likely on general rules for collective choice than on the later choice to be made *within* the confines of certain agreed-on rules... Essential to the analysis is the presumption that the individual is *uncertain* as to what his own precise role will be in any one of the whole chain of later collective choices that will actually have to be made. ....[T]he individual will not find it advantageous to vote for rules that may promote sectional, class, or group interests because, by supposition, he is unable to predict the role that he will be playing in the actual collective decision-making process at any particular time in the future. He cannot predict with any degree of certainty whether he is more likely to be in a winning or losing coalition on any specific issue.. ...His own self-interest will lead him to choose rules that will maximize the utility of an individual in a series of collective decisions with his own preferences on the separate issues being more or less randomly distributed. (Buchanan and Tullock, 1962, p. 78; emphasis in original).

There is a striking difference between this conception of fairness and that defined by Rawls (1971: 61). The Rawlsian "distribution of primary goods" has a much more permanent and deterministic flavor. There are two steps: the liberty principle applies to choices about employment and production allocations, and then the difference principle is applied in limiting, or justifying, distributions of income, wealth, and power.

Clearly, Buchanan and Tullock are imagining a more dynamic and fluid process than what Rawls had in mind. The constitutive moment is a jumping-off point for a set of rules that will guide a society through political conflict, with groups coalescing and dissolving over time, in both cases by voluntary consent. Buchanan and Tullock wanted to foster the capture of mutual gains from exchange and cooperation in a social, group setting, while minimizing conflict, and conferring legitimacy on outcomes even when people disagree.

Rawls is rightly credited with developing the "original position" in a way that gave him analytical purchase of the problem of justice as fairness. Nevertheless, there were important precursors. Tomasi (2012), for example, calls Rawls's use of the idea "the unoriginal position" and points to a passage in Hayek that takes much the same logic and applies it to fairness in laws.[19] An even earlier "original position" can be found in Montesquieu.[20]

Every day one hears it said that it would be good if there were slaves among us. But, to judge this, one must not examine whether they would be useful to the small, rich, and voluptuous part of each nation; doubtless they would be useful to it; but, taking another point of view, *I do not believe that any one of those who make it up would want to draw lots to know who was to form the part of the nation that would be free and the one that would be enslaved.* Those who most speak in favor of slavery would hold it the most in horror, and the poorest of men would likewise find it horrible. Therefore, the cry for slavery is the cry of luxury and voluptuousness, and not that of the love of public felicity. Who can doubt that each man, individually, would not be quite content to be the master of the goods, the honor, and the life of others and that all his passions would not be awakened at once at this idea? Do you want to know whether the desires of each are legitimate in these things? Examine the desires of all. (Montesquieu, 1750 / 1989; Book XV, Chapter 9, p. 253; emphasis added).

Regardless of whether Rawls' "original position" was original with him (it appears it was not), the Rawlsian emphasis on "justice as fairness" is important. If the institutions of society, or the rules of a group, clearly are chosen to benefit some members and harm others, that constitution will not be seen as legitimate. Moreover, illegitimacy means that the contract cannot be enforced without great expense and constant turmoil. This has been recognized for thousands of years: Roman law asserted the principle that *Nemo iudex in causa sua*, or "no one can be a judge in his own case."

THE SOUL OF THE STATE

"the constitution is in a figure the life of the city."

Aristotle, *Politics*, Book IV, Part XI.

The Greek word that sometimes is translated to the English word "constitution" is *politeia*, but that simple translation is not correct. The meaning of *politeia* is better expressed as the self-defined identities, obligations, form of government, and rights of a citizen in a community, or *polis*. Some translators, in trying to capture the sense of the word, have claimed that the *politeia* is to a *polis* as the soul is to an organism, something that both organizes and animates the body. A town without a *politeia* is just a bunch of people and is not a community at all.

Aristotle illustrates the concept by exploring the effects of time. Is the nation the individual people, the physical space occupied by those people, or the *politeia*? What changes, and what stays the same?

…shall we say that while the race of inhabitants, as well as their place of abode, remain the same, the city is also the same, although the citizens are always dying and being born, as we call rivers and fountains the same, although the water is always flowing away and coming again? Or shall we say that the generations of men, like the rivers, are the same, but that the state changes? For, since the state is a partnership, and is a partnership of citizens in a constitution, when the form of government changes, and becomes different, then it may be supposed that the state is no longer the same… And if this is true it is evident that the *sameness of the state consists chiefly in the sameness of the constitution* [politeia], and it may be called or not called by the same name, whether the inhabitants are the same or entirely different. (*Politics*, Bk III, Part I; emphasis added).

Aristotle's proposal, that the group is the same so long as it acts and chooses according to the same *politeia*, is a useful benchmark. Nevertheless, to judge whether several constitutions are the same or different, we need a clear definition.

A *constitution* is both an agreement on principles, rules, and the structure of government, and (often) the document that records that agreement and makes it formal and visible to the world. A group can be constituted without a formal document, but a formal document without an actual agreement is never a constitution, no matter what it is called. There are five analytical problems with constitutions that we will address repeatedly. In the briefest possible terms, the key analytical problems of constitutional design are:

The fundamental transformation
Agenda manipulation
Revelation manipulation
Constraining domain
Inherited disequilibrium

We will briefly discuss each of these, as a means of illustrating the problems groups face in constituting themselves.

The fundamental transformation

Oliver Williamson (1979) first proposed this phrase in transactions costs economics, though the problem has been recognized for centuries. Starting from a situation of pure competition, both buyer and seller have many alternatives. But once the parties sign a contract, there is a "fundamental transformation" of the strategic situation. Each party to the contract is now one part of a bilateral monopoly with all the associated problems of hold-up and ex-post recontracting.

Government may fail to provide promised services, taxes may go up, and citizens may be arrested. Similarly, citizens or corporations may conceal income and assets, pollute the environment, cheat on the rules agreed on for deciding, and routinely break laws that citizens said in the constitution they wanted the government to enforce. Before the constitution was signed, there were many different arrangements possible, but after the constitution is in place, all sides may take considerable advantage of the costs of exit facing their partners.[21] That is the reason why one so often hears some version of "Well, if you don't like it, just leave!" from groups who are forcing change within a system.

One party can threaten not to perform as agreed without some additional payment or consideration, something that is not part of the signed contract. The damaged party can object ("But that's not what we agreed!"), of course. The problem is that monitoring and enforcement of the "agreement" is expensive. The damaged party is free to leave, or sign a new contract with someone else, but either of these actions would be even more expensive than conceding to the first party. In any case, while the disagreement is adjudicated, or a new agreement signed, the damaged party has no means of obtaining services, which may be the most expensive outcome of all. A "good" constitution limits the incentives to engage in ex post recontracting by making dispute resolution transparent and predictable.

Agenda manipulation

As we will see in later chapters, the rules governing voting can change the outcome of voting, even with a fixed set of individual preferences. Consequently, and in certain situations (for example, if citizens all vote sincerely), choosing a chair or parliamentary officer can be tantamount to choosing a dictator. For this reason, voting procedures that look good on paper may cause a constitutional system to collapse in war and recrimination.

That is exactly what happens to many constitutional systems: The problem of design is as much engineering as ethics. Although the *politeia* must embody the ethical and normative "soul" of the people, it also must be engineered to prevent manipulation and control of the agenda. Ideally, the "best" voting system would be like Caesar's wife: above reproach.[22] The problem, as we will see in Chapters 3 and 4, is that this is literally impossible: All voting systems can be manipulated; no voting system is strategy proof.[23] The "best" voting system may simply be the one that people understand and trust.

Revelation manipulation

Voters are not helpless. When faced with agenda manipulation or even the suspicion of it, citizens can practice a deception of their own: revelation manipulation, or strategic voting. It would be naïve to expect people to vote their honest preferences when strategic voting is more likely to satisfy those preferences. When the French Academy of Sciences made Napoleon an "honorary" member, he immediately recommended a change in its voting procedure. The system they were using was based on the ideas of Jean-Charles, Chevalier de Borda (1733–1799). The "Borda Count" was much more open to revelation manipulation than most types of voting, because voters were asked to rank each candidate. Borda allegedly defended his system by sniffing, "My scheme is intended only for honest men."[24]

Interestingly, revelation manipulation is more than simple dishonesty. It blunts the power of agenda manipulation, unless (as we shall see) the agenda controller can eliminate certain options. If choosers can vote strategically, the agenda controller can no longer reliably achieve his most preferred new outcome. However, the agenda controller may still be able to prevent change, privileging the status quo.

Constraining domain

Democracies are not simply nations with majority rule constitutions. Any democracy must balance responsiveness to the will of the majority against protection for fundamental rights of individuals. In modern terms, laws, not majorities, rule a democracy. But this is not just a modern problem. The balancing of law versus mass will has been one of the core difficulties of constitutional design for thousands of years. Consequently, morals and traditions (the "law") and the legislative will of the people may be different, perhaps even opposed. If the majority is always able to act on its impulses, there is no constitution at all, only a mob.

The interests of the parties to the constitutional contract are in conflict, looking across the time divide before and after the fundamental transformation. *Before* the constitution is agreed upon, each citizen tries to design a set of rules that offer general protections, because no one knows what his or her interests will be. *After* the rules are adopted, groups of citizens try to use strategies within – and possibly even outside – the rules to impose their will on others.[25]

Consider the "right" to freedom of speech. By definition, a democracy is unlikely to interfere with the rights of the majority to free speech. The protection, if there is one, also must shelter the speech rights of minorities. Interestingly, two of the first attempts to frame this right – balancing majorities and individuals – were written just a few weeks apart, in the late summer of 1789.

In August of 1789, the French were wrestling with the problem of stating the basic rights all citizens had and that no one could legitimately take away. Their version of the freedom of religion, speech, and the press (from the "Declaration of the Rights of Man"[26]), passed August 26, 1789, looked like this:

10. No one is to be disquieted because of his opinions, even religious, *provided their manifestation does not disturb the public order established by law*.
11. Free communication of ideas and opinions is one of the most precious of the rights of man. Consequently, every citizen may speak, write, and print freely *subject to responsibility for the abuse of such liberty in the cases determined by law*.

We have added italics to clarify just how odd the language is. Number 10 says that citizens can have any religious opinion they want so long as it is not against the law. Number 11 says that citizens can say or print anything they want, again so long as it is not against the law. That does not seem like much protection, for if the right is a fundamental *individual* right, citizens should be able to exercise the right, *even if the majority wants to pass a law* against it.

The U.S. House of Representatives passed an alternative just four days earlier, on August 22, 1789. Due to distances and delays in communication, a conference committee revised and finalized the U.S. version on September 25, 1789. The U.S. version of the fundamental right is the First Amendment:

Congress shall make no law respecting an establishment of religion, or prohibiting the free exercise thereof; or abridging the freedom of speech, or of the press; or the right of the people peaceably to assemble, and to petition the government for a redress of grievances.

That is an explicit protection against the majority. France said "Don't break the law," but the U.S. said "Don't *make* the law." Since this restriction was an amendment added directly to the Constitution, some individual choices about what to say or write are protected from government interference even in those in instances where the majority of people would disagree with those choices. The paradox lies in the fact that democratic constitutions must contain anti-majoritarian elements while circumscribing the domain appropriate for collective choice, preserving and protecting everything outside that domain for private choice.[27]

Inherited disequilibrium

Earlier, we noted that revelation manipulation might be an effective curb to the power of agenda manipulation. However, there is a deeper problem: A fundamental disagreement about the desirability of outcomes can be transported into fundamental disagreements about the institutions through which outcomes will be chosen.

Citizens have beliefs – right, wrong, or simply confused – about the structures of choice (presidential system versus parliament, first past the post versus proportional representation, and so on) that lead to their most desired outcomes. If there is no substantial agreement about outcomes, the debate over the institutions to place into the constitution will "inherit" this indeterminacy. Riker (1980) reached this conclusion:

> In the long run, outcomes are the consequence not only of institutions and tastes, but also of the political skill and artistry of those who manipulate agenda, formulate and reformulate questions, generate "false" issues, etc., in order to exploit the disequilibrium of tastes for their own advantage. And just what combination of institutions, tastes, and artistry will appear in any given political system is, it seems to me, as unpredictable as poetry. (p. 445).

ANALYTICAL POLITICS

In this book, we look at how *groups* choose. For many important political processes, that means we are starting in the middle. The analysis is useful for collections of people who have already constituted themselves as a group: those who have decided to make a group choice and are now trying to decide just how to do that. For many societies, as with Lewis and Clark, it is clear that the group must stay together and choose. But for other situations – those that have occurred throughout human history– there are other options, which include leaving the group or fighting within the group for control (Hirschman, 1970). We will not take up those questions – not because they are unimportant, but because they represent a different approach to politics.

TERMS

Agenda Manipulation
Amendment Process
Citizenship and Citizen Obligation
Collective Domain
Constitutions
Constitutive Moment
Constraining Domain
Decision Rule
Epistemology

Exit
Fundamental transformation
Groups / Collective Choice
Inherited Disequilibrium
Ontology
Organization Chart
Original Position
Revelation Manipulation
Roving Bandit
Sovereignty
Stationary Bandit

PROBLEMS FOR CHAPTER 2

2.1 What are the minimal elements for a set of rules to be a "constitution?" What do you think is the best decision rule for adopting the constitution in the first place? What is the best rule for changing the constitution? What else should a constitution contain, beyond the minimal "deciding how to decide" components?

2.2 What circumstances might lead a roving bandit to become a stationary bandit? What are the differences between a stationary bandit and a legitimately constituted government?

2.3 Imagine that you were a member of a group of four people whose job it is to make up a new board game. After you make up the game, four people have to play the game every day for a year. How would you decide how to choose rules, and to resolve disagreements over what the rules should be? Does it matter if the four people making up the rules will also be playing the game, or if the players are a different four people from the rule-makers?

3

Choosing in Groups: An Intuitive Presentation

The general will rules in society as the private will governs each separate individual. Maximilien Robespierre (attributed, 1791)

From the point of view of seeking a consensus of the moral imperative of individuals, such consensus being assumed to exist, the problem of choosing an electoral or other choice mechanism, or, more broadly, of choosing a social structure, assumes an entirely different form from that discussed in the greater part of this study. The essential problem becomes that of choosing our mechanism so as best to bring the pragmatic imperative into coincidence with the moral. It is from this point of view that Rousseau discusses the relative merits of different forms of government.

In this aspect, the case for democracy rests on the argument that free discussion and expression of opinion are the most suitable techniques of arriving at the moral imperative implicitly common to all. Voting, from this point of view, is not a device whereby each individual expresses his personal interests, but rather where each individual gives his opinion of the general will. Arrow (1963: 85)

WHAT DOES "ONE" WANT? WHAT DO "WE" WANT?

Imagine that three people – Eugene, Justin, and Willow – want to have lunch, and they are a *constituted* group, so they want to have lunch *together*. The group finds itself in the wholesale produce district. There is not enough time to leave and return before one group member has an important appointment. There are no restaurants or retail grocers nearby, and all they can do is buy a bushel of *one kind* of food. If (but *only* if) they pool their money, they will be able to buy a bushel of one of the three types of food available: apples, broccoli, or carrots. If they cannot agree, they cannot buy anything; if they do agree, they can buy only that one thing.

How might our three hungry, rational people approach this problem? The first step for each is personal: What do I want? To decide this, each person consults an inner guide to choice (called "preference"). Before continuing with our example, we must take a moment and define what we mean by preference.

PREFERENCES

For the analytical political theorist, preferences are one of the building blocks of any theory. A "thin" preference is an unspecified ordering, from best to worst, of the possible alternatives, possibly allowing for the possibilities of ties or indifference. This conception of preferences is so useful partly because the actual subjective content of the preference is arbitrary, so describing preference in this way means no loss of generality.

In our three-person food bushel example, this would mean that each person has a favorite food, a least favorite food, and other foods ranked in between, if there are no ties. We do not need to know what those are; we just call this ordering "preference." It is important that the "thin" preference is rational, but the content of the preference itself is not important to the general problem. All that is required for rationality is that the person can (a) choose between any two alternatives, calling one or the other better, or calling them equally good, and (b) order all the alternatives from "best" to "worst" (with ties possible) without the contradictions or "loops" that we will later call intransitivities.

"Thick" conceptions of preference fill in the content of the ranking or ordering with the idiosyncratic, subjective preference of the chooser. Where do such preferences come from? Nearly everywhere: inherited from your parents, learned from the people who raised you, acquired through experience from your peers, and absorbed from school, newspapers, and the internet. Your political preferences are the entire complex of tastes, judgments, attitudes, prejudices, and beliefs that make you who you are. Where preferences come from and how they change (or do not) is one of the core questions in the social sciences.[1]

Analytical political theorists often tackle this problem by assuming preferences are "exogenous," coming from outside (and before) our analysis, and are relatively fixed. We start with a *group* – already somehow constituted – whose members have *preferences* defined over a fixed set of *alternatives*. Each of the three implicit problems (How was the *group* constituted? Where did these *preferences* come from? How were the *alternatives* defined, and limited, and why are some alternatives considered and others excluded?) is an interesting question in its own right. However, the problem we focus on assumes those three sets of questions are already answered. Then we ask: How do members of a group express their preferences through some kind of decision rule that results in the selection of a single legitimate "choice" from a given set of alternatives?

If there were three alternatives, say A, B, and C, an analyst would ask you to "order" them, meaning, "rank them from best to worst." You might say you like B best, then C, and then you like A least. Therefore, your preference would be B is better than C, B is better than A, and C is better than A. These rankings may be complex and based on several considerations; for example, our chooser might prefer donuts to broccoli, in terms of taste and enjoyment. However, taking everything (nutrition, calories, diabetes, etc.) into consideration, that chooser picks broccoli over donuts.

Storing your ranking in the form of a preference ordering is simple, but extremely useful. We do not need to know your *reasons*; we just know how you rank alternatives. Therefore, when we say "preferences," all we mean is "a ranking over alternatives." Of course, this means that two people who have the same preference (say, "B is better than C is better than A") might have completely different reasons. This fact is one of most important aspects of group formation, coalition building, and politics generally: preferences may be contingent on many other factors. If many of us agree that one alternative is better than another, we have a possible basis for cooperative action. That is why we use "ranking" as a way of thinking about "preference," which is actually a much more complex subject.

USING PREFERENCES TO PREDICT GROUP CHOICES

Our goal here is to move from individual preference to group choice. It turns out that to define *group choice*, we really only need three things: an expression of the *individual preference orderings* of the members of the group, the *choice set* (or the list of alternatives that might be feasibly chosen), and the *decision rule* that the group will use. As we discussed earlier, it would be a mistake think these three things define *group preference*; all we can do is represent *group choice*. The following example will illustrate the difference.

Recall our three friends – Eugene, Justin, and Willow – trying to decide on lunch. They can buy only a bushel of one kind of food, so they must pool their money and act as a group. There are three types of food available: apples, broccoli, and carrots. If they cannot agree, they can't buy anything and they will all go hungry.

The problem would be easy, of course, if they all agreed that carrots were best. The group choice problem rests on solving problems of *disagreement* in a way that everyone agrees is legitimate. So, imagine that these are the thick (e.g., fully described) preference orderings for each person.

EUGENE: Apples are best, Broccoli is okay, Carrots are not good.
JUSTIN: Broccoli is best, Carrots are okay, Apples are not good
WILLOW: Carrots are best, Apples are okay, Broccoli is not good

If we combine these in one table, the preference rankings look like the columns in Table 3.1:

TABLE 3.1. *Three choosers rank alternatives*

Chooser	Eugene	Justin	Willow
Best	A	B	C
Middle	B	C	A
Worst	C	A	B

We now have the first and second elements of the group choice problem settled. The only *alternatives* are apples, broccoli, or carrots. The table above contains the individual *preferences* (the ranking of alternatives). All we need to know now is the *decision rule*. This is the tricky part, unless the group already has well established rules and procedures. If the group has not decided how to decide, it is not fully constituted. The group must decide how to decide how to decide.

Any discussion based on individual preferences will quickly prove futile. If, for example, Eugene tells Justin, "Apples are good," Justin will hear "I, Eugene, like apples!" Since Justin has his own tastes in food, Eugene's claim will not persuade Justin to change his view of apples, which he detests. "*Eugene* likes apples" is not a persuasive argument for the problem "Does *Justin* like apples?" if Justin thinks the answer is "no."[2]

A philosopher might say that the problem in such cases is that there is no "fact of the matter." When it comes to taste in foods, it makes no sense to say that something is universally "better" than something else. Preferences depend on taste, and people have different tastes.

We cannot answer the question "what is the best choice for the group?" using purely a priori reasons, because the choice will be based on tastes, and people disagree.[3] After arguing for a while, our three choosers might decide to do resort to a way of resolving the disagreement. They might put it to a vote.

In the first round, they might each cast one vote for their first choice. But this would result in a three-way tie, since each alternative would receive one vote. They must choose in some other way. Suppose someone suggests the "Vegetable, Then Fruit, Agenda:"

Carrots and Broccoli are both vegetables. Let's choose the vegetable we like best, as a group, and then we will vote that food against the fruit, Apples. The winner of that second vote will be our favorite, our group choice.

That seems reasonable, and fair. The vote for the "best vegetable" is taken, and it comes out 2–1 in favor of Broccoli.

Broccoli	Carrots
Eugene	Willow
Justin	

All that remains is to settle the contest of Broccoli, the better vegetable, against Apples.

Broccoli	Apples
Justin	Willow
	Eugene

Apples! The group pools its money and buys a crate of apples. This is a fair outcome, because each alternative had a fair chance. The group used standard democratic procedures to choose, and so even Justin, who detests Apples, must accept the outcome. They agreed on rules, therefore no one can complain just because he or she does not like the outcome. Everyone agreed to be part of the group that constituted itself to choose via the "Better Vegetable, then Fruit, Agenda," and now the choice is binding on everyone. The group choice is Apples.

PROCEDURES COUNT AS MUCH AS PREFERENCES

The previous example is unsettling. Is it really so easy to generate consensus out of fundamental disagreement? After all, the three people disagreed about as much as was humanly possible, and yet it was easy to find a group choice. We used the *individual* preferences, and *majority rule*, along with a *particular agenda* – first Broccoli versus Carrots, then the winner against Apples – to come to the decision. Was anything about the agenda odd? Would a different agenda lead to a different outcome?

Obviously, a different set of preferences would lead to a different outcome. So the real question is, could changing the procedure change the result even though the preferences are held constant? Yes: Different procedures often yield different outcomes, even if preferences stay the same. The members' preferences alone do not constitute the group. *The constitution of the group must also specify the decision rule,* and that decision rule can have as big an impact on outcomes as the preferences of group members. Different members make for a different group. Different procedures make for a different group. Members and procedures characterize groups.

We hypothesized that someone might logically suggest the above "Vegetable Proposal." Perhaps it *seems* logical. But a look at the table gives you a hint about who probably proposed that rule, which led to a group choice of Apples. Who was it? It is likely the person whose individual choice would be Apples, from Table 3.1.

Eugene! If he knew everyone's preferences from the table, he knew that if Broccoli is voted against Carrots, Broccoli wins. Then Apples will beat Broccoli. Choosing this *agenda* – assuming everyone votes honestly – is the same as choosing the *outcome*, Apples.

The point is that there are many "logical" reasons, and many different agendas. Each chooser has self-interested reasons for choosing an agenda because different agendas lead to different outcomes. Therefore, it really was too easy to generate a consensus after all, because there is no consensus. With full information and sincere voting, agenda control is tantamount to dictatorship.

To see this, suppose someone proposes a different, though still logical, decision rule: "Air First, Then Dirt."

Apples and Broccoli both grow above ground, while Carrots are root vege-tables. Let's choose the food that grows up in the air that we like best as a group, and then we will vote that food against the one that grows in the dirt, Carrots. The winner of that second vote will be our favorite, our group choice.

The first vote is between the choices that grow up in the air, Apples v. Broccoli. It comes out 2–1 in favor of Apples.

Apples	Broccoli
Eugene	Justin
Willow	

Then we vote the "air" winner, Apples, against the below ground alternative, Carrots.

Apples	Carrots
Eugene	Justin
	Willow

Now, the group – the same group, with the same preferences – chooses Carrots. Who proposed the "Air First, Then Dirt" agenda? Probably Willow, since Carrots are her first preference. She may have proposed it earnestly, with a straight face, and marshaled evidence for why this decision rule, and no other, was ethical and logical. She may even have honestly believed the argument that she was making. But that agenda led to her most-preferred outcome, just as if she were dictator.

A justification for the third agenda, voting Apples against Carrots, with the winner facing Broccoli, is an exercise at the end of this chapter.

STRATEGIC VOTING

The requirement that people vote *honestly* – that they sincerely represent their preferences in the way they vote – is not innocuous. In the previous chapter, we recounted how Borda insisted that people would be "honest." Given the simple analysis we just went through, it should be easy to see why Napoleon laughed at the idea that people could be reliably honest.

It is not clear that dishonesty is a bad thing, however. Consider the first example we gave earlier of the power of an agenda choice. The rationale was "Vegetable First, Then Fruit," so Broccoli was voted against Carrots in the first round, with the winner facing Apples.

What would happen in the first round if we actually tried this, and if the choosers had read up to this point? Look at Table 3.1, and assume that all three choosers know their own preferences and everyone else's preferences: [4] Justin really hates Apples. He would like to have Broccoli, of course, but he also cares about avoiding Apples, so Carrots are not a bad outcome for him.

When the vote for the "best vegetable" is taken, Justin thinks ahead, and realizes that if he votes for Broccoli over Carrots, as his *honest* preference dictates, the result in the second round will be that Apples will win. In effect, a vote for Broccoli is *really* a vote for Apples. Therefore, in the first round he changes his vote to Carrots:

Broccoli	Carrots
Eugene	Willow
~~Justin~~	Justin

Carrots are now the "best vegetable," and, just as Justin foresaw, when the final vote is taken, Carrots wins.

Carrots	Apples
Willow	Eugene
Justin	

What this means is that when Eugene announces the agenda, it appears that the electorate faces a choice between Broccoli and Carrots. However, everyone knows that there will be another vote of the first-round winner against Apples. Two of the choosers, Willow and Eugene, have no opportunity to behave strategically. However, Justin, as Figure 3.1 illustrates, can vote strategically:

It makes no sense to vote strategically in the final round, because then all votes are for actual outcomes. However, for any vote before the last, the choice is more complex. Justin must look down the decision tree that each choice implies, and then work by backward induction to select the best *vote* (from his perspective) rather than the best food. If Justin votes honestly, that will result in Apples being chosen for certain, assuming that Willow and Eugene vote in their own self-interest in the final round. So Justin might vote strategically (dashed line) rather than sincerely (solid line) in the first round.

But that means that Eugene, who made the seemingly logical – but actually strategic – "Vegetable Proposal," is thwarted in his attempt to dupe the group into choosing Apples, and ends up losing because Justin can use

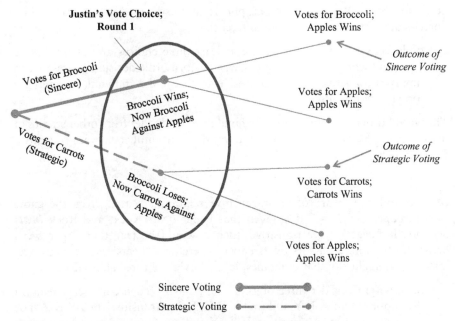

Justin's Vote Choice; Round 1

Votes for Broccoli; Apples Wins

Outcome of Sincere Voting

Votes for Broccoli (Sincere)

Broccoli Wins; Now Broccoli Against Apples

Votes for Apples; Apples Wins

Votes for Carrots (Strategic)

Outcome of Strategic Voting

Broccoli Loses; Now Carrots Against Apples

Votes for Carrots; Carrots Wins

Votes for Apples; Apples Wins

Sincere Voting ●━━━━━●

Strategic Voting ●— — —●

FIGURE 3.1. Strategic voting in the "Vegetable first, then fruit" agenda

the counterstrategy of voting for Carrots instead of Broccoli in the first round. Once the agenda is set, there is nothing Eugene can do about it. Changing his vote in either round cannot benefit Eugene. Therefore, the group choice is Carrots. Unfortunately, that is the *least* preferred outcome from the perspective of Eugene, who proposed the tricky agenda in the first place.[5]

THE PARADOX OF CONDORCET

The above analysis is generic; it is not true only for Apples, Broccoli, and Carrots. You can substitute any other set of alternatives for A, B, and C and the possibility of this kind of indeterminacy arises. Under what circumstances can these kinds of outcomes arise? Three conditions are required:

- Three or more choices
- Three or more choosers
- Disagreement of a particular kind, when neither persuasion nor compromise is possible

Under these conditions, it may not be possible for a group to make a determinate, ethically defensible choice from a set of alternatives using majority rule. Some people refer to this finding as "Condorcet's Paradox" after the Marquis de Condorcet (1785, 1788). To paraphrase, and using modern language (Condorcet's understanding was quite different):

> **Condorcet's Paradox:** If there are at least three choices and at least three choosers who disagree, then pairwise majority rule decision processes can imply intransitive group choices, even if all the individual preference orders are transitive.

The word "transitive" above may be familiar to the reader from other studies of mathematics. Relations of numbers along the real number line are transitive, for example:

$$7 > 5 \text{ and } 5 > 3 \text{ so } 7 > 3$$

Most people are aware of an intransitive relation, "beats," from the game "Rock, Paper, Scissors." It is given that Paper *beats* Rock, and Rock *beats* Scissors. If "beats" were transitive, then it would be true that Paper *beats* Scissors. Of course, Scissors *beats* Paper. Therefore, "beats" is not transitive. Instead, we might say that outcomes "cycle" over the three alternatives.

> **Transitivity:** Consider three objects X, Y, and Z. Then consider a relation R. Suppose that X R Y and that Y R Z. If R is transitive then X R Z. For example, equality is transitive: If X=Y and Y=Z, then it must be true that X=Z.
>
> **Cycle:** If the relation among three alternatives X, Y, and Z is such that X R Y, Y R Z, and Z R X, then the relation among the three alternatives defines a cycle.

It is clear why this is called a cycle: X R Y R Z R X RY R Z...forever, round and round, like Rock, Paper, Scissors. Zach Weiner, who draws the web cartoon *Saturday Morning Breakfast Cereal*, recognized the problem, and also the problem of agenda control (Figure 3.2).

The young woman is trying to change the rules of the game, by assuming that the aggregate choice over Rock, Paper, and Scissors should be transitive. Of course, if we take her reasoning seriously, then every play both beats, and is beaten by, every other play, because Rock, Paper, Scissors describes a cycle. Each play both beats, and is beaten by, *itself*, if you follow the cycle around. If you think group decisions should be "rational," this is disturbing: there is no "best" alternative, and – worse –each alternative is strictly better than itself.

INDIVIDUAL PREFERENCES ARE TRANSITIVE, BUT GROUP CHOICES NEED NOT BE

Condorcet's Paradox is a problem with the transitivity of the pairwise choices expressed by a *group* over a sequence of decisions. There is no cycle in the preference of any individual – because each individual's preferences are

FIGURE 3.2. An example of Rules and Cycles

transitive – but there is a *cycling majority*. If you think democracy is "rule by the majority," you have to ask which majority. One majority prefers X to Y, another majority prefers Y to Z, and a third majority prefers Z to X. If you accept the will of one or two of these majorities, you must violate the will of the other majority. It is impossible to make a single determinate choice and respect the "will" of all three majorities.

There is no reason, however, to conclude that such a group is in any way "irrational," because there is no particular reason to expect that the overall "preference order" constructed from the pairwise choices of the group would be a transitive *preference ordering* in the first place. Groups are different from individuals, because groups are collections of individuals who can disagree.[6]

It is worth pointing out that although we call the result "Condorcet's Paradox," Condorcet himself was working on a different problem, which he called "inconsistencies." He was interested in decision rules that would always select a special kind of alternative if the alternative existed: an alternative that would defeat all other alternatives in a sequence of pairwise votes. In his honor, we now call such an alternative a "Condorcet winner."

Condorcet winner: An alternative X which, when compared with any other feasible alternative Y, is preferred by at least half of the voters.

Given that definition, we can restate the problem: Condorcet was concerned with identifying a decision rule for democracies such that the Condorcet winner always would be selected if the Condorcet winner exists. If there is no Condorcet winner, then the outcome depends on the decision rule, which Condorcet did not think was very interesting.

Condorcet's intuition (and it is still plausible nearly 250 years later) is that "Choose the Condorcet winner if it exists" is a useful standard for judging decision rules. If a Condorcet winner does exist, then we should select that outcome, regardless of how the choice is carried out. To put it differently, voting procedures that fail to discover the Condorcet winner, if one exists, are bad voting procedures and should not be used.

However, much of the more recent research has focused on the opposite concern: how to choose when there is *no* Condorcet winner. Given that there is no Condorcet winner, what does it mean for the legitimacy of group choice?

In our example, Apples defeats Broccoli defeats Carrots defeats Apples in pairwise majority-rule elections. There is no Condorcet winner. What that means is that although all the preference orderings of the choosers are transitive, the ordering of the choice itself is intransitive.

A majority is opposed to every feasible alternative, but there is no alternative that all majorities prefer. That is the essence of what we now call Condorcet's Paradox. [7]

Were it not for the work of intellectual historians investigating the origin of the idea, Condorcet's advances might have been lost in the cobwebs of antiquity. Duncan Black, while researching his *The Theory of Committees and Elections* (1958), discovered the contributions of Condorcet, Borda, Nanson, and Dodgson, among others.

Interestingly, though, it turns out that Condorcet was not the first to lay out the problem, though we now credit it to him. In a remarkable piece of scholarship in the history of ideas, McLean and London argue:

the theory has in fact been discovered four times and lost three times. Ramon Lull (c1235–1315) proposed a Condorcet method (should we now call it a Lull method?) of pairwise comparisons; Nicolas of Cusa (1401–1464), also called Nicolas Cusanus, proposed a Borda (Cusanus?) method. Both writers discuss the problem of manipulation, Cusanus extensively. (McLean and London, 1990, p. 99).

McLean and London make an interesting argument: Representative democracy as we now think of it did not begin with the Greeks because they made most of their decisions, at least for selecting officials, by lot (chance) or by simple voting procedures. The constitution of the Athenian voting assembly, for example, only allowed for "up or down" votes on questions of policy; there were no amendments, or votes among competing alternatives. The Greeks were uninterested in what we now think of as "social choice," or devising fair rules for making complex choices. However, they never faced the "three alternatives, three choosers, disagreement" conditions where voting rules become crucial.

The problem of choosing among three or more alternatives, however, was well established by the Middle Ages, and McLean found evidence that people worried about the problem in a variety of medieval contexts, including choosing Holy Roman emperors, popes, and doges of Venice. Orders of monks and nuns had to "constitute" themselves as groups by choosing decision rules, and a study of their writings reveals a deep understanding of the problem of indeterminacy.

Lull assumed that the problem was epistemological, discovering a hidden truth – for the monks, understandably, that meant, "God's will," – that all choosers believed existed. His first effort to describe the problem, written in Mallorca between 1273 and 1275, was actually called, "The Art of Finding the Truth,"[8] assuming that there is an objectively best candidate or right policy.

We now know things may be more complicated than that. The problem may not be reducible to epistemology, because no objectively "best policy" or "best candidate" may exist. Situations with three choices and three choosers who disagree lead to two much larger problems, problems that will be important parts of our explanations of institutions and their value in later chapters. The two problems are *manipulability* and *chaos*.

SOCIAL CHOICE: DISCOVERING THE GENERAL WILL,
OR MAKING A DECISION?

It is a common belief that aggregating preferences by majority rule yields an outcome that is a social optimum, provided the decision rule used by the group is the correct one. But what if the problem is not the *discovery*, but rather the *existence*, of a "general will"? That is the question raised by Condorcet's Paradox, most usefully thought of in "if-then" form:

If there is no Condorcet winner or otherwise determinate or morally defensible choice among alternatives based on preferences:

Then outcomes will be either imposed (a result of agenda control or political power, i.e., manipulation) or arbitrary (an idiosyncratic product of essentially random institutions, i.e., chaos).

Cycling and Manipulability: Many groups would likely accept the decision process ("Vegetable First, Then Fruit") outlined above. Perhaps a parliamentary officer, a chairperson, or some respected citizen is in a position to impose an agenda (agenda control). Alternatively, perhaps there is long custom, or even a formal rule, that requires that the votes be conducted in this order (structural or institutional equilibrium). The essential thing to recognize is *there is no uniquely defensible mapping from preferences into outcomes.*

Influencing the agenda or strategically misrepresenting preferences can manipulate any decision rule other than unanimity. (Gibbard, 1973; Satterthwaite, 1975). If people do not vote strategically, the agenda controller as a kind of dictator may impose the outcome. But if people do vote strategically, fibbing about what they want as a way of avoiding what they hate, the information being aggregated is based on lies and deception. Either way, it is hard to call such results "democratic" in the way that normative political theorists use the term.

Indeterminacy: The second, deeper problem is that democratic choice is fundamentally indeterminate. This indeterminacy metastasizes into the choice of voting mechanism. There are many possible ways to add up votes, mapping preferences into outcomes, and there is no obvious way to select one over the other on purely procedural grounds. Assessing analytical political theorists' discoveries about voting processes, William Riker (1982) put it this way:

> We should never take the results of any method always to be a fair and true amalgamation of voters' judgments. Doubtless the results often are fair and true; but unfortunately, we almost never know whether they are or not. Consequently, we should not generally assume that the methods produce true and fair amalgamations. We should think of the methods, I believe, simply as convenient ways of doing business, useful but flawed. This gives them all a place in the world, but it makes none of them sacrosanct. (p. 113)

No matter how an outcome is chosen – and the group must do *something*, even if only because failing to make a choice is still something – an actual majority will favor some other feasible alternative. This is not the same as cycling. It is fundamental chaos, which opens up the process to violence and civil unrest. The difference between cycling and indeterminacy has been recognized in the literature for some time. As Przeworski (2003: 10) puts it:

> The word "cycling" is banned from this book. Nothing "cycles" here. This paragraph does not describe how proposals will be made but only a property of the function that transforms individual preferences into a collective one. All that we have learned is that this function fails to pick a unique equilibrium.

Gerald Mackie (2004) goes further. He argues that the reliance on the problem of "cycles" is intellectually dishonest, because cycles are rarely (Mackie would say almost never) observed in real democracies of large or small scale. Mackie would credit Buchanan's claim that the problem of choosing in groups is not the same as adding up separate, self-interested preferences. But Mackie is much more optimistic about the ability of groups to make choices, because the nature of choosing in groups is for him fundamentally different from simply adding up preferences of individuals.

The problem is deeper than choosing the best rule; it lies in the fundamental indeterminacy of choosing in groups: In a cycle, a majority opposes every alternative. Justice, fairness, whatever rules you want to impose, do not change the fact that the group has to choose *something*, just one something, from the set of alternatives. Once they have chosen, no matter the decision rule selected, there will be a majority that wanted something else and is likely to blame the current winners for cheating. The cycle of revolution and new winner, revolution and new winner, has no logical stopping point. Given the conditions defined above, where people form alliances to choose something, there is by definition a majority opposed to every alternative. Democracy can lead to chaos, and societies do not like chaos. In fact, they dislike it so much that they might even look to a dictator to take command.

Consider the period of the "Convention" in post-Revolutionary France, from September 1792 through September 1795. There were three factions contending for power, none of whom controlled a majority. In the early portion of the Convention, until June 1793, the Girondins, the conservative (by revolutionary standards) faction from the southwest, dominated the government. However, the radical Jacobins, based in the Paris Commune, engineered a takeover of the assembly by forming a majority coalition with the more passive liberals. This "Terror" lasted from June 1793 through July 1794.

Then, on the Ninth of Thermidor (after the Convention had renamed the months, and modestly reset the calendar from year 1791 to 0), the coalition shifted again. The majority turned on the Jacobins, arresting and executing Robespierre and his supporters. Because the Jacobins themselves did not constitute a majority, their excesses and abuses of power enabled a new majority coalition to form and remove them from power.

In the period after Thermidor, factional discord destroyed any coherence in political conflict. The stakes were too high because winning one day almost certainly meant revolution and execution in a few months as the cycle of politics turned.

By the end of 1795, a new Constitution had been written. The Convention was dissolved, and a new governing body called the Directory was constituted. An ambitious general named Napoleon Bonaparte began to consolidate power. The number and complexity of intrigues and power struggles over the next three years are almost without precedent in political history (outside of Italy) as leaders and coalitions rose to power only to be swept away and new rules were constantly rewritten to secure the outcomes desired by those temporarily in control. In effect, the chaotic cycle was turning repeatedly, in shorter periods.

By the end of 1799, Napoleon and his brother Lucien effectively controlled all the organs of power, and France was, for all practical purposes, no longer a democracy. Many of its citizens seemed quite pleased by this development. Many of the rest were dead: killed by an experiment with pure democracy. In fact, the surest way to be killed was to have a momentary grasp on power. The situation seemed chaotic to observers, but the chaos was in part a result of the inability of democratic institutions to deal with disagreement and factional discord.

It is common to lament the prevalence and seeming robustness of dictatorship as a form of government. The United Nations states, in Article 29, Section 2 of the Universal Declaration of Human Rights:

In the exercise of his rights and freedoms, everyone shall be subject only to such limitations as are determined by law solely for the purpose of securing due recognition and respect for the rights and freedoms of others and of meeting the just requirements of morality, public order and the general welfare in a *democratic* society. (Emphasis added)

Could it be that the explanation for the frequency and durability of dictatorship as a form of government is due to the difficulty of constructing stable democratic institutions? The *Economist* (2012) entertains the possibility: "Mr. Putin [is surprisingly popular] with ordinary Russians, most of whom preferred the stability that he brought to the more democratic chaos of Boris Yeltsin."

The design of institutions and the form of the constitution must above all other things *survive,* and produce predictable outcomes through consistent rules. Once disagreement about outcomes leads to a violent cycle in institutional arrangements, the choice of a Napoleon is much more understandable.

CLOSING THOUGHTS

One could certainly object that it is implausible for every participant in a decision process to know the preferences of all other participants, and in a one-time decision that might be true. But in any setting where participants are together for long periods of time (such as a social club, a faculty department, or a legislature), the assumption that preferences are known, or at least mostly known, makes good sense.[9]

Finally, as we have seen, the key information may not be the first preference in the ordering; it may be difficult to hide first choices. However, if a politician can disguise his or her views from other members, or – even better, deceive them – effective agenda manipulation becomes next to impossible. This leads to another strategy in a kind of arms race for power. Since agenda control is difficult and can be defeated by disguising preferences, groups are forced to bargain to form coalitions. If the group has a number of meetings over time and votes on choices that are well anticipated, then some majority coalition is likely to caucus in advance, and then hold together for the sequence of votes at the meetings.

One type of "long coalition" (Aldrich, 1995, 2011; Schwartz, 1986) that seems particularly useful in organizing political choice in this way is called a "party." Though we cannot rely on the existence and selection of a stable, determinate outcome just from adding up preferences, it is quite possible – in fact, common – for institutions based on parties and constitution to select stable, determinate outcomes. The properties of those institutions are the core object of study in analytical politics.

TERMS

Agenda Control
Condorcet's Paradox
Condorcet winner

Cycling / Cycling Majorities
Elections
General Will
Groups / Collective Choice
Manipulation
Preference Orders
Strategic Voting
Transitivity
Voting

PROBLEMS FOR CHAPTER 3

3.1 Give the following configuration of preferences:

Chooser	Eugene	Justin	Willow
Best	A	B	C
Middle	B	C	A
Worst	C	A	B

Suppose Justin is the agenda controller and gets to propose the sequence of pairwise votes that will result in an outcome.
  A. What agenda should Justin propose?
  B. What persuasive justification (along the lines of "Vegetables, then Fruit") can you think of? Can you think of another, different justification?
3.2 Suppose that four people, Lyle, Michelle, Nancy, and Orville, have to choose one alternative from among four alternatives, W, X, Y, and Z.
  A. Write down a set of preference orders for the four people that does not result in a cycle (i.e., that creates a determinate choice).
  B. Write down a different set of preference orders for the four people that results in a cycle. What are the key differences between the two configurations of preferences?
3.3 Determine if the following preference profile yields a Condorcet cycle:

ONE	TWO	THREE
A	D	C
B	A	D
C	B	A
D	C	B

If not, why not? If so, what elements of the choice set are involved?

4

The Analytics of Choosing in Groups

An iron rule exists in genetic social evolution. It is that selfish individuals beat altruistic individuals, while groups of altruists beat groups of selfish individuals. The victory can never be complete; the balance of selection pressure cannot move to either extreme. E.O. Wilson. *The Social Conquest of the Earth*.

In Chapter 3, we presented the conceptual problem of choosing in constituted groups. This problem often is called "social choice theory," and it uses individual preference orderings as data to arrive at an aggregate ordering over alternatives or states of the world. Social choice theory is an analytic approach to the tension highlighted by E. O. Wilson in the quote above: Individuals *want* things, but groups *do* things. A selfish individual will die without a group, but effective groups have to solve the problem of satisfying the needs of selfish individuals. The trick is to choose rules that enable the group to perform *as if* it were composed of individuals who want to cooperate, when in fact at least some group members might cheat on the agreement if they could.

Wilson developed his logic as evolutionary theory, primarily in non-human species (his special interest, in fact, was insects). Animal and even plant species that "cooperate" do so by being rewarded in terms of differential fitness, meaning survival and reproduction. Such species do not choose their rules; the rules choose them! Good rules are those that increase fitness and groups or species that have good rules survive. Humans, by contrast, do choose rules. But humans evolved in settings where the need to cooperate and yet still achieve essentially selfish goals was important. There are arguments about whether humans have an ethical or moral sense because of evolution, expressed through emotions, or whether humans developed a moral sense through reason.[1] Either way, choosing in groups is the key social problem faced by communities of humans, in the Stone Age and today.

In this chapter, we will cover some of the same topics examined in Chapter 3, but we will do so with more attention to precise definitions and technical aspects of the problem of preferences, and representing preferences. We then turn to the peculiar problems of representing political preferences, and two key difficulties: failure of completeness and internal bliss points. We then take up the problem of public goods, and look at how public goods change the problem of group choice, regardless of whether one's primary interest is economic or political.

DEFINITIONS

We will need five definitions to distinguish related concepts at an introductory level. Readers who wish to have a deeper, and more rigorous, introduction should consult Austen-Smith and Banks (1999), Schofield (2008), or Schwartz (1986)

Preference: A ranking over bundles of alternatives (commodities, services, states of the world) from better to worse, allowing for indifference among some bundles and strict preference when comparing other bundles. Preference orders are *rational* if they are *complete* and *transitive*. A "preference profile" is a set of preference orders of the enfranchised choosers.

Utility Theory: The use of a mathematical function whose independent variables are commodities, services, or states of the world. The dependent variable, or value returned by the function, is an index number. Larger index numbers indicate higher utilities. Utility functions can, under some circumstances, stand in for or "represent" the preference ordering.

Representation: The mapping of a preference profile onto a family of mathematical utility functions, if this is possible. The utility function then is said to "represent" the preference order, and the individual's utility function is therefore an analytic proxy for the person. The utility function can "represent" the preferences of the individual.

Binary Relation. Formally, a binary relation $\mathfrak{b}$ is an ordered triple. For our purposes, this means $\mathfrak{b}$ is defined on (X, X, S), where X is the set of all possible choices in n-space $(X_1 \times X_2 \times X_3 \ldots \times X_n)$, including all possible contingencies. That is, X is created by calculating the Cartesian product of all dimensions of choice. This seems confusing, but the kind of binary relations we are going to use take an element of the choice set X and compare it to some other element of X (or to the same element), and the comparison will be defined by $\mathfrak{b}$.[2] S is the set into which $\mathfrak{b}$ maps X. Generally, the specific binary relations $\mathfrak{b}$ we will use have to do with *preferences*, such as "at least as good as," "preferred to," or "indifferent to," though many other kinds of mapping relations are possible. So, for example, we might say a particular alternative x_A "is preferred to" x_B, and

the "is preferred to" part would be represented as a binary relation ♭. And
we use x_A to represent an element of X (the first part of the three-tuple)
and then compare to another element x_B of X (the second part of the three-
tuple). In this case, both x_A and x_B are elements of the same set, X. But that
is not a general property of binary relations, though it usually is true for
preference representation. We are choosing two alternatives x_A and x_B
from the set of alternatives X, and deciding which (if either) is preferred.
Social Choice Function: A social choice function maps the preference profiles
of many (or at least two, to be "social") into an aggregate or social utility
function, or social welfare function. Where a utility function indicates
whether an *individual* likes one, or the other, of two alternatives, the
social choice function can indicate whether the *society* or group chooses
one, or the other, of two alternatives.

The intuition behind the notion of "preference" is straightforward: Given two
alternatives, you like one more, or you like them equally well. In principle, you
could do this for all pairs of alternatives. If we could record all of these pairwise
or binary comparisons in a database, and if those "preferences" were stable, we
would not need the chooser to stick around. An observer could predict what the
chooser would do, based on what was in the database. In fact, the observer, in a
sense, could choose for you, *because that preference order is you*, or at least all
of you that is necessary to know how you would choose.

Of course, sometimes you might choose based on what seems like a whim.
Alternatively, you might choose based on history ("I had the snails in white
wine sauce yesterday, today I'll have an empanada"). There might be contingencies ("It is cloudy and cold, so I'll have soup instead of salad").

However, there is no particular reason that history and other contingencies
could not be built into the process. Analysts use a *Gedankenexperiment*, a kind
of mental simulation. Suppose that a person had an arbitrarily large amount of
time and found herself in an indefinitely large warehouse. In the warehouse are
grocery carts of unbounded size. In each cart is some bundle of goods and
services and a setting for every contingency that could affect choice (weather,
history, etc.).

The subject picks one market basket and compares it to every other market
basket; the subject continues to do this until all the market baskets have been
compared, one at a time, to all the others. Yes, this would take forever, but that
is why our mental simulation assumes time is unlimited.

There are many ways to present the comparison. For simplicity, let's begin
by using capital letters (A, B, and so on) as alternatives or possible choices. That
is, let x_A just be "A," and so on. The simplest way to write down a comparison
is to define a binary relation, until now referred to generically as ♭, with a
specific binary relation "$\geqslant$", which means "at least as good as":

*If $A \geqslant B$, that means A "is at least as good as" B, from the perspective of
the chooser.*

The comparison operator $\geq$ is going to be applied to points such as A∈X and B∈X, where ∈ means "is/are elements" of the set of alternatives X. Then the set **S** is the result of applying $\geq$, typically either A $\geq$ B or B $\geq$ A, or both.

From $\geq$ it is possible to derive two additional binary relations: $\succ$ (strictly preferred to) and $\approx$ (strictly indifferent to). These are defined as follows:

$\succ$ *(strict preference): If A $\succ$ B then A $\geq$ B but B $\not\geq$ A*   (4.1)
$\approx$ *(strict indifference): If A $\approx$ B then A $\geq$ B and B $\geq$ A*

There are four useful properties summarizing binary relations that we should define: reflexivity, symmetry, transitivity, and completeness.

Reflexivity: A binary relation is reflexive if the relation is defined on the same elements for all $x_i \in$ X. Take an element A; can we compare A to itself, using our binary relations? You can see that $\geq$ and $\approx$ are reflexive (A $\geq$ A and A $\approx$ A), but $\succ$ is not (A $\succ$ A is not possible).

Symmetry: A binary relation is symmetric if a comparison in one "direction" is also valid for the opposite comparison. Thus $\geq$ and $\succ$ are not symmetric (A $\succ$ B means B $\succ$ A is *never* true; A $\geq$ B does not imply that B $\geq$ A, and in fact that is true if and only if B $\approx$ A, meaning that $\geq$ is not symmetric). On the other hand, $\approx$ is clearly symmetric (A $\approx$ B implies that B $\approx$ A, and vice versa).

Transitivity: A generic binary relation ♭ is weakly transitive if the following is true: If A ♭ B and B ♭ C, then C ♭A. If the relation is *strictly* transitive, then it must be true that A ♭ C. We will generally assume that the binary relations $\approx$, $\succ$ and $\geq$ are all transitive, for individuals. Why is this important? If $\succ$ were intransitive that would allow A $\succ$ B $\succ$ C $\succ$ A, which would in turn mean that A $\succ$ A, violating the nonreflexive nature of $\succ$.[3]

Completeness: If preferences are complete, then for all $x_A \in$ X and $x_B \in$ X, it must be true that either A $\geq$ B or B $\geq$ A, or both. To put it slightly differently, there can be no instances where both A $\not\geq$ B and B $\not\geq$A are true. Substantively, this could happen if the citizen/consumer does not know which of the above is true, because of lack of information or a lack a defined preference between the alternatives. This is one reason we start with use $\geq$ instead of $\succ$. The $\succ$ relation is never defined for comparing a bundle to itself, so both A $\not\succ$ A and A $\not\succ$A are true. Therefore, $\succ$ cannot be, by itself, complete. Furthermore, it is quite possible for A $\not\succ$ B and B $\not\succ$A to be true, whenever A $\approx$ B, so again $\succ$ is not complete. Focusing only on $\succ$ is always incomplete. So, we use $\geq$ to avoid that problem.[4]

There is a particular kind of ordering, the weak order defined by the binary relation $\geq$ applied to the entire set of alternatives X, that we will depend on for representing preferences. We can connect this weak order to the intuitive approach we already used in Chapter 3:

TABLE 4.1. *General Pattern of Preferences*

A ? B	A ? C	A ? D	A ? E	B ? C
B ? D	B ? E	C ? D	C ? E	D ? E
A ≈ A	B ≈ B	C ≈ C	D ≈ D	E ≈ E

TABLE 4.2. *A Possible Set of Preferences*

A ≻ B	A ≻ C	A ≻ D	A ≻ E	B ≈ C
B ≻ D	B ≻ E	C ≻ D	C ≻ E	D ≻ E
A ≈ A	B ≈ B	C ≈ C	D ≈ D	E ≈ E

A **weak order** is a binary relation ≽ that is complete and transitive, defined over a set of alternatives and representing the preferences of a given individual.

Weak orders are cumbersome if the number of alternatives is large, but for small numbers of alternatives, weak orders are very useful and convenient.

For example, imagine there are five alternatives, A, B, C, D, and E, and we are working with the binary relation "at least as good as", or ≽. Remember, ≽ can be decomposed into "strictly preferred to" (≻) and "indifferent to" (≈).

Since there are five alternatives, there are fifteen pairwise comparisons we need as data to construct the preference ordering.[5] Table 4.1 summarizes these comparisons.

We have filled in the bottom row of the table, because ≽ is reflexive, and therefore a rational consumer is indifferent between an alternative and the same alternative. But how are the "?" comparisons to be filled in? The answer is any combination is possible which expresses the preferences of the chooser, subject only to completeness and transitivity. In this case, completeness implies that no "?" can remain. Each must be replaced by ≻ or ≈.[6] In addition, transitivity is a requirement imposed on three-part chains of comparisons.

Suppose we ask our chooser to complete a kind of survey filling in the data of her pairwise preference for each comparison in Table 4.2. It might look like this.

From these data, we can construct the preference profile – weak order – for the chooser. She ranks the alternatives as follows: A ≻ B ≈ C ≻ D ≻ E.

Of course, there are many ways to put data in the table. How many? Assuming that every pair has a direct comparison (i.e., preferences are complete), there are three possibilities for each cell: I ≻ J, J ≻ I, and I ≈ J (or J ≈ I, which is the same thing, because indifference is symmetric and need not be written out as a separate possibility). Since there are ten cells (not counting the cells that simply show in effect that each alternative is at least as good as itself), that means that there are 3^{10}, or 59,049 possible preference profiles.

TABLE 4.3. *An Alternative Set of Preferences*

A ≻ B	A ≻ C	~~D ≻ A~~	A ≻ E	B ≈ C
B ≻ D	B ≻ E	C ≻ D	C ≻ E	D ≻ E
A ≈ A	B ≈ B	C ≈ C	D ≈ D	E ≈ E

But many (in fact, almost all) of these possible profiles would be intransitive. For example, imagine that the table looked like Table 4.3, where we reverse just one entry, the comparison between A and D in Row 1, Column 3, which we have highlighted with a dark line.

The problem is that in this table there is a cycle over some of the elements. Specifically, A ≻ B ≻ C ≻ D ≻ A. This is not a weak ordering, and is not a valid rational preference.

Alternatively, the form of the intransitivity could involve indifference. If A≈ B and B≈ C, but A≻ C, that is not a weak order. Either for reasons of logic, or because of natural selection (a person with such preferences would not survive, though he would be very, very happy!), we restrict consideration to transitive preferences.

Obviously, there are many, many ways to change one or more of the binary preferences and make the resulting ordering intransitive. Calculating the number of transitive profiles, for five alternatives and then for N alternatives, is an end-of-chapter problem for the reader. A hint can be found in Muravyov and Marinushkina (2013).

UTILITY FUNCTIONS: REPRESENT!

With the idea of "preference" nailed down more clearly, we can proceed to the experiment with infinite market baskets, in an infinitely large warehouse, with infinite time. The reason to go to all this trouble is that the orderings of all the binary comparisons that make up "preference" can be used to fit a mathematical function that *represents* those preferences. To represent, in practical terms, means that there exists a function that returns, for every market basket in the set of alternatives, some index number that is an element of the real numbers $\mathbb{R}$. That is an enormous convenience, analytically.

Remember that the two bundles, $x_A \in X$ and $x_B \in X$, are points in an n-dimensional space:

$$x_A = (x_{a1}, x_{a2}, x_{a3}, \ldots x_{an}) \quad (4.2)$$
$$x_B = (x_{b1}, x_{b2}, x_{b3}, \ldots x_{bn})$$

Now the problem of "representing" weak orders with a mathematical function is complex, relying on results in topology. However, the conceptual problem is simple. Assume that the chooser has finished her task of recording all pairwise comparisons among feasible alternatives in our warehouse. (Just remember that when we say "A" we mean "$x_A \in X$").

Then a family of mathematical "utility functions" U can be said to *represent* a given weak ordering if the following statement is true, for all alternatives A, B, and C:

Any function U(A) mapping A∈X => ℝ is a "utility function" that *represents* the preference relation ≽ for an individual, *provided* that for all A∈X and B∈X both of the following are true:

A ≽ B implies U(A) ≥ U(B)

and   (4.3)

U(A) ≥ U(B) implies A ≽ B

If you have studied economics, you have seen utility functions, with indifference curves and the smoothly analytic properties that (some) mathematical functions allow for. So long as the idea of preference over market baskets containing varying amounts of divisible goods and services is sensible, this technique is very useful.[7]

The problem is that the preferences we have considered so far are defined over *private* goods (like Apples or automobiles or smart phones). If I buy something, it is mine. I can eat it, live in it, or use it. It is not obvious this sort of preference representation scheme would work for group choice, or for "political" preferences. Moreover, it turns out they *don't* work, at least not in the same way. This is neither good nor bad, as a result. It is just a property of group choice.

REPRESENTING POLITICAL PREFERENCES

The solution to the problem of representing preference for the consumer – in the realm of economics – largely is solved. [8] Under general assumptions of the form of preferences, such as diminishing marginal utility and non-satiety, and some topological conveniences such as compactness and continuity, utility functions that represent preferences always exist. Even under more perverse circumstances, some mechanism for mathematical representation exists for broad classes of preferences.[9]

But this cannot easily be said of preferences on political issues. There are two serious complications: the failure of "completeness," and modelling an internal bliss point or optimum.

Representation Complication #1: Failure of the completeness axiom: The completeness axiom is problematic even when dealing with the private sector. There may be foods, or cars, or computer software the consumer has never heard of and cannot evaluate. All completeness really means is when presented with a pair of choices, the consumer can think, decide, and be sure of the comparison. This is a stretch, but not entirely ridiculous.

In politics, the set of alternatives is complex, and the dimensions of evaluation are manifold. Worse, voters have only limited incentives to acquire information about alternatives, because their chance of affecting the outcome is negligible. Therefore, instead of completeness, political preferences in elections are likely to suffer from what political scientists call "rational ignorance."[10]

There is an important distinction, however, between two different contexts for the application of political preferences to alternatives.[11] One context is *committee voting*, and the other is *mass elections*. Committee voting is a decision setting where there are few voters, participants can propose new alternatives, the implications of the decision for the individuals choosing may be very large, and participants are well informed about the alternatives. School budget votes by a county commission or voting on a budget bill in a legislative committee are examples of committee voting. In the setting of committee voting, "completeness" is not so implausible, because individual votes matter and the difference in the outcome can be significant.

In mass elections, completeness is much less plausible. In fact, it is ridiculous. Mass elections are situations where a very large number of voters participate, making the impact of any one vote negligible. Furthermore, the choice is among candidates, rather than alternatives, and mass voters have little direct say in what (who) the alternatives are. It may be that each candidate can be seen as a "bundle" of policies, but it is hard to know either what candidates actually intend when they make promises, or what they are competent to do. Worse, candidates have strong incentives to be ambiguous, and most voters have only very limited access to information of any kind. So voters have little incentive to find out about alternatives, and the "alternatives" are often ambiguous – even delusional – candidates, not policy proposals. U.S. Presidential elections are one example of mass elections, but even much smaller elections such as city council or state house of representatives are best conceived as mass elections.

To summarize, there are three parts to the analytic politics account of whether voters' preferences can be thought of as "complete."

- First, each citizen is motivated to seek his or her own self-interest, though many citizens may care about a conception of the "public good." The problem is not that they are selfish, but rather that their self-interest prevents them from learning many details about what alternative is better for the public good. They do not know much about what policy is best, even from their own selfish perspective. They are likely to be taken in by simplistic platitudes about caring rather than complex, pragmatic proposals about solving problems.
- Second, the citizen has access to limited information, and acquiring more accurate information is quite expensive in terms of effort and time. So, in addition to not really knowing what they want (as in #1 above), they don't know much about what candidates are promising or if those promises are credible.
- Third, political elites know this, and (as Downs 1957 argued) use advertising and simple slogans to attract votes.

The problem with completeness is that it relies on adequate information to be able to say whether I like A, I like B, or I am indifferent between them. Buying a car is a private good, and consumers have solid reasons to learn about cars. Third parties publish reviews and evaluations of consumer products, the products are comparatively homogenous and discrete, and "good" and "bad" are largely objective. Whether these comparisons are fully "complete" is debatable, but it seems at least likely that consumers have some way to judge the alternatives, given their preferences.[12]

However, acquiring accurate information and then voting for the best candidate is a public good, and private action will underprovide it. Even if (some, many, all) voters are motivated by the public interest in terms of their *preferences over outcomes*, they still have selfish interest reasons to free ride and be influenced by strategic political messages from consultants and political operatives, whom Downs called "persuaders." All the parties and groups trying to attract votes have their own reasons to distort information.

What does this problem imply for political preferences? Citizen voters may have reasonably well defined preferences over outcomes or states of the world. But the "alternatives" actually presented are ambiguous candidates, parties, or other choices that map into outcomes in ways that are obscured by a lack of information on the part of voters and incentives for obfuscation on the part of political elites. Even voters interested in the public good will have great difficulty deciding which of the feasible alternatives is most preferred. Unlike the consumer market baskets in the warehouse, the choices in politics are few and fuzzy.

Representation Complication #2: Internal satiation, or bliss point: In consumer problems with private goods, it generally is assumed "more is preferred to less," or non-satiation. At worst, we can generally assume free disposal. What this means is that if you have more hamburgers (for example) than you can eat, you can sell them at zero price or throw them away at no cost. In a situation where resources have positive prices and consumption is private, this situation would never happen because I would not buy that many hamburgers in the first place.

But politics is different. Many of the issues decided on by voting are ideological,[13] meaning that there is a single right answer in the voter's mind. Abortion, same sex marriage, capital punishment and other such issues have, in each voter's mind, a correct answer. A deviation from this correct answer makes the voter worse off, but having "more" of the correct answer, whatever that even means, does not make her better off.

Further, for many non-ideological issues, especially regarding spending and taxation, the voter has an ideal policy that occupies a point in the interior of the set of alternatives. The voter has an "ideal point," or most preferred budget, and is unhappy if spending is either more or less than this ideal. If you think, for example, that the ideal number of "garbage days" is one per week, you will be unhappy if there are four pickupos each week or if there is only one pickup

TABLE 4.4. *Four Types of Goods*

	Excludable	Non-excludable
Rivalrous Consumption	Private Goods (Apples, Oranges)	Common Pool Resources (Fisheries, Atmosphere)
Non-Rival Consumption	Club Goods (Swimming Pools)	Public Goods (National Defense)

every month. It is not true that you think, "More is better," because tax burden of the additional services has increased.

These two difficulties, limited information and internal bliss points, are daunting obstacles to doing analytical politics using the preference–based approach. The problem of preference representation in politics is different from economics, because the preferences, information constraints, and institutional settings are so different. As we shall see, it is still possible to discuss preferences, and to offer useful representations. However, we will have to rework things a bit.

PUBLIC GOODS

It is useful to start with basics: gains from *group* action, many of which are public goods. Public goods are different from private goods, and we need to account for the difference if we want to represent political preferences.

A private good is a service or commodity with two features: low-cost excludability – if you don't pay, you can be prevented from consuming – and rivalrous consumption – if you consume something, there is less for everyone else. Some goods lack one or the other of these attributes, and so are neither pure private goods nor pure public goods. Goods that are *both* non-excludable and non-rival are pure public goods. Table 4.4 gives examples to makes the distinction clear.

Rival/Excludable: If I want an apple, then in a private property system an applecart owner can withhold the apple until I pay for it (excludability). If I eat the apple, it is not available for anyone else (rival consumption). Excludable in provision, rival in consumption goods are private goods.

Rival/Nonexcludable: If I want to catch a fish, it costs very little at the margin once I have the equipment, the ship, and the location. On the open ocean, outside national boundaries, I cannot be easily stopped from fishing, so the good is non-excludable. But each fish I take reduces the stock available for anyone else to take, so consumption is rivalrous. This is a common pool resource that causes problems for market provision, but is not a public good.[14]

Non-rival/Excludable: If I want to be able to swim in a pool, a fence surrounding the pool can prevent me, with a guard at the gate who accepts a fee or membership card in exchange for access. Therefore, the pool is excludable. But a large pool has little rivalry in consumption up to the point where the pool is crowded. One more person jumping in has very little impact on my enjoyment of the pool (non-rival). This is a club good, which is similar to a public good except that its excludability means that a voluntary neighborhood association or club can provide it.[15]

Non-rival/Non-excludable: If a large group wants to defend its territory, that group faces both problems. Effective defense will protect all residents of the area, even if they did not pay (non-excludability). In addition, if a new family joins the group, or a new baby is born, there is no increased demand for border defense (non-rival).

It is important to consider the nature of the goal when the group makes its "deciding how to decide" choice. The simplest distinction in deciding how to decide is whether to choose individually or collectively. But notice that there is no necessary relation between the goods in Table 4.4 and the choice of how to allocate those goods, or how much to produce, and how to pay for them. The decision of whether to choose individually or collectively is a *political* choice, not an economic one. There is nothing to prevent tyrannous groups from dictating individual choices, and controlling activities that are in no sense "public" goods. On the other hand, there is nothing to ensure that goods (or bads, like pollution) are placed within the jurisdiction of the group. Individuals who can impose costs on the group without penalty are a kind of tyranny, also.

Large groups – nations, for example – generally allow some individual choices, while other choices are exclusively made collectively. Between those two extremes, nations exhibit substantial variation in the scope of individual autonomy versus collective control. This means the group may decide who can marry whom (which seems private), or an individual can cut down trees on public land and sell the timber without asking anyone's permission. Table 4.5 depicts some options.

The problem of "market failures"[16] is largely outside the scope of this book, but it is worth noting that they are the result of a misalignment of property rights, incentives for action, or revelation of information that results in a misallocation of resources. Consulting the table above, we see that leaving private good choices up to individual consumers, the top left cell has good results. Market failures tend to crop up in the other three settings, if choices are private or individual:

- With *club goods*, individuals on their own will generally supply, and therefore enjoy, less of the club good (such as a pool, athletic facilities, or park) than they would prefer, and be willing to pay for.
- With *common pool resources*, the misallocation of property rights results in overuse of the commons, whether it is overgrazing a pasture or overfishing a seabed. Some collective action may be required to fix the property rights

TABLE 4.5. *Types of Goods, and Types of Choices*

Type of Good			
Choice Type	Private	Club	Commons	Public
Private Collective	Consumer Sovereignty	Market Failure: Underprovided	Market Failure: Overprovided	*Market Failure:* Underprovided Goods, Too Much Pollution
	Government Failure: Tyranny of the Group	Private Clubs	Fix Property Rights	Classic Public Good

problem. In this case, the good is overprovided, because the price is too low for the individual.

- With *public goods*, the individual faces both misallocations: If any of the good is provided, no one can be excluded. Additional people can be served with any amount of the good, so no individual has an incentive to produce any of the good (hoping instead to "free ride" on the productive activity of others). In a private choice setting, public goods are underprovided, so some group or collective choice is required.[17]

At least one solution to the problem of public goods, and consequent market failure, has been found. It is often called "Lindahl Equilibrium" after Erik Lindahl (1958) the economist who first solved the problem.

PUBLIC GOODS AND LINDAHL EQUILIBRIUM*

The solution requires us to work through some algebra, deriving an equilibrium for the consumer and the citizen.[18]

The Consumer's Problem – Private Goods Only

Imagine there are two private (excludable and rival) goods, Apples (A) and Broccoli (B). Each is available at a price in the marketplace: A costs P_A and B costs P_B. The consumer has an income equal to I. We will assume no saving, so the consumer will spend I on the combination of A and B – given P_A and P_B – that maximizes her utility. In other words, the consumer's problem is:

$$\text{Max U} = f(A,B) \text{ subject to } I = P_A A + P_B B \qquad (4.4)$$

The problem can be rewritten using a LaGrangean multiplier λ:

$$L = f(A,B) + \lambda (I - P_A A - P_B B)$$

Taking partial derivatives of this function and setting them each equal to zero yields the first order conditions of the problem.

$$\frac{\partial L}{\partial A} = \frac{\partial f}{\partial A} - \lambda P_A = 0$$

$$\frac{\partial L}{\partial B} = \frac{\partial f}{\partial B} - \lambda P_B = 0 \qquad (4.5)$$

$$\frac{\partial L}{\partial \lambda} = I - P_A - P_B = 0$$

Rearranging these first order conditions yield the following necessary condition for maximizing consumer welfare:

$$\frac{\frac{\partial f}{\partial A}}{\frac{\partial f}{\partial B}} = \frac{P_A}{P_B} \qquad (4.6)$$

This condition is familiar to anyone who has taken a course in microeconomics. It implies that the consumer should allocate her funds for expenditures on private goods until the last dollar spent on Apples gives the same *marginal* satisfaction as the last dollar spent on Broccoli. Graphically, it means the slope of the highest feasible indifference curve would be equal to the slope of the budget line, implying a tangency.

Consumption of private goods precludes their consumption by others. Assuming no externalities in production or consumption, we can "add up" the quantities desired by each consumer, at prevailing prices, and then see if producers will produce enough (not too much, not too little) at that price. The French economist Walras famously invoked the idea of an "auctioneer" to determine if everything "added up" in this way using a process he called "*tâtonnement*" (*par tâtonnement* is French for "by trial and error").

The job of the "auctioneer" is to facilitate price adjustment: If there are more Apples being produced than people want to buy at the prevailing price, then the price is too high. There will be pressure on the price to fall, as producers try to rid themselves of excess inventories. Then, all the actors in the economy adjust their actions given the new price. At the lower price, producers produce less and consumers buy more. The auctioneer calls out a price, and everyone adjusts on quantity. At some point, the price falls (or rises) enough to equate the quantity supplied with the quantity demanded, and everything "adds up."

In private goods markets, under some special assumptions (including "many price takers" on both the supply and demand sides of the process), an equilibrium can be shown to exist. Under the direction of the auctioneer, the process of *price* adjustment, with the consequent changes in individual choices about production and consumption, can create a tendency toward equilibrium, at least in principle. To the extent this process of *tatonnement* can be relied on also to redirect resources from less valued toward more valued production, the results of general equilibrium theory in economics can be derived.

Do these rather optimistic results, implying both the *existence* of an equilibrium and a tendency in market processes to *move toward* that equilibrium, still obtain in conditions where there are public goods? Can we represent preferences for public goods in the same way as preferences for private goods?

The Consumer/Citizen Problem with Public Goods

In private good markets, the auctioneer "adjusts" prices. It is not obvious there exists a similar conceptual *tâtonnement* process to achieve equilibrium if public goods are thrown into the mix. After all, the *tâtonnement* process for private goods was based on individual quantity adjustments to aggregate price changes. Each person purchases a different amount, and all that needs to happen is the aggregate quantity supplied and the aggregate quantity demanded sum to equality.

Public goods are not like that at all. If any national defense is provided, all "consumers" have to accept exactly the same amount with no room for individual quantity adjustment, with some people consuming more and some less, because public goods are non-rival. If any amount is provided, that is the amount all citizens must "consume." Further, it is hard to know how to think of "price" since each person can pay a lot, a little, or nothing, and still receive whatever amount of national defense is produced. If any is produced, all that is produced is available to everyone, because public goods are non-excludable.

Then what can we say? Let us continue the previous example with A and B but add a third (public) good called D for defense. Since we need more than one person if we are to model choosing in groups, let's consider the choices of Mr. 1 and Ms. 2.

The total amounts of the three goods, A, B, and D that the society can produce are described by a transformation function T:

$$T\,(A,\,B,\,D) = 0$$

Where:

$$A_1 + A_2 = A$$
$$B_1 + B_2 = B \qquad\qquad (4.7)$$
$$D_1 = D_2 = D$$

The reason for the difference between the equations for the private goods (A and B) and the public good (D) is Mr. 1 and Ms. 2 consume (possibly) different amounts of A and B, but by definition, each must "consume" the same amount of the public good D.

A number of scholars have addressed this problem in a general equilibrium context. The three most important for our purposes, however, were Bergson (1938), Samuelson (1954, 1977), and Arrow (1963). What follows is a simplified adaptation of their work. Bergson, Samuelson, and Arrow all make use of a "social welfare function," or SWF:

$$SWF = w(u_1, u_2, \ldots u_n) \tag{4.8}$$

Each of the u_i's is the utility of the *ith* citizen/consumer, and "social" welfare is some function of the aggregation of all of the individual utilities of all citizens. One could imagine many SWFs. If the utility measures were cardinal, it might be the sum of utilities or the weighted sum of utilities, or the SWF could focus on the utility of just one person (the dictator).

In our little society of two people, we can write the social choice problem this way combining the SWF (the objective function) and the transformation function (the constraint):

$$\text{Max } SWF = w(u_1, u_2) \text{ subject to } T(A, B, D) = 0 \tag{4.9}$$

Again, we form a LaGrangean multiplier, for just our two-person society:

$$L = w(u_1, u_2) + \lambda\, T(A, B, D) \tag{4.10}$$

Again, we take the partial derivatives of the LaGrangean, this time with respect to the six decision variables (amounts of A for 1 and 2, amounts of B for 1 and 2, amount of D for everyone, and the value of λ, the marginal social utility of an extra unit of productive resources):

$$\frac{\partial L}{\partial A_i} = \frac{\partial w}{\partial u_i}\frac{\partial u_i}{\partial A_i} + \lambda\frac{\partial T}{\partial A} = 0,\ i = 1, 2$$

$$\frac{\partial L}{\partial B_i} = \frac{\partial w}{\partial u_i}\frac{\partial u_i}{\partial B_i} + \lambda\frac{\partial T}{\partial B} = 0,\ i = 1, 2 \tag{4.11}$$

$$\frac{\partial L}{\partial D} = \frac{\partial w}{\partial u_1}\frac{\partial u_1}{\partial D} + \frac{\partial w}{\partial u_2}\frac{\partial u_2}{\partial D} + \lambda\frac{\partial T}{\partial D} = 0$$

$$\frac{\partial L}{\partial \lambda} = T(A, B, D) = 0$$

The term $\partial w/\partial u_i$ is the "weight" each citizen has in the SWF; a plausible weight is 1/n, where n is the number of people in the group, but this is not necessary for a SWF. In a dictatorship, as noted above, the value might be 1 for the dictator and 0 for everyone else. That might an unjust SWF, but mathematically there is nothing to rule it out. These weights are one of the core problems of "constitution" for a group, as noted above.

For the two private goods, A and B, the conditions for each individual are basically as before if one manipulates the terms in the first order conditions:

$$\frac{\dfrac{\partial w}{\partial u_i}\dfrac{\partial u_i}{\partial A_i}}{\dfrac{\partial w}{\partial u_i}\dfrac{\partial u_i}{\partial B_i}} = \frac{P_A}{P_B} = \frac{\dfrac{\partial T}{\partial A}}{\dfrac{\partial T}{\partial B}},\ i = 1, 2 \tag{4.12}$$

The transformation function is standing in for price in terms of the opportunity cost of resources used to produce either of the private goods. The cost of a unit of A can be expressed as the number of units of B foregone. The equilibrium, if there is one, has to have the feature that the price ratio is equal to the marginal rate of substitution, both in terms of the individual utility functions and the SWF.

But notice the $\partial w / \partial u_i$ term appears in both the numerator and denominator of the ratio in the equilibrium condition. It cancels out! While the weight received in the SWF may be of great personal interest to the individual citizen, it has no impact on the marginal equilibrium allocation of resources in private goods markets.[19]

The result for the public good D looks odd, because the first order condition for D is very different. Written with respect to A for Mr. 1 (the equations with respect to B and for Ms. 2 look similar), it looks like this:

$$\frac{\dfrac{\partial w}{\partial u_1}\dfrac{\partial u_1}{\partial D} + \dfrac{\partial w}{\partial u_2}\dfrac{\partial u_2}{\partial D}}{\dfrac{\partial w}{\partial u_1}\dfrac{\partial u_1}{\partial A_1}} = \frac{\dfrac{\partial T}{\partial D}}{\dfrac{\partial T}{\partial A}} \qquad (4.13)$$

This expression shows why representing preferences for public goods in the same setting where we represent preferences for private goods is so difficult.

There are three quite distinct problems:

1. The weight terms $\partial w / \partial u_i$ *do not* cancel. The correct level of public good depends not just on the technical trade-offs, but on the constitution of the group.
2. Quite separately, the implied equilibrium levels of the public good are the sum of marginal evaluations of the public good by each of the citizens. We cannot talk about our private preferences for the public good without immediately focusing on the political choice of groups. There is no purely individual component to selecting public good production levels; it's all about the politics.
3. Since the optimal level of the public good selected – call it D^* – depends on the sum of *all the marginal valuations* of all citizens, who pays and how much? It is clear from the first order conditions the total cost should be proportionate to the price ratio embodied in the transformation function. But what are the appropriate individual "prices," or tax shares?

For private goods, the ratio of marginal utilities equals the price ratio, and consumers can make different, idiosyncratic choices to ensure this condition is met. For public goods, on the other hand, the *sum* of the marginal utilities of all citizens is the determining factor, and all citizens must consume the same amount.

Remember, for private goods, we imagined an auctioneer varying the price, and people responded by varying their private levels of consumption and production. The equilibrium is found *par tâtonnement*. The auctioneer continued to call out different prices until the quantities supplied at that price exactly equaled the quantities demanded.

That will not work for public goods, though. People cannot adjust their quantities idiosyncratically in response to changes in price, because all the quantities have to be the same if any of the public good is produced. Consequently, for public goods, we have to vary the aggregate quantity everyone must share, because the public good must be supplied at the same level for everyone.

To be clear, the problem is that individuals cannot adjust the quantity they can consume as with private goods, with aggregate demand simply being the sum of the individual demands at a single price. What is necessary for public goods is to propose an overall quantity and then let citizens propose the *personal share* (tax) they would be willing to pay, and then see if the total bids add up to the cost of providing that level of public good.

The auctioneer would call out quantities of the public good and note the level of *cost* to the state associated with producing that quantity. Then, every citizen would announce his or her value, or willingness to contribute tax payments, for that level of D. The auctioneer would sum the bids, and if the sum of the bids exceeded the cost of the proposed level of public good production, the auctioneer would propose a new *higher* level of D. If the sum of the bids falls short of the total cost of production, the auctioneer would propose a *lower* level of D. Eventually, as the auctioneer keeps calling out production levels, the two sides of the equation will match: The *total bids* of all citizens will sum to the *total cost* of the level of the public good D the citizens are bidding on.

As we said at the outset, the economist who first understood this possibility for equilibrium in the market for public goods was Erik Lindahl (1958), who in turn owed quite a bit to the work of Wicksell (1958). If it were true that this approach, like the *tâtonnement* process for private goods, was simply a metaphor for understanding a very complex but workable adjustment process, the problem of representing public sector preferences would be solved. Sadly, it is not so simple for three reasons: demand revelation problems, impossibility theorems, and failure of "induced" public sector preferences.

Demand revelation: Any production of the public good benefits all citizens, but the amount paid in taxes depends on how much each citizen is willing to pay. Each citizen has a strong incentive to underrepresent his or her demand for the public good. Others will bid for public good production, in which case the non-bidder can free ride. Alternatively, no one else may bid, and then it makes little sense for any one citizen to play the sucker.

As a result, public provision through voluntary demand revelation fails in just the same way (and for a similar reason!) as private provision failed: The public good is produced at a level much lower than the Pareto optimal level. Everyone would be better off if they revealed their preferences truthfully; but each citizen can even be better off if he or she alone reveals a false valuation, either zero or close to it, and pays only a tiny share of taxes. Since this is true for each citizen, if the number of citizens is large it would not help even if a singular citizen resolved unilaterally to be honest and pay a full share. The fact that others are free riding means the increment to the total production of the public good would be negligible, while the cost to the solitary honest individual would be punitive.[20]

Impossibility theorems: Kenneth Arrow (1963), along with a variety of scholars since, showed that a SWF cannot represent public preferences, as was assumed by the model depicted above. The problem of representation of private preferences, as this chapter has argued at some length, has a solution in most cases. But the problem of public good preferences *never* has a solution if the requirement is a robust and ethically defensible SWF. We will discuss this again in Chapter 6, but it is easy to see the lack of a determinate SWF derivable from individual preference orders renders the public goods preference revelation problem impossible to solve, even on its own terms.

Failure of "induced" public sector preferences: A plausible strategy for modeling public sector preferences was proposed in the 1960s: treat public goods as an entirely separate, independent sector of choice. The division seemed promising, as a number of decisions on "ideological" grounds (such as abortion, marriage, and capital punishment) are likely separate from consumer choice.

However, many decisions are not separable. For one thing, each consumer's budget for private goods is dependent on her tax share, which is dependent on the quantity of public goods "demanded." But the quantity of public goods certainly depends on the mix, scope, and price of private goods available. Because the tax cost of the public good determines the quantity of private goods foregone, "induced" public sector preferences may depend strongly on how the public good is financed.

The first attempt to embed public sector preferences in a model with both public and private goods was Barr and Davis (1968). A number of empirical applications (Borcherding and Deacon 1972, and Bergstrom and Goodman 1973) using the median voter approach (a concept we will consider extensively in the following chapters) were quite successful.

The problem is the nonseparability of public and private sector preferences requires that citizens make choices simultaneously with consumers – they are, after all, the same people. The original work, done independently by Denzau and Parks (1975, 1977, 1979, 1983) and Slutsky (1975; 1977), showed there is no mathematically consistent means of "representing" public sector preferences as microeconomic utility functions. This result is reviewed and explained at some length in Milyo (2000).

These authors demonstrated that if consumer preferences are "economic" (that is, reflexive, connected, transitive, and weakly convex), those attributes will be "inherited" by the induced public sector preferences. Those public sector preferences, however, do not exhibit convex upper contour sets or indifference curves that enclose regular convex sets. In particular, circular or ellipsoidal indifference curves for public sector preferences were not implied, and are not derivable, from "rational" private sector preferences. This is important because it requires that we consider "political preferences" as being inherently spatial, as we will see when come to Chapters 5 and 6.

Later, Coughlin and Hinich (1984) derived necessary and sufficient conditions under which it is possible to represent public and private sector preferences, but those conditions are highly restrictive. They showed public sector preferences would be "single-peaked" (a concept important in spatial representations of utility functions) only if the mapping from the space of possible public policy alternatives in actual states of the world is linear. Therefore, despite considerable advances in the study of public goods, a universalizable and mathematically convenient way of representing individual preferences over *both* public and private goods in one combined utility function does not exist.

Does that mean preferences for public goods cannot be modeled? Fortunately, the answer is no. One avenue of attack is the "weak order" approach discussed earlier. Various social choice problems are amenable to treatment simply by writing down the entire weak ordering and using the implied binary comparisons to represent the preferences of the chooser. No representation problem needs to be solved, because the weak order is used directly. The portion of analytical politics theorists who study this question is significant; for two excellent recent reviews, see Nitzan (2010) and Taylor (2005).

An alternative approach will allow the analyst to preserve the convenience and portability of the utility function concept. That approach is to drop the notion of modeling derived or induced public good preferences as economists have sought to do and instead model preferences for collective choices directly as analytic primitives. There is a long history of this approach, and it has been quite fruitful.

The reason, as we saw in Table 4.4, is the key distinction for many types of group choices has little to do with whether the *underlying good or service* is public or private. The key determining factor for the modeling approach is instead whether the *choice mechanism itself* is individual or collective. It makes sense to model collective choice, rather than public goods, because this way, our focus is much more directly on the institutions and consequences of people choosing in groups rather than the abstract world of ideal levels of production and tax shares for public goods.

This approach, with foundations in the work of Downs (1957) and Black (1958), has gone through many versions and extensions. The extension to multiple dimensions effected by Davis and Hinich (1965, 1966) and Hinich, Ledyard, and Ordeshook (1972) dramatically expanded the applications for which this model of "spatial politics" could be used.

THE FUNDAMENTAL PROBLEM OF AGGREGATION

The problem of aggregating possibly disparate individual preference orderings into a legitimate and accepted consensus is the core of the "social choice" problem. One reason we have spent so much time on representing preferences is it enables us to analyze political institutions. Plott's fundamental equation of politics illustrates the importance of the ability to separate preferences and institution:[21]

Preferences * Beliefs * Feasible Set * Institutions => Outcomes

This "equation" is conceptual, not literal. One cannot multiply these concepts together in any quantifiable way. Still, laying out how all these factors interact to produce outcomes is quite useful.

Two parts of Plott's fundamental equation are (mostly) beyond the scope of our analysis in this book. *Beliefs* are an important element of strategic interaction, and belief formation is an important part game theoretic models. The problem of the *feasible set* is an important one, but a complex combination of technology, culture, and resource constraints usually exogenously determines the feasible set in politics. .

That leaves *preferences* and *institutions*. Plott's equation illustrates two of the most important principles of analytical political theory:

- If preferences change, outcomes can change, even if institutions remain constant.
- If institutions change, outcomes can change, even if preferences remain constant.

One might argue, of course, preferences and institutions are often both changing. However, keeping the two types, or sources, of change distinct analytically is fundamental to an understanding of politics. Further, as Plott's equation shows, changes of one type interact with changes of the other type. Relatively small changes in preferences, if multiplied by a change in the way those preferences are counted, may change policy outcomes dramatically.

FINAL WORDS

This chapter summarizes the problem of "representing" preferences. We discussed the general problem of deriving weak orders using binary comparisons of alternatives, and we introduced the use of a mathematical utility function to stand in for this mass of pairwise relations.

Such an approach has been developed in the elegant economic theory of purely private choices. It is important to recognize "private" in this sense actually has two distinct meanings: The first is "private goods" with no externalities, common pool problems, and so on; the second is "private choice," where individuals choose for themselves rather than having people choosing in groups.

But this is a book about people choosing in groups. Pure private market institutions do not handle well the problem of public goods, externalities, and common pool resources. Analytical tools more appropriate for the study of markets are not useful for the problem of collective, or political, choice.[22] A variety of scholars has demonstrated that an integrated model of private choice and "induced" public sector choice is not (yet?) mathematically feasible.

Groups face the particular problems inherent in representing *political* preferences, which may be defined over *public goods*. There are two means of handling political preferences: *weak orders* and some form of *utility function*. Standard utility functions, of the form used in economics, are generally not appropriate for use in representing political preference. This explains why a particular kind of utility function approach, or spatial theory, is commonly used in political science. We will take up spatial theory in the next section.

TERMS

Aggregation
Altruism
Auctioneer
Binary relation
Club good
Common pool resource
Demand revelation
Indifference
Lindahl equilibrium
Preference Order
Private good
Public good
Reflexivity
Representation
Selfish
Selection
Social choice
Symmetry
Transitivity
Utility Function
Weak Order

EXERCISES

4.1 Consider a binary relation β. You are given the following information as true:

$A\beta B \quad B \text{ not } \beta A \quad B \text{ not } \beta B \quad B \beta C \quad C \text{ not } \beta A$

Which of the following properties does β possess?

a. Reflexive

b. Transitive
c. Symmetric

4.2 Prove that the indifference relation ($\approx$) is reflexive, symmetric, and transitive.
4.3 Prove that all complete preference relations must be reflexive.
4.4 (adapted from Austen-Smith and Banks, 2004)
Statement: A binary relation $\geq$ is transitive on the choice set $\mathbf{X}$ if and only if three conditions all hold for sets of three alternatives (i.e., $\forall\{A, B, C\}$ $\subseteq \mathbf{X}$).

(1) $x \succ y$ and $y \succ z$ implies $x \succ z$
(2) $x \approx y$ and $y \approx z$ implies $x \approx z$
(3) $x \approx y$ and $y \succ z$ implies $x \succ z$, and $x \succ y$ and $y \approx z$ implies $x \succ z$
    a. Prove the above statement
    b. Prove that if $\geq$ is complete (but not necessarily transitive), then statements (1) and (2) imply (3), making (3) redundant.

4.5 Consider the following table of five alternatives, with unknown data for pairwise comparisons.

A ?? B	A ?? C	A ?? D	A ?? E	B ?? C
B ?? D	B ?? E	C ?? D	C ?? E	D ?? E
A ≈ A	B ≈ B	C ≈ C	D ≈ D	E ≈ E

The chapter showed that there are 3^{10} possible ways to fill out the table, if intransitivities are allowed. But if intransitive preference profiles are deleted, how many allowable preference profiles remain?
4.6 What is the general answer to the question posed in 4.5 above, assuming the number of alternatives is N?
4.7 Fill in the Table in problem 4.5 above with some preferences that yield different weak orders for three people, ONE, TWO, and THREE. Given your weak orders, which of the following agendas should ONE choose if he knows the preference orderings and knows that TWO and THREE know, and are likely to vote strategically?

- A versus B - the winner against C - the winner against D
- A versus B - the winner against D - the winner against C
- A versus C - the winner against B - the winner against D
- A versus C - the winner against D - the winner against B
- A versus D - the winner against B - the winner against C
- A versus D - the winner against C - the winner against B
- B versus C - the winner against A - the winner against D
- B versus C - the winner against D - the winner against A

- B versus C - the winner against A - the winner against D
- B versus D - the winner against A - the winner against C
- B versus D - the winner against C - the winner against A
- C versus D - the winner against A - the winner against B
- C versus D - the winner against B - the winner against A

II

SPATIAL THEORY

5

Politics as Spatial Competition

Froth at the top, dregs at bottom, but the middle excellent.

Voltaire

The most perfect political community is one in which the middle class is in control, and outnumbers both of the other classes.

Aristotle

Mathematical utility functions make the idea of preference portable and generalizable. If the "utility function" happens to have nice properties, including differentiability, then calculus can be brought to bear on many problems describing responsiveness and rates of change, and a wide variety of intuitive results can be discussed and debated.

Economic theory gave birth to the basic spatial model of politics. The problem, as we noted in Chapter 4, is that economic utility functions cannot be used for public goods and collective decisions. The idea of a spatial utility function to "represent" political preferences was laid out by Black (1948), Black and Newing (1951), Downs (1957), and Black (1958).[1] However, the modern spatial theory of political competition betrays very little of its mitochondrial DNA from economics. Spatial theory has become a stand-alone tool for representing political preferences, analyzing competition, and predicting outcomes.

The tools we have developed in the previous section, based primarily on weak orderings, are useful if the number of alternatives is small and the choosers are in a "committee" setting. It is now time to develop tools more suitable for analyzing elections or complex committee votes, such as budgets. These are votes where the alternative space is of very large dimension and at least some dimensions are measured as continuous numbers. For mass elections, both the number of voters and the number of possible alternatives is very large, because the alternatives are points in space. In these circumstances, the spatial model offers a variety of analytical conveniences.

Still, the convenience of the model – while real enough – is not the best argument for using the spatial approach. As Austen-Smith and Banks (1999) point out:

> For many applications it is natural to think of the feasible set of alternatives as representable by some subset of Euclidean space. *Indeed, a spatial metaphor is common in the everyday language of politics:* Political parties are discussed as being "centrist," "leftist," "extreme right-wing"; candidates for office are described as "moving to the left" or attempting to capture the middle ground"; and so on and so forth. In many collective choice environments, therefore, the spatial model is *both* intuitively appealing *and* technically convenient. (p. 151; emphasis added).

The primary assumption is that policy positions of candidates or parties can usefully be conceived as points in a "space." Policy space can encompass one issue, several, or many. Each issue is associated with a dimension in the space, where a "dimension" is an ordered set of alternatives. Then, alternatives are conceived as points in the multidimensional space formed by the Cartesian product of the dimensions.

For the idea of "spatial preferences" to make any sense, it must be possible to approximate the preferences embodied in the ordering of all those market baskets, in the large warehouse, formed from chaining up all the pairwise comparisons conducted by the chooser we introduced in the previous chapter. We will do this by creating a function that "represents" the preference ordering, using a continuous, monotonically increasing set of numbers.

This is not difficult for budgets, because money has standard ratio measurement properties, and is (approximately) continuously divisible: $4 is twice as big a budget as $2, and $3 lies between $2 and $4. Then $3.50 lies between $3 and $4, and $3.75 lies between $3.50 and $4.00, and so on.

The spatial model allows the analyst to integrate three separate components of the dynamics of political competition.

- *The Nature of Voter Preferences:* Each voter prefers candidates or policies that are "closer" to that voter's highest and best moral and material values for government. In other words, preferences are represented by a weighted function of distance on many issues, accounting for the salience and interdependence of issues in the space.
- *Endogenous Platform Selection:* Political parties can estimate, with some error, how voters choose and what each voter wants. Election-motivated actors make proposals (or choose candidates) that attract the most votes, given the nature of voter preferences postulated in the spatial model. Under some circumstances, these platforms may converge until they are nearly indistinguishable. In other circumstances, the platforms may diverge or become unpredictable.

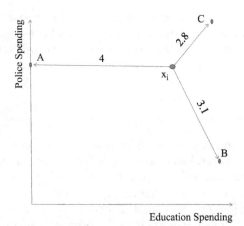

FIGURE 5.1. C is "closest" to x_i

- *Predictions about Outcomes:* If an analyst knows the preferences of voters and locations selected by candidates, parties, or the writers of a referendum, and if the analyst knows the decision rule used to aggregate these preferences over these alternatives, it is often possible to make predictions about the outcome. These predictions may be inaccurate in cases of low information about voter beliefs, or in cases where the turnout decision of voters complicates the problem. The useful thing about spatial theory is that it allows simulations, or questions about counterfactuals: "what if?" The quality of outcomes has normative import, as well, of course. Elections are a means of making public policy responsive to voter desires. Simulating the results of different forms of voting institutions allows analysts to draw at least tentative conclusions about government responsiveness and accountability.

Before going any further, it is useful to consider a simple numerical example that will clarify the nature of choice and utility in the context of spatial utility functions as a way of representing preferences. Keep this example in mind as we go through the nuts and bolts of representation later in the chapter.

Consider four actors: a voter who has an ideal point x_i and three candidates ("market baskets") A, B, and C. There are two dimensions of interest in our example, spending on education (the horizontal axis) and spending on police protection (the vertical axis). The utility function of voter i is spatial, meaning that she likes candidates who are "closer" to her ideal point.

All that is required, then, is to locate the four points (i's ideal point, and the candidate platforms) in space, and let the voter choose the candidate who is closest to her ideal point. The graph of the problem appears in Figure 5.1.

The graph allows you to "measure" the distances with your eye, but it also gives the exact distances from the x_i to each of the platforms. The voter is "closest" to candidate C. But notice that candidate A is *exactly* where the voter wants on police protection. If the voter was deeply concerned about police protection, much more than education, she might choose A. Some "single issue" voters do choose this way, as we will discuss below. But in our example the voter cares about each of the issues equally – we will say the issues have "equal salience" – and she chooses C.

SPATIAL THEORY

The idea of spatial competition as an analytic strategic problem is often traced to Hotelling (1929). Later, Lerner and Singer (1937), and Smithies (1941), used "space" to describe economic competition with costly transportation. But it is more plausible to credit von Thünen (1966) with a variety of important foundational contributions in spatial theory in 1826. One could go further back; Hinich and Munger (1997) claim the original median voter result is at least visible in outline, if not in detail, in Aristotle's *Politics*, Book IV, Part 11.

Spatial theory was adapted for analytical *politics* by two pioneers: Anthony Downs, in *An Economic Theory of Democracy* (1957), and Duncan Black, in *The Theory of Committees and Elections* (1958). Their work laid out two of the most important theoretical contributions of analytical political theory. The spatial approach is different from the "weak orderings" approach used by social choice theorists, because spatial theorists use an explicit utility function to represent preferences. That utility function is closeness, augmented by representation of differences in saliences and nonseparability. The two core conclusions of the spatial model are these:

- Political power lies at the "middle" of the distribution of citizens effectively enfranchised by the society's political institutions. Under some circumstances, there is a single pivotal median voter whose vote determines the outcome of the election or political choice. It may not matter much what anyone out on the extremes wants, because if they become even more extreme, the median – if it exists – still decides.
- Under some circumstances, the self-interested strategic choices of parties or candidates can cause alternatives to converge toward the center of the distribution of preferences. To the extent that this outcome conforms to norms or moral intuitions about "good policy," then democratic processes can deliver on their promise of good government. But under other circumstances, the outcomes can be polarized, or indeterminate. Thus, the stability of political systems is a variable, determined by the structure of individual preferences and the institutions used to aggregate those preferences.

The contribution of the spatial theorists who have built on the work of Downs and Black has been to state these two principles of political power very precisely. Most importantly, analytical politics works to distinguish situations where the principles are true, false, or conditionally true based on other variables outside the model.

The Foundations of the Spatial Model of Politics

The spatial model is not conjectural or unrealistically abstract. Human beings actually think this way and routinely use the words "left," "right," and "center" as if those words mean something, and as if the listener will attach the same understanding to the words when they are used to discuss politics. This belief that the listener will attach a predictable meaning to a candidate's "spatial" position is important. People use the metaphor of space because it helps them understand politics. Communication requires that some part of the understanding of these terms be shared. We will begin with the simplest possible set of assumptions about information and behavior before moving to more realistic but more complicated models in later chapters.

The first clear use of the left-center-right spatial metaphor was just after the French Revolution of 1789. It is remarkable, given the extensive treatment historians have accorded this period, that so little attention has been paid to the contribution of the Revolution to our everyday language of politics. Earlier, in Chapter 2, we discussed some of the dynamics of the Revolution and its aftermath. Now, it is useful to consider the rhetorical legacy of those events.

The extreme differences in power and prestige in the French political system caused tensions. The novelty of the idea of democracy, and its requirement of equality in the form of "one person, one vote," required profound conceptual changes. It is perhaps not surprising that people started to use the idea of political space as a way of organizing the conflict.

"Left" and "Right" were the physical positions of political groups in the National Assemblies (1789–1791), and later in the National Convention (1792–1795). Groups that disliked each other sat as far apart as they could. Radical allies of Robespierre sat in the "Mountain," the high benches against the top wall.

From the perspective of someone entering the hall, these radical deputies were on the far left. The independent deputies (the "Marsh," or the "Plain") occupied the debating floor in the lower center of the hall. The Girondin deputies held most of the ministries that ran the government, and consequently controlled most of the practical power in the Assembly. They gathered in the far "right" corner of the hall (Schama, 1989: 648). Over time, it became clear that those on the left (Jacobins) wanted radical change. Those on the right (Girondins) defended the status quo because they had control of the government.

These meanings have changed only slightly in being transformed into the modern language of politics: "Left" still generally means those who want change, with the extreme left seeking revolutionary change. The right is conservative, either defending the current policies against change, or advocating a return to previous policies and norms.[2]

The "left-center-right" image has led social scientists to develop models that capture spatial political competition. In the next three sections, we will consider spatial models that formal theorists use to analyze democracy.

These three sections each describe one component of the general model outlined above: voter choices, endogenous platform choices, and predictions about outcomes.

SPATIAL UTILITY FUNCTIONS AS A REPRESENTATION OF PREFERENCE

The starting point for voter choice is preference. The spatial model uses a particular kind of utility function to "represent" preference: The candidate or alternative *closer* (*-est*) to the voter's own views receives that citizen's vote. Both the voter's ideal point and the candidate/alternative can be defined in a Cartesian coordinate plane, as we saw earlier in this chapter in the space "education × police." This notion of closeness can be made quite precise: Utility is some inverse function of the distance from the voter's ideal point to the alternative in question, so that farther = worse.

But what function? There are many possible functions that might "represent" distance. The absolute value of the difference between the voter ideal and the platform, the square of the difference, and square root of the distance are all possibilities. Further, how to handle platforms that have several characteristics ("How much spending on education? How much spending on police")? How does a voter balance these different considerations?

We will answer these questions more fully in the following chapter, presenting a model that can handle both salience (different weights in terms of utility) and nonseparability (issues must be considered together). For now, the important thing is that spatial theory uses "the voter" as a mathematical simulation that embodies useful and tractable answers to the two questions posed above. Specifically:

(i) The voter perceives each candidate as a platform, or point in a "space" formed by the Cartesian product of all the individual issues at stake in the contest. The voter then evaluates each platform by comparing it with her own ideal set of positions on these issues. Other considerations, such as valence, or affective reaction to the candidate, can be added to the model.[3] Alternatively, the nature of issues themselves can be "directional," that is, having to do with the changes or direction voters prefer, rather than a point position or fixed location.[4]

(ii) The salience – the relative importance of each issue, in the voter's mind – is captured by a set of weights. A large weight means the voter thinks that issue is more important than issues with smaller weights. If the voter doesn't care at all about some issue, that issue has zero weight. Pundits and government officials often bemoan the fact that something they care about is not "an issue" in the election. But that's not quite right; it is an issue, but in voters' minds, it has zero weight, either because they are unaware of it or because they genuinely do not care.[5]

The notion of a "spatial" utility function as a representation of preference is actually quite complex, and it is important to keep in mind that any order-preserving transformation of the representation is equally valid as a "utility function." The reason this property of utility functions introduces complexity into the analysis is that the equilibrium properties of voting systems may depend on which specific functional form is selected. At a minimum, one might choose from among city-block, linear distance, or some nonlinear loss function (such as the quadratic commonly used in single-dimensional spatial theory). We are restricting consideration to the linear distance representation and the quadratic, but the comparison with city-block (see, for example, Macartan and Laver, 2010) raises a number of other possibilities. It is possible to generate a general representation of spatial preferences (Eguia, 2011, 2013) that includes all these types of utility functions as special cases, but this is beyond the scope of the present inquiry.

In Chapter 3 we introduced a distinction between quite different contexts for voting, committees (few voters, high stakes, liberal amendment rules, good information) and mass elections (many voters, voting on candidates instead of proposals, and costly information). It is useful to give an example of how each context shapes the problem of spatial voting. In this example, we will consider a decision, by a group, choosing a budget.

Example 1 (Committee voting). "Committees" are small groups of choosers selecting a policy directly. Imagine there are three people on a committee charged with choosing an entertainment budget for their club. Suppose we believe that each person would prefer budgets closer to his or her idea of the best budget. Let shy guy A think the club should spend $250, let moderate woman B favor $375, and let party man C be stoked to spend $1,250 so they can hire a band, which costs at least that much. Each chooser has an idea of the best amount of spending for the party budget. This is the voter's *ideal point.* The core assumption of spatial theory is that people prefer alternatives that are closer to their ideal point.

So A, who wants a budget of $250 if it were up to him, likes $225 more than $210, and likes $265 more than $290. One possible utility function to "represent" these preferences appears in Figure 5.2, for Mr. A, on the left of the diagram.

Notice that A while prefers $250 to any other alternative, he is indifferent between $40 less ($210) and $40 more ($290). This means that he has "symmetric" preferences. The property of symmetry is preserved by any affine transformation of the utility function, which might make it taller or shorter (since the units of utility are arbitrary).

Ms. B has an ideal point of $375. However, her utility function is much shorter and wider than that of Mr. A. Thus, while B's utility function is also symmetric, like A's, her intensity of preference is less. She wants $375 for the party budget, but she wouldn't care that much if the group spent slightly more or less.

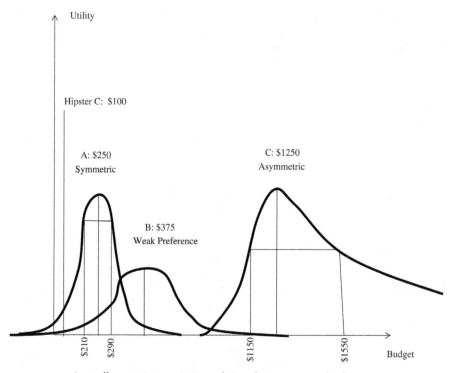

FIGURE 5.2. A small committee – A, B, and C – choose a party budget

How can we square the interpersonal utility comparison (A has a more intense commitment to his most preferred budget than B has to hers) with the fact that the units of any utility function are arbitrary? The answer is that if we are going to place both utility functions on the same graph, we are assuming they have the same units and are therefore comparable. A pure subjectivist viewpoint would rule this out, of course, because the claim that A "cares more" is hard to measure or prove. But intensity of preference is commonly measured in politics, and so spatial utility functions are often drawn on the same graph. It is still true that the utility functions are not unique and could be transformed in a variety of ways. So long as all the spatial utility functions are transformed in the same way, however, it will always be true that A will care more about his ideal point, and resist compromise, more than the relatively more indifferent Ms. B. will.[6]

Person C has an ideal point of $1,250 because he really wants to hire a band. For C, there is a qualitative difference for any budget less than $1,250, because not even a terrible band will play for less than that. C's preferences are still monotonic, in the sense that he likes $1,000 more than $970, and likes $1,500 more than $1,600, and so on. But his preferences are *asymmetric*: C is much happier with spending $50 more than his ideal point than he is with spending $50 less. This is illustrated in Figure 5.2 by choosing an arbitrary "level" of utility, and asking what budgets above and below C's ideal point of $1,250 would make him indifferent. At the level of utility chosen here, C would be indifferent between $1,150 ($100 less than his ideal point) and $1,550 ($300 more than his ideal point). Clearly, the implication of asymmetry is that equal deviations from the ideal point on opposite sides are not valued equally by C, unlike A and B, whose preferences are symmetric.

These three individuals, A, B, and C, have decided they want to have a party. But to be a constituted group they have to choose a decision rule, and then unanimously agree that they will be bound by the outcome of that decision rule, even if that particular outcome is not one that each individual would have selected.[7] For the sake of example, let's assume that the decision rule they have selected is majority rule, with free proposal power for all members.

That is all we need to know to make a prediction about what the committee will decide as a group: ideal points (if preferences are "spatial," where closer is better) and the decision rule (in this case, majority rule with free proposal power). The prediction is that the outcome will be a budget of $375, because the center or median position rules.

It is easy to see why the center has such power. Committee members are free to propose their own ideal points; suppose the status quo budget is $0 (no party), and that someone is chosen to make the first proposal. What will happen? It seems to depend on who goes first, but that is deceptive (the specifics are left as an exercise to the reader at the end of the chapter). A new status quo budget would be established each time a majority voted for the change. However, the process would not go on indefinitely. As soon as B proposes her ideal point, $375, the process will be stable, and $375 will be the outcome.

The reason is that no alternative can defeat the median in a pairwise majority rule contest. The $375 proposal will defeat any proposal it is matched against, so it becomes the status quo. A and B prefer $375 to any proposal larger than, and B and C prefer $375 to any proposal less than, $375. So $375 is an "equilibrium," or stable result of the voting process.

An interesting property of the median, unlike the mean or other concepts of the "center" of the distribution of voter preferences, is that it is stable with respect to changes in the preferences or ideal points of other committee members out on the extremes (as long as they remain members of the constituted group; if one or more people quit the median changes). Suppose that C decided that he wanted a top band, at a cost of $25 million, for the party. Would the result change? Not at all, the median would still be $375. On the other hand, if C became a hipster and decided that cover bands weren't cool, and switched his preference from $1,250 to $100, then the median of the "new" committee would be A's preference of $250.

Example 2 (Mass elections). "Elections" are quite different from committee votes. Elections are activities of large groups of voters who do not know each other, choosing a candidate or voting up or down on an initiative or other policy choice. Such citizens are unlikely to have any kind of proposal power,

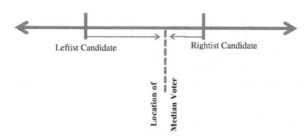

FIGURE 5.3. An Election with a single spatial dimension – ideology

and they may be poorly informed about the nature of the choices that are available. Figure 5.3 is an illustration of the "classical" left-right dimension. The specific meaning of "left" and "right" will depend (Hinich and Munger, 1994) on the particular political culture of the electorate, and the time.

The logic of spatial theory implies that the location of the specific voter ideal points in a large population is not important. What matters is the "center," in particular the median, of the distribution of voters, and the location of the candidates. The candidate closer to the median is the predicted winner. In this case, that happens to be the candidate on the right.

There are several problems with this conception, which is the reason that the spatial theory of mass elections is a separate topic from committee voting. We will discuss these problems at greater length later. One can immediately see, however, that the units of the ideological "dimension" are not obvious; the notion of "location" on such an ill-defined dimension is likewise problematic, and in any case it is not clear what it means for a candidate to move or choose a location; the location of the median voter(s) (there may well be a lot of voters at the median position!) is not clearly defined; and the whole analysis assumes that either everyone votes or that the turnout decision is predictable from the perspective of the analyst. In fact, in most mass elections, the particular dimension(s) in the contest are not well defined, the location of the median position is unknown, and turnout is hard to predict.

ASSUMPTIONS

There have been several assumptions underlying the examples above, and it is important to make those assumptions clear and precise. The spatial approach to specifying utility functions for citizens or committee members is being applied in a particular way. We will expand the application in the following chapter. But for now, we will work with the following assumptions.

(a) The choice is *unidimensional*: There is only one issue, and committee members or citizens like their own ideal point best.
(b) Preferences are *single peaked*: Each member likes new proposed budgets more the "closer" they are to the member's ideal. More precisely, utility

declines monotonically the greater the distance between a proposal and the ideal point of the member.

(c) Voting is *sincere*: The member votes for the more preferred alternative in the contest or comparison immediately presented. This is true even if other proposals will be raised further down the agenda. More intuitively, sincere voting means that the member does not look ahead, but considers only the two alternatives being voted right now.

There is an additional property of spatial preference functions that we will sometimes find useful to invoke:

(d) *Symmetry.* A preference function is symmetric if equal departures from the ideal in opposite directions yield equal declines in satisfaction.

The intuition of the spatial model is deceptively simple: *political power rests in the middle of the distribution of preferences effectively enfranchised by the institutions of society.* This result is commonly called the median voter theorem (MVT). The MVT implies that the median position, if at least one exists, will be a Condorcet winner.

More Careful Definitions

The foundation of spatial theory is the use of a utility function to capture and represent preferences. Consider a *representative citizen i,* who can be anyone in the set of N people (named 1 through n) that we call "enfranchised," or citizens with the power to vote. Assume i has an *ideal point* x_i, or a unique[8] position strictly preferred to any other alternative. (Notice that for ideal points, and for most other purposes, we will use subscripts to identify people, so x_1 is person 1's ideal point, and x_i is i's ideal point.)

Finally, let $|z|$ denote the *absolute value* of a number z. For example, $|-31| = 31;\ |6| = 6.$

We are now in a position to be able to offer a statement of the MVT as a contingently true proposition, or theorem. Consider two alternatives y and z, where both y and z are on the *same side of i* (making symmetry irrelevant). We can now define the two familiar binary relations, "preference" ($\succ_k$) and "indifference" ($\approx_k$) in spatial terms. (Note that the subscript on the relation symbol denotes the particular citizen whose preference is being represented, so "k prefers" and "k is indifferent.")

PREFERENCE

$$y \succ_i z \text{ if and only if } |y - x_i| < |z - x_i| \tag{5.1}$$

INDIFFERENCE

$$y \approx_i z \text{ if and only if } |y - x_i| = |z - x_i| \tag{5.2}$$

The only innovation in these definitions is that now preference declines mono-tonically with distance. Unlike more abstract preference functions, both these definitions clearly require that the issue being considered be ordered along a single dimension. For the example we have been considering, the dimension is budget size, but the model is equally applicable to other settings where units are divisible and ordered.

Symmetry is not assumed in these formal definitions. Without assuming symmetry, we can define preference and indifference only for the case where y and z are on the same side of the ideal point. If preferences are symmetric, then (5.1) and (5.2) also describe an evaluation of y and z when y and z are on different sides of x_i. This seems a powerful statement, but the power of the claim derives from the restrictiveness of the assumption of symmetry.

Now that indifference and preference have been defined for individual i, we can consider these same relations, and the distribution of ideal points $\{x_1, x_2, \ldots, x_n\}$ for many citizens, and see what happens when they vote. To make our prediction, we need to define a "median position" more carefully.

It is the nature of pairwise majority rule elections that a proposal preferred by one half $(N/2)$ of the voters is guaranteed to be at least a tie. If an alternative receives more than $N/2$ votes, it wins outright. This property suggests that the median captures an important part of what is meant by the "middle" in politics.[9] Simply put, the median value beats or ties all other alternatives in pairwise majority rule elections.

To see this, consider the definition of a median position:

• Choose an arbitrary citizen i's ideal point x_i
• Let N_L (the number to the left) be the number of citizens j for whom $x_j \leq x_i$
• Let N_R (the number to the right) be the number of citizens k for whom $x_i \leq x_k$

In words, then, citizens with the subscript j have ideal points less than x_i. Citizens with the subscript k have ideal points greater than x_i. N_L is the number of j's. N_R is the number of k's.

Then a median position can be defined as follows.

Median position. A position x_i is a median position, or x_{med}, if and only if:

(1) $N_R \geq N/2$

and

(2) $N_L \geq N/2$.

The "and" seems confusing; how could both N_L and N_R be greater than $N/2$? The reason is that the citizens actually at the median position are counted twice. They are part of N_L and they also are part of N_R, because N_L and N_R both include the median.

So what a median position x_i requires is that at least half of the citizens have ideal points greater than or equal to x_i, and at least half have ideal points less than or equal to x_i. In general, then, $N_L + N_R \geq N$

This definition, adapted only slightly from Duncan Black's formulation,[10] is cumbersome. But it is useful because it encompasses odd N, even N, and situations where several voters share an ideal point. Thomas Schwartz gives a more intuitive definition (1986, p. 87):

x is a median position if no majority of individuals has ideal points (peaks) to the left or to the right of x

The difference between Black's definition and Schwartz's has to do with the treatment of ideal points that lie at the median position itself. In our definition, N_L and N_R both include the ideal point(s) at the median position, so $N_L \geq N/2$ and $N_R \geq N/2$. In Schwartz's definition, no majority of citizens can all want *strictly* more, or *strictly* less, than the median position. The advantage of Black's approach is that it measures directly the vote that the median position will receive in a majority rule election. For any proposal strictly to the left of x_i, the median will receive N_R (or more) votes. For any proposal strictly to the right of x_i, the median position will receive at least N_L votes.

Odd N, even N, and uniqueness of the median position

In some cases, such as for the party budget example (Figure 5.2) the median ideal point was easy to identify. There were two members (A and B) who had ideal points less than or equal to x_{med}. There were also two (B and C) with ideal points at least as big as x_{med}. B is a median position, since

$$N/2 = 1.5 \qquad N_L = 2 > N/2 = 1.5 \qquad \text{and} \qquad N_R = 2 > N/2 = 1.5.$$

The median is not always so easy to identify. For one thing, the median may not be unique. Suppose that B was absent on the day of the vote. Now $N = 2$, and *all positions between 250 and 1,250* (including $x_A = 250$ and $x_C = 1,250$) are "medians." Consider, for example, $x = 1,000$. There are, because of B's absence, one ideal above 1,000 and one below 1,000. The same is true for 300, or 671, or 1,198. The "median position" is a range of points, not a single point.

If assumptions (a)-(c) are met then at least one median always exists. If N is odd, there is always a unique median. If N is even then the median may be unique, or it may be a closed line segment between (and including) two ideal points.

But the fact that the median position is unique does not mean that there is a single median voter. Several voters may share the ideal point at the median position, so while the median point is unique the median voter may not be. Let's add some voters to the party budget committee problem, to illustrate these claims.

N even, no shared ideal points: Consider the three citizen/ideal point combinations we had before, plus one more, person D with an ideal party budget of $1,500. That means we have:

$$x_A = 250, x_B = 375, x_C = 1,250, x_D = 1,500$$

(a) Four unique ideal points, with a median interval (dotted line)

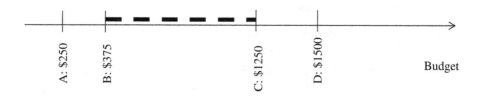

(b) Five non-unique ideal points, with a unique median position (large dot)

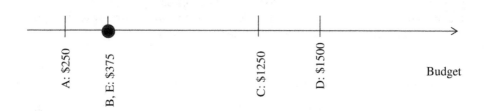

(c) Four non-unique ideal points, with a unique median position (large dot)

FIGURE 5.4. Examples of median positions and intervals

as depicted in Figure 5.4, panel (a). The median is therefore an interval containing x_B and x_C, and all the points between them.

N odd, shared or non-unique ideal points: Add a fifth committee member, E, who happens to share an ideal point with B at 375. Then the unique median (you know there is a unique median position, because the number of committee members is odd) is located at 375.

N even, shared or non-unique ideal points: Imagine that C drops out to become a heavily tatooed barista, and the other four members remain. Now that there is again an even number of voters the median could be unique or an interval. In this instance, the median position is unique, at 375. This is important to recognize: Once we allow citizens to share ideal points, it turns out that a unique median *can* exist even if N is even. There is only one median position (though there are two median voters), even though the number of voters is even.

It is worth summarizing what we know about the existence and nature of median points, given the distribution of voter ideal points:

- If preferences are single-peaked, and the issue space is one-dimensional, then at least one median position always exists. The results below all assume that preferences are single-peaked and the issue space is one-dimensional. These two assumptions are sufficient, but not necessary, for existence of at least one median position.
- If N is odd, then the median is always unique, or a single point in the policy space. This is true even if ideal points are shared. (See Exercise 5.8.)
- If N is even and no ideal points are shared, there is a *closed interval* of medians.
- If N is even and some ideal points are shared, then there may be either a unique median or a closed interval of medians.

THE MEDIAN VOTER THEOREM

We can now state and prove the median voter theorem and a corollary. The MVT result is based on the two assumptions discussed earlier:

(1) There is a single issue. This means that all the alternatives can be represented as points on one line, and each voter i has an ideal point x_i on this line.

(2) Preferences are spatial (single-peaked utility function, utility monotonically declining (though perhaps not symmetrically) with distance from the ideal point).

Median voter theorem. Suppose x_{med} is a median position for the society. Then the number of votes for x_{med} is greater than or equal to the number of votes for any other alternative z.

Proof. A "median position" has been defined as a point (it may or may not be unique) that has the property that $N_R \geq N/2$ and $N_L \geq N/2$. Now, suppose $z < x_{med}$ (z is to the left of x_{med} as we normally draw the line). All ideal points to the right of x_{med} are closer to x_{med} than to z. All voters with ideal points to the right of x_{med} vote for x_{med} versus z, by assumption (2). Likewise, all voters with ideal points exactly equal to x_{med} vote for x_{med}. Since x_{med} is a median position, there are at least $N/2$ voters such that $x_i \geq x_{med}$. So x_{med} receives at least $N/2$ votes, ensuring it cannot be strictly defeated by any alternative to the left. The same reasoning applies if $z > x_{med}$.

To paraphrase: A median position can *never* lose in a majority rule contest. It can tie other alternatives if there is a closed interval of medians, since any two median points will by definition each receive $N/2$ votes, but it cannot lose. This version of the statement and proof of the MVT probably is best attributed to Duncan Black.

COROLLARY TO THE MEDIAN VOTER RESULT

The corollary requires two extra assumptions:

(3) The society has exactly one median position x_{med}.
(4) Voter preferences around each x_i are symmetric

Corollary. If y is closer to x_{med} than z, then y beats z in a majority rule election. If y and z are on the same side of x_{med}, it is not necessary to invoke symmetry. But if y and z are on opposite sides of x_{med}, symmetry is required.

Proof. Again, let $z < y$ and assume that $z < x_{med}$. Since y is closer to x_{med} than z, $(y + z)/2 < x_{med}$, whether y and z are on the same side of x_{med} or not, and $(y + z)/2$ is equidistant from y and z. Thus, all ideal points to the right of $(y + z)/2$ are closer to y than to z, whereas all ideal points to the left of (less than) $(y + z)/2$ are closer to z than to y. Since x_{med} is unique, the number of ideal points equal to or to the right of x_{med} is greater than $N/2$. These ideal points are closer to y than to z, because $(y + z)/2 < x_{med}$. Since preferences are symmetric, y receives a majority of the votes.

The MVT says that if the median position itself is one of the alternatives being compared, the median always wins (or ties if the median position is not unique). The corollary implies that for any other pair of proposals, the alternative *closer* to the median wins if preferences are symmetric, or if both proposals are on the same side of the median.

What if Preferences Aren't Single-peaked?

There is an important question we have not yet answered: Does at least one median position always exist? The existence of even one median position rules out majority rule cycles, because cycles require that a majority oppose every feasible alternative. But no majority opposes a median position, by definition.

It turns out that this intuition, that the middle must hold power, comes quite close to our modern conception of the technical conditions that promote electoral stability. This type of instability is observed when some people's preferences are not single-peaked. That means, in spatial terms, that at least *some people like the middle alternative least.*

If a substantial proportion of voters have preferences that are not single-peaked, there may be no median voter, or median position, even if the other assumptions of the MVT are met. Riker (1982) argues that the possibilities for genuine "popular rule" may be sharply circumscribed by the structure of preferences among voters. If preferences are not single peaked, it may be strictly impossible to arrive at a nonarbitrary outcome, or collective judgment, by majority rule. This is not some minor mathematical curiosity, because it means that claims about the existence of the middle are only conditionally true. To see how preferences that are not single-peaked can affect democratic choice in spatial voting, we will consider an example.

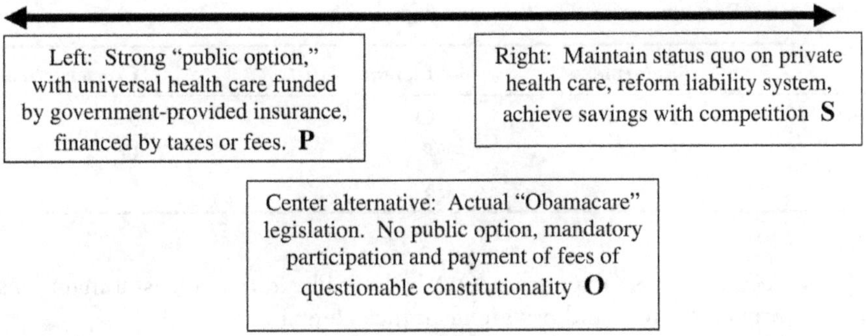

FIGURE 5.5. Health care reform alternatives

EXAMPLE: U.S. HEALTH CARE REFORM

Imagine that there are three options for health care policy, arrayed along the "left-right" dimension shown in Figure 5.5.

For the sake of the example, assume that there are only three preference profiles, radical reformers, incrementalists, and conservatives:

I. *Radical Reformers:* P ≻ S ≻ O
   - These people want to reform the system of health care delivery in the U.S., and to provide as close to 100 percent coverage as possible. To do this, they would like to ensure passage of a strong "public option," and their first choice is P.
   - Second best, from their perspective, is S. Better to leave things as they are than to choose an expensive half measure that will discredit reform that has no public option.
   - The worst outcome would be what actually was done, derisively called "Obamacare." This reform does not go nearly far enough, and it leaves out a "public option," the key objective of reformers. Therefore, the problem with Obamacare is not that it goes too far, but that it does not go far enough. Still, for reformers, O is worst option.

II. *Incrementalists:* O ≻ P ≻ S
   - Slow, gradual change (O) is best. Sure, Obamacare is not perfect, and there is more to be done. Better not to make a mistake than to do too much at once.
   - Second best is a large reform, with a public option, P.
   - Our health care system is too damaged to do nothing, and thus S is the worst alternative, entirely unacceptable.

III. *Conservatives:* S ≻ O ≻ P
   - S is the best we can do. The U.S. has the finest health care in the world. Sure, some people aren't covered, but socializing our medical system is too high a price to pay.

TABLE 5.1. *Preferences on Health Care Reform*

	Reformers	Incrementalists	Conservatives
Best	P	O	S
	S	P	O
Worst	O	S	P

- Second best is Obamacare, O. We don't like it, but at least it maintains private doctors and private insurance companies.
- The worst outcome would be socialized medicine, or the so-called "public option," P. That must be defeated at all costs.

We can depict the preference profile for the American political controversy over health care in 2009 in Table 5.1.

What actually happened? The Democrats in the U.S. Congress managed to eliminate S as a viable option, because of their massive victory in 2008 and their large majorities in the House and Senate. By trumpeting their support for P, the Democratic leadership got the impression that P could win, because P defeats S. (Reformers and Incrementalists say P ≻ S, Conservatives say S ≻ P, so P wins.)

But that meant that P was put up against the remaining alternative, O. Conservatives prefer O ≻ P, and so do Incrementalists, Blue Dog Dems and others in swing districts. The majority in favor of P, which the Democrats had been so sure of, evaporated.

Tactically, the Reformers made a mistake. They needed to portray the choices as P vs. S. If they had done that, they might have gotten P, their most-preferred outcome. But the opposition cleverly portrayed the choices as being O vs. P, and the result was that O, the least preferred outcome for the reformers, was the result. There were many causes of the 2010 election backlash against the Democratic majority. However, a major part of the explanation is likely to be that the Democrats in Congress exhausted themselves achieving a policy victory that angered two majorities: The majority that favored P over S, but got O instead, and the majority that favored S over O, but still got O.

The new Republican majority in the house in early 2011 liked to support their attempts to repeal Obamacare by claiming, "The majority of Americans are opposed to Obamacare." This is not just the result of biased sampling – the *Wall Street Journal*'s published percentage of Americans who support Obamacare in January 2011 was 41 percent. By December 2013, 56 percent of Americans viewed Obamacare "at least somewhat unfavorably."[11]

However, there is a problem here, one our readers should now be able to identify. *There is a majority opposed to* all three alternatives. The claim that a majority of Americans are opposed to Obamacare is true, but it does *not* imply that the status quo is the way to go. These survey data imply that, in the case of

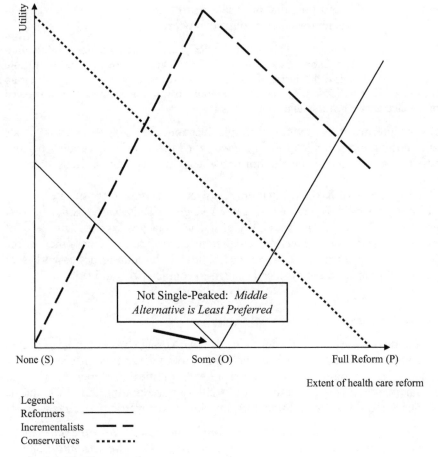

Not Single-Peaked: *Middle Alternative is Least Preferred*

None (S)   Some (O)   Full Reform (P)

Extent of health care reform

Legend:
Reformers ———
Incrementalists — —
Conservatives ·······

FIGURE 5.6. Health care reform

healthcare reform, preferences are not single-peaked – thus, theory predicts that indeterminacy and sensitivity to voting order might be observed.

The technical reason for this instability is the fact that there are three different contradictory majorities: The majority that prefers O to P, the majority that prefers P to S, and the majority that prefers S to O. The explanation is easy to see in terms of the spatial model.

As Figure 5.6 shows, the reason that there is no median voter is that a substantial proportion of the electorate (the radical reformers) like the "middle" alternative (in this case, O) least. Since the assumption of single-peakedness is violated, a majority is opposed to every alternative.[12]

The discussion in this section represents a slightly different statement of the thesis advanced in William Riker's (1982) *Liberalism against Populism*. In this famous book, Riker argues that political theorists have placed too much faith in the power of participatory, or populist, democracy:

> What is different between the liberal and populist views is that in the populist interpretation of voting, the opinions of the majority *must* be right and *must* be respected because the will of the people is the liberty of the people. In the liberal interpretation, there is no such magical identification. The outcome of voting is just a decision and has no special moral character. (p. 14: emphasis in original)

Riker's interpretation of voting is simple: Elections are a way to control officials and nothing more. Some observers have called this conclusion unduly pessimistic or have objected that the normative conclusions make citizens skeptical about government.

This critique of Riker's conclusions, however, ignores the positive character of his argument.[13] The nonexistence of a single best alternative is not of itself good or bad. Rather, the possibility of indeterminacy is a generic property of majority rule decision processes, under some circumstances. This is the just the sort of contingent truth, with a specific isolation of the contingency at work, that analytical political theory is ideally suited to characterize and identify.

FINAL WORDS

Spatial theory is based on the intuitive idea that voting choices can be predicted by comparing distances from an ideal point to an alternative. It uses a utility function based on difference to "represent" political preferences. We can summarize the two basic results of this chapter by restating the MVT and its corollary requiring the additional assumption of symmetric preferences.

Median voter theorem: *A median position cannot lose to any other alternative in a majority rule election. If the median position is unique, it cannot even tie any other alternative.*

The MVT implies that the middle of the distribution of citizen preferences in a society holds a privileged position in political competition. If the median position is unique (identified with just one voter), we call this very important person the median voter.

Corollary: *In a comparison of alternatives that are not median positions, the alternative closer to the median wins.*

The corollary shows that under certain conditions (unique median and symmetric preferences), closeness to the middle is the basis of political power. Consequently, even if the status quo is different from the median, there are pressures for new alternatives to move toward the center until a median position is reached. And even if the median voter does not "win," the median selects the winner.

Together, these two conditions establish an important benchmark in what we can say about the likely outcomes of political conflict. More important, we have given some formal support for the intuitive claim that the "center" of the society is where political power lies. As we have pointed out repeatedly, this notion of the center as the source of political power is widely held; media and political operatives both take it for granted.

We have seen in this chapter the problems posed by the lack of single-peaked preferences. In the next chapter, we will generalize the MVT to allow for more than one dimension. It will turn out that the simple intuition about distance and voting that led us this far is not reliable. In two or more dimensions, the "center" may not exist at all, even if preferences of individuals are single-peaked.

TERMS

Cartesian policy space
Committee
Convergence
Distance metric
Endogenous platform selection
Girondin
Jacobin
Left-Right dimension
Mass elections
Median position
Median voter theorem
Middle
Platform
Representative citizen
Sincere voting
Single-peaked
Spatial model
Symmetry
Unidimensionality
Uniqueness
Voter preference

EXERCISES

5.1 For a given issue, let $x_1 = 2$, $x_2 = 6$, $x_3 = 9$, $x_4 = 9$, and $x_5 = -2$. What is the median position of the five voters? What is the mean, or average, position?

5.2 Suppose this five-member committee (from Exercise 5.1) is asked to vote (sincerely) on two alternatives, $y = 8$ and $z = 3$. If preferences are symmetric, which alternative will win?

5.3 Suppose $x_6 = 7$ is added to the committee. What is (are) the median position(s) now? If the new, six-member committee is asked to choose between $y = 8$ and $z = 3$, what happens?

5.4 For another issue, let $x_1 = -3$, $x_2 = 21$, $x_3 = 7$, $x_4 = 6$, and $x_5 = -4$. What is the median position and mean ideal point of these five voters? Suppose x_3 is replaced by $x_3' = 25$. Which changes more, the mean or the median position'?

5.5 Given Aristotle's discussion of the distribution of citizens that makes for the best society, is "mean" an accurate description of what he meant'?

5.6 Three different measures of the central tendency of a distribution were discussed in the chapter: mean, mode, and median. For what sorts of distributions are these three concepts identical?

5.7 The median income for a family of four in the United States is about $48,000. The mean income for a family of four is about $64,000. Which is a better measure of "middle class," as you understand that term? Draw a distribution of income in which the mean is larger than the median. Do you think this type of distribution also describes the patterns of incomes in other countries?

5.8 * Prove the following statement: "If N is odd, the median is always a single point, and not an interval." (*Hint: Assume an interval of ideal points exists, and then use the median voter result proved in this chapter to show that an interval of medians implies N is even. It may help to remember that any integer multiplied by two is even.*)

Note: Exercises marked * are advanced material.

6

Two Dimensions: Elusive Equilibrium*

The nature of man is intricate; the objects of society are of the greatest possible complexity; and, therefore, no simple disposition or direction of power can be suitable either to man's nature or to the quality of his affairs. When I hear the simplicity of contrivance aimed at and boasted of in any new political constitutions, I am at no loss to decide that the artificers are grossly ignorant of their trade or totally negligent of their duty...

The rights of men are in a sort of middle, incapable of definition, but not impossible to be discerned... Political reason is a computing principle; adding, subtracting, multiplying, and dividing, morally and not metaphysically, or mathematically, true moral denominations.

Edmund Burke, *Reflections on the Revolution in France*, 1790, Part IV

EQUILIBRIUM AND THE MIDDLE

The previous chapter introduced the idea of "spatial" utility functions for choices along a single dimension, and laid out the solution of equilibrium at the median position. Now, we ask whether this notion of the "middle" also is a plausible result in more complex political spaces, with two or more dimensions. Burke's claim is intriguing: Is the "middle" in complex political choices really "incapable of definition, but not impossible to be discerned"? Is the middle a *general* concept, or is it restricted to policy choices of one dimension?

To introduce the logic of the multidimensional spatial model, it is useful first to consider an example of a legislative committee. We will call this the "Appropriations Committee;" it is responsible for choosing a budget with two line items. That is, the budget will be sum of the spending on Policy 1 and spending on Policy 2. The choosers may have preferences on each policy, prefer one policy to another, or have a complex preference regarding how the two policies go together.

TABLE 6.1. *Subcommittee ideal points on two projects*

Member	Project 1 (millions of $)	Project 2 (millions of $)
Mr. A	150	120 (Median Project 2)
Mr. B	50	40
Ms. C	100	70
Ms. D	10	200
Mr. E	80 (Median Project 1)	150

THE APPROPRIATIONS COMMITTEE

Suppose there are five committee members, named A, B, C, D, and E. They must make budget recommendations for two projects. Their ideal points for Project 1 and Project 2 appear in Table 6.1.

Assuming that preferences are spatial (single-peaked, with utility declining monotonically with distance), let us imagine that committee members vote one issue at a time. The median voter on Project 1 is Mr. E, favoring a budget of $80 million, and the median voter on Project 2 is Mr. A, favoring a budget of $120 million, assuming that the committee members can separate the two issues. Technically, this means that the utility function is *separable*, so that the preference for one project does not depend on the expected level of spending on the other project.

This result, the vector of dimension-at-a-time medians, is important. To help the reader visualize the problem, we graph the two dimensions, the ideal points, and the one-issue-at-a-time solutions in Figure 6.1.

Having two (or more) projects changes the choosers' problem significantly, in at least three ways.

- *Salience:* Members' assessments of the relative importance of the two projects may differ markedly, because each project serves different groups of people or different national needs.[1]
- *Separability:* The level of spending or intensity of regulation for one project may affect preferences for the other project. This is "nonseparability." Preferences about spending levels for Projects 1 and 2 may be related in a way that makes the idea of fixed, independent dimensional "ideal points" untenable. If my preferences are nonseparable, I cannot tell you how much I want to spend on Project 1 unless I can at least estimate how much we will spend on Project 2, and vice versa. For each expected level of project 1, I have a *different conditional ideal point* for project 2.[2]
- *Multidimensional Amendments:* Proposals can now take the form of changing along both dimensions at once. This means that the nature of equilibrium must account for the increased dimension of the space of political conflict. Even if preferences are single-peaked, the configurations of preferences that generate stable equilibria are different once there is more than one dimension.

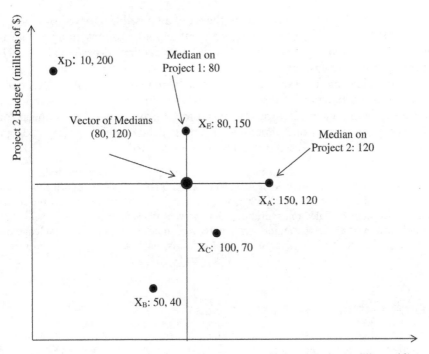

FIGURE 6.1. Ideal points of committee members and the results of voting one issue at a time

The first thing we will need to do is expand our conception of "preference" using the spatial utility function. We have to account for the complexities we have discussed – salience and nonseparability – and then use the resulting augmented utility function to explore the problem of multiple dimensions.

We will continue to use capital letter subscripts to differentiate committee members. From now on, we will also use number subscripts to distinguish projects (here, Projects 1 and 2). Continuing with the example in Table 6.1, A's ideal point on Project 1 is $x_{A1} = 150$; D's ideal point on Project 2 is $x_{D2} = 200$.

Some readers will recognize this two-dimensional space $\mathcal{P}$ as a Cartesian product, which we talked about previously in Chapter 3 when we took up binary relations. The Cartesian product is the space that is created by "multiplying" the two dimensions[3] together:

$$\mathcal{P} = P_1 \times P_2 \qquad (6.1)$$

What this means practically is that we can define budget proposals and member ideal points along both dimensions at the same time. Ms. B's ideal, for example, is

$$\mathbf{x}_B = (x_{B1}, x_{B2}) = (100, 70)$$

(Note: **bold** indicates a "vector")

Her ideal point is the element of $\mathcal{P}$ (the set of all possible budgets for Projects 1 and 2) that Ms. B likes best. B prefers any other point less. Assuming an "ideal point" this way requires that the voter's preference is singled-peaked along each of the separate dimensions.

The key element in the spatial approach is the representation of preference as some weighted function of distance (Davis and Hinich, 1966; Davis, Hinich, and Ordeshook, 1970). Before we can go any further toward the concept of distance in more than one dimension, we must define carefully a key concept that until now we have used only loosely: equilibrium.

Equilibrium in political decision-making is a status quo position in the policy space that – once selected – cannot be defeated by any other feasible position. In principle, such a position could defeat (or tie) all other proposals. Another possibility is that the status quo is protected by rules or institutions that prevent consideration of proposals that would defeat it if a pairwise majority rule vote were to be conducted. The problem with voting, unlike much of the analysis in economics, is that a unique equilibrium rarely exists.

REPRESENTING SPATIAL PREFERENCES

Neither salience nor separability matter if voting is "one-issue-at-a-time," provided preferences are single-peaked (Kadane, 1972; Kramer, 1972). Under these assumptions, the corollary to the MVT proved in the preceding chapter applies. More complex deals or side payments (such as "log-rolling") might still be possible, of course.[4]

Consequently, assuming free proposal power for all members, the vector of single-dimension medians will be the outcome. The median position on Project 1 is $80 million ($x_{E1}$), and the median on Project 2 is $120 million ($x_{A2}$). Thus, the committee will pass two bills, and the vector of median points ($80m, $120m) will be an equilibrium. However, our goal is to consider the possibility that two (or more) issues are voted together, rather than one-issue-at-a-time.

INDIFFERENCE, PREFERENCE, AND SPATIAL UTILITY FUNCTIONS

In earlier chapters, we defined preference and indifference, using both orderings and spatial utility functions. We defined preference as a function of closeness, so that the closer of two alternatives is preferred. Indifference required (for symmetric preferences) that two alternative budgets were equally close to the member's ideal budget.

But in a two-dimensional policy space, where every point represents both a Project 1 budget and a Project 2 budget, indifference is more complicated: There are many points equally "far away" from each ideal point. The graph

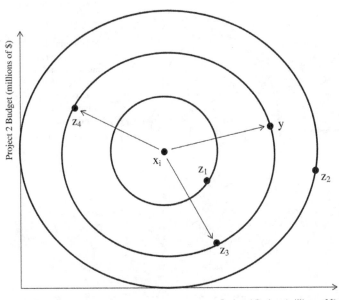

Project 1 Budget (millions of $)

FIGURE 6.2. If issues are equally salient and preferences are separable, indifference curves are circles

of the points a chooser likes equally well is an *indifference curve*. There are three cases to consider.

Case 1: *Preferences are separable and issues have equal salience.*

In this case, indifference curves are *circles*. This case, illustrated in Figure 6.2, is intuitively the closest to the definition of indifference with symmetric preferences in one dimension. A circle has the property that all the points are an equal distance (the "radius") from the center, which is the member's ideal point. Thus, the member is comparing other proposals with budget y based on their *distance* from his ideal point x_i. The member likes budget z_1 better, because it is closer than proposed budget y. He likes budget z_2 less since it is farther away. He likes budgets z_3, z_4, and y the same, because they are all the same distance from x_i.

Case 2: *Preferences are separable and issues have different salience.*

In this case, indifference curves have an *elliptical* shape, with major axis parallel to the policy the voter cares about least. The indifference curves still connect all the budgets that a member likes equally well, as in the simple case, but the curves are no longer circles. If the horizontal issue is more salient, the indifference curves are narrow. If the vertical issue is more salient, the indifference curves are wide. These are illustrated in Figure 6.3.

Case 3: *Preferences are not separable and issues have the same or different salience.*

Panel (a) Project 1 is more salient

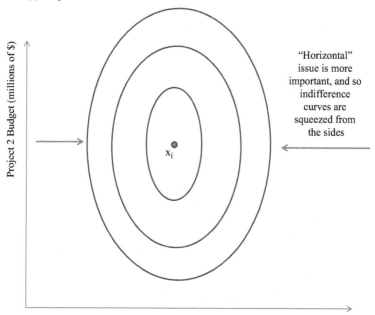

Project 2 Budget (millions of $)

"Horizontal"
issue is more
important, and so
indifference
curves are
squeezed from
the sides

x_i

Project 1 Budget (millions of $)

Panel (b) Project 2 is more salient

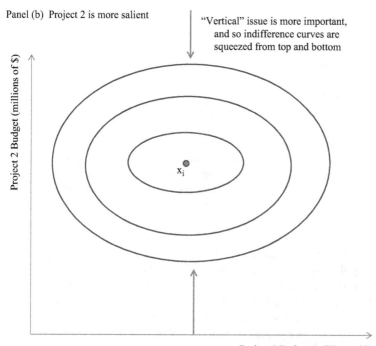

"Vertical" issue is more important,
and so indifference curves are
squeezed from top and bottom

Project 2 Budget (millions of $)

x_i

Project 1 Budget (millions of $)

FIGURE 6.3. If projects are separable, but projects have different salience, indifference curves are ellipses

Nonseparability complicates the very idea of "preference" because the utility or satisfaction the chooser derives from a position along each dimension depends on the *expected* policy on the *other* dimension. If we allow simultaneous consideration of both issues, with nonseparable preferences, it is possible to draw indifference curves. However, they can take many different forms.

NONSEPARABILITY: POSITIVE AND NEGATIVE COMPLEMENTARITY

Recall from the definition given earlier that nonseparability means that the *ideal* or *most-preferred level* of the on one policy depends on the *expected level* of the other policy. We can characterize two important kinds of nonseparability: positive complementarities (something like complementary goods in economics) or negative complementarities (something like substitutes).

The simplest indifference curves associated with each type of nonseparability appear in Figure 6.4. Panel (a) depicts "positive complementarity," and panel (b) depicts "negative complementarity." The easiest way to recognize the type of preferences is to look at the slope of the major axis (the longest diameter of a particular elliptical indifference curve). If the major axis has a positive slope, as in Panel (a), then those preferences exhibit positive complementarity. If the major axis has a negative slope, as in Panel (b), then those preferences exhibit a negative slope.

The best way to understand the meaning of negative and positive complementarity is to give an example of each:

Positive complementarity: A city council member has to decide how many new officers to hire and how much money to spend on new laptop computers for them to use in investigations. Suppose the member believes that each officer who has a car also needs a computer to be effective. Imagine that the city council as a group has already decided, based on the recommendation of the police chief, to hire more officers than this board member thinks prudent $(y_1 > x_{i1})$. He disagrees with the decision, but accepts the choice. He might then vote to support a proposal to buy each of the new officers a laptop. The conditional ideal represents more computers than his package ideal, because (from his perspective) too many officers have been hired. Nevertheless, since each officer needs a computer he votes for the increase in computer purchases, also. Consequently, $x'_{i2} > x_{i2}$.

Negative complementarity: A city council member may have individual policy ideal points for garbage and parks budgets for next year; together these form the package ideal point in two space. But suppose the council votes first on a parks budget that is larger than councilperson i's ideal $(y_1 > x_{i1})$. How will she react? Suppose she does not want to raise taxes, but cares strongly about a balanced budget. The council member knows that the budget is fixed at a total of $B = y_1 + y_2$, so if she doesn't want to run a deficit, and if y_1 is already set,

Panel (a) Positive Complementarity

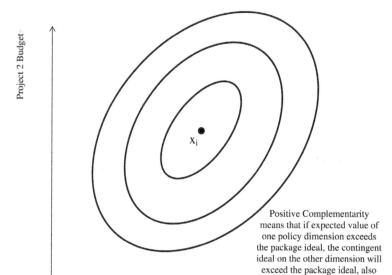

Project 2 Budget

X_i

Positive Complementarity
means that if expected value of
one policy dimension exceeds
the package ideal, the contingent
ideal on the other dimension will
exceed the package ideal, also

Project 1 Budget

Negative Complementarity
means that if expected value of
one policy dimension exceeds
the package ideal, the contingent
ideal on the other dimension will
be less than the package ideal

Panel (b) Negative Complementarity

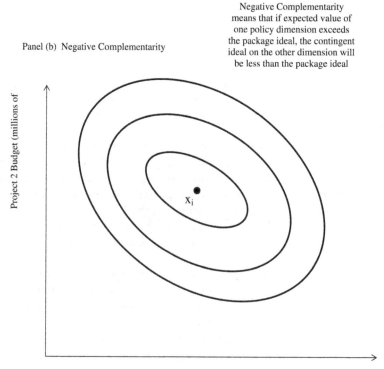

Project 2 Budget (millions of

X_i

Project 1 Budget (millions of $)

FIGURE 6.4. Negative and positive complementarity

then $x'_{i2} = y_2 = B - y_1$. The council member calls for cuts in garbage collection budgets down to x'_{i2}, below her "ideal" level x_{i2}.

But this is a constrained choice, *contingent* on the budget for spending on 1 being already decided. If she could, the councilperson would like to take some money budgeted for parks and use it to increase money spent on garbage collection. This may not be an option, either for parliamentary reasons or because other members would oppose her.

Alternatively, if a regulatory authority ordered that more money be spent on garbage collection, *every* council member might favor cuts below his or her package ideal point on parks if they also want the budget to be balanced. In general, if complementarity is negative, having to accept *more* of one project means the member wants *less* of the other project (compared with the most preferred budget if he or she could choose on both dimensions simultaneously).

In each of these examples, it appears that preferences are not really "fixed."[5] The reason is that a member's goals for one policy depend on what he or she expects to happen in another budget area. It is important to recognize, however, that the *preferences are actually fixed*. It is just that the preferences are nonseparable.

Are nonseparable preferences irrational? After all, the Corollary to the MVT is broken, because the member likes points further away from her ideal point *better*, at least over a sizable interval; does that mean that nonseparable preferences are also not single-peaked?

Not really. Remember, *separability does not matter at the ideal point*: No matter the form of the complementarity between projects, if $\tilde{y}_1 = x_{i1}$ then the implied ideal point on the second issue is also the level contained in the package ideal point. And vice versa. Separability only matters *away from* the package ideal point.

This is true in large-dimensional problems also, of course. If the budget on any dimension is fixed at a level different from that most preferred by the voter, all the other "ideal" budgets of the voter may change. The direction of the change depends on whether the voter perceives the complementarities in the activities as positive or negative.

Figure 6.5 illustrates the problem for projects exhibiting positive complementarity. As the figure shows, the voter can approve of movements *away from* his one-dimensional ideal if preferences are not separable. In the example in Figure 6.5, the voter's ideal level of spending for Project 1 is the status quo. But the budget for Project 2 is fixed at a level different from (in this example, above) his ideal point. He votes for an increase in the Project 1 budget, away from his ideal point. *With nonseparable preferences, the order in which issues are decided affects the final decision.*[6]

Earlier, we saw that the agenda, or order of voting, can determine the outcome if preferences are not single-peaked. However, cycling is relatively rare, and in any case, voters can vote strategically in response to attempts at agenda control. Nonseparability is different: The order matters even if there are

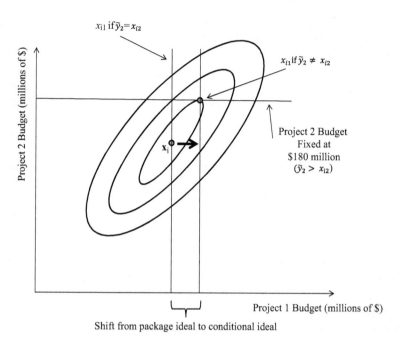

FIGURE 6.5. The "paradox" of nonseparable preferences: The case of positive complementarity

only two issues, and even if preferences are single-peaked, because the order affects the *conditional* ideal points. Accounting for nonseparability is difficult, though it may be important for understanding the nature of real-world voting and decisions, and even survey responses.[7]

VOTING ON COMPLEX PROPOSALS: CHANGING ALONG BOTH DIMENSIONS AT ONCE

Let us return to the relatively simple problem of a legislature or other small "committee" voting on two issues with separable preferences. Kadane (1972) and Kramer (1972) demonstrated that if preferences are separable and issues are voted one-at-a-time, voting sequence is irrelevant, and the result will be the vector of dimensional medians.[8]

What happens if this extreme "germaneness" rule is relaxed, so that proposals can reflect changes in both projects simultaneously?[9] Imagine that there are two projects and three committee members with circular indifference curves. To evaluate the likely solutions, it useful to establish some solution concepts.[10]

Pareto set (named after the Italian economist and sociologist, Vilfredo Pareto, 1848–1923). The Pareto set is the set of all Pareto efficient allocations, meaning that for these allocations it is impossible to move from the status quo position and make anyone better off without making at least one person worse off.

In the two (or more) dimensional spatial model the Pareto set is the smallest closed set of points that contains all ideal points, and the line segments connecting them.[11] Status quo points outside the Pareto set are *unanimously inferior* to at least one point in the Pareto set.

Condorcet winner (named after the French mathematician and social scientist, Marie Jean Antoine Nicolas Caritat, Marquis de Condorcet, 1743–1794). A policy position that beats or ties any other alternative in majority rule contests. We have discussed the Condorcet winner in the context of preference orders in Chapter 3. And we have an example of a *spatial* Condorcet winner: the median position in one dimension when preferences are single-peaked.

Win set (Black and Newing, 1951, Section II). The "win set" of an alternative z (written $W(z)$) is the set of alternatives that will garner more votes than z in a pairwise majority rule election without abstention. More formally, let $R_i(z)$ be the set of alternatives x such that $x \succcurlyeq_i z$; we will call this the "preferred to" set, because it is the set of points that voter i likes at least as well as z. Then $W(z)$ is the set of points in all the intersections of (at least) a majority of the members' $R_i(z)$ sets. That is, the win set is the *union* of the *intersections* of all the *preferred to* sets $R(z)$ of all groups of voters at least large enough to majority prefer (MP) another point to z:[12]

$$MP(z) = \cap_{i=1}^{(n+1)/2} R_i(z) \tag{6.2}$$

$$W(z) = \cup[MP(z)]$$

There is a particular kind of set, called the "null set," or set with no elements, often denoted "∅." This suggests a definition for equilibrium:

z is an *equilibrium* of a majority rule decision process if and only if $W(z) = ∅$

Of course, z might be an equilibrium because there are no alternatives that a majority of voters prefer (*preference induced* equilibrium), or z might be an equilibrium because the points that could defeat it in a majority rule vote are ruled out by veto or institutional rule (*structure induced* equilibrium).[13]

One possible configuration of ideal points for three voters (A, B, and C) appears in Figure 6.6. In addition to the ideal points, Figure 6.6 highlights the set of unidimensional medians, the Pareto set, and $W(x_{med})$, the win set of the intersection of the unidimensional medians, x_{med}.

The win set of any point x is the collection (union) of the overlaps (intersections) of the sets of alternatives preferred by (at least) a majority of members to x. In this case, with three members, we start by drawing each member's indifference curve through the presumed status quo, x_{med}. Then $W(x_{med})$ is the set of all alternatives where two (or more) of the indifference curves intersect or overlap.

We saw that x_{med} is a Condorcet winner under the special agenda restriction that issues are voted one-at-a-time. Is this also true when both issues can be voted simultaneously? No, not in this example and not in most examples. The reason is that $W(x_{med})$ is not empty for most possible configurations of ideal points. *In fact,*

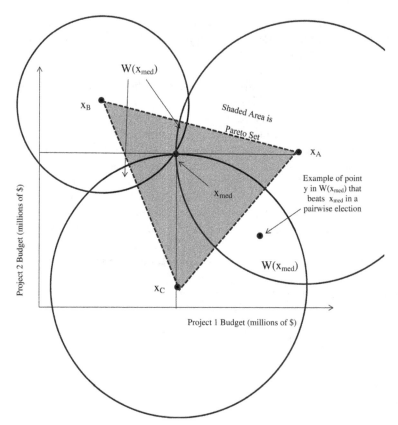

FIGURE 6.6. The win set of the intersection of unidimensional medians is generally not empty

for almost any arbitrarily selected set of ideal points of three or more voters, there is at least one point in $W(\mathbf{x}_{med})$. Since any point in $W(\mathbf{x}_{med})$ beats $\mathbf{x}_{med}$, by definition, then if the set $W(\mathbf{x}_{med})$ is not empty then $\mathbf{x}_{med}$ is not a Condorcet winner.

CHAOS

Is there *ever* a Condorcet Winner in spaces of more than one dimension, even assuming that preferences are separable and single-peaked? The answer is "yes," but it is not likely. The so-called chaos theorem shows that for most multi-dimensional spaces the standard spatial model has few predictions about the possible outcome.[14]

The chaos theorem implies that, in the absence of restrictions on (a) the configuration of ideal points or (b) the sequence of proposals (such as voting one issue at a time), majority rule processes are indeterminate.[15] Still, it is possible to rule out those outcomes that lie outside the Pareto set, if the group can solve the collective

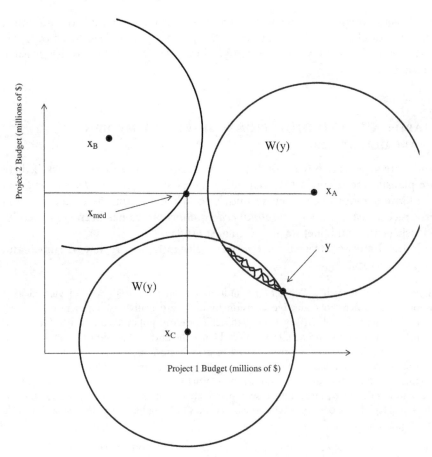

FIGURE 6.7. The win set of almost any arbitrary point y is generally not empty

action problem of assigning particular benefits.[16] Edmund Burke's "computing principle," from the beginning of this chapter, seems to have some merit.

Suppose one point in $W(x_{med})$ is selected as the new status quo for the committee depicted above in Figure 6.6. This point in our example is the point **y**, which is outside the Pareto set, but is preferred to x_{med} by voters A and C. This is a useful illustration of the "chaos" result: If voting is sincere and proposals are generated randomly, then the trajectory of voting processes can lead outside the Pareto set, and in fact can lead anywhere.[17]

If we redraw the indifference curves and recalculate the win set of the new status quo, we will once again find (as in Figure 6.7) that $W(y)$ is not empty. This process, for most arbitrarily selected sets of ideal points, could continue endlessly, if for some reason this (endless proposal power, no stopping rule) were the decision procedure the group had selected.

Figures 6.6 and 6.7 illustrate that there is no guarantee that the outcomes that are selected as a result of such a chaotic process satisfy even the most basic requirements of value: $W(x_{med})$ and $W(y)$ can quite easily contain points that are not elements of the Pareto set. Majority rule may lead to an outcome that the entire society, *unanimously*, thinks is worse than other feasible alternatives.

STABILITY IN TWO-DIMENSIONAL SPACE: THE MEDIAN IN ALL DIRECTIONS

There are at least two ways out of this predicament. The first is to ask if there are plausible restrictions that can make the existence of a *preference-induced equilibrium* more likely. The second is to ask if institutions of the decision process can lead to a *structure-induced equilibrium,* as has been suggested by Shepsle (1979) and Shepsle and Weingast (1981).[18]

Jeffrey Banks contrasted the two views elegantly, in a review of Hinich and Munger (1997):

[T]he absence of such a "center" in multidimensional models [can be] viewed as a serious impediment to collective decision making, especially in conjunction with the Chaos Theorem... [which says] one can get from any policy to any other (and back again) via the majority preference relation. Hence the authors' pessimistic conclusion: in two or more dimensions "there is not necessarily a 'middle' that we can depend on to lend stability to democracy: majority rule processes can be arbitrary" (p. 63). In this judgment, the authors are certainly in the majority, as can be seen by the subsequent "structure-induced equilibrium" research, which rationalizes various political institutions (e.g. legislative committees) as the barricades holding back the otherwise inevitable onslaught of chaos.

An alternative perspective, though, is that these core nonexistence and chaos theorems do not predict (as it is commonly phrased) "anything can happen"; as nonequilibrium results they do not predict anything at all. Rather, what these negative results demonstrate is the impossibility of any general theory of political behavior based solely on the notion of preference aggregation under majority rule, and therefore the necessity of additional structure in order to have a well-posed equilibrium model. From this perspective, then, the lesson to be learned is one for the modeler of political processes, rather than one about the political processes themselves. (Banks, 1998: 1506).

To put it simply, "we don't know what will happen" does not imply that "anything can happen." We just do not know. We will talk more about randomness, prediction, and the perspective of the observer in Chapter 8.

SUFFICIENT CONDITIONS

Plott (1967) demonstrated that conditions sufficient to guarantee the existence of equilibrium are possible, but these conditions are highly restrictive. Later work, including that of Davis, DeGroot, and Hinich (1972), Enelow and Hinich (1983a, 1984b), and especially McKelvey and Schofield (1986, 1987) expanded the set of ideal point configurations for which a Condorcet winner exists, but the conditions are still highly restrictive. The sufficient conditions, sometimes called the "Plott conditions," require an ordinal pairwise symmetry of all voters along any vector passing through the status quo. One configuration of preferences for which there is a Condorcet winner is depicted in Figure 6.8, panel (a). For each voter whose ideal point x_i is different from the dominant point (Condorcet winner, in this case x_D), there must be another voter j whose ideal point x_j lies on the same line through x_i and x_D, and lies the same distance as x_j, on the opposite side of x_D.

If the Plott conditions are met, then a unique equilibrium always exists. However, the conditions are not necessary for equilibrium. In panel (b) of Figure 6.8, we see an illustration of a configuration of ideal points that imply a Condorcet winner, but which fail Plott's symmetry conditions. The question is, just what is the *general* principle that determines whether a given committee, represented by a set of ideal points in a multidimensional policy space, will come to a unique and determinate outcome by other than arbitrary means?

The answer is best summarized as follows. First, we define a "median in all directions," and then give a different definition of Condorcet winner.

An alternative is a *median in all directions* if every line drawn through it, at all angles, divides the ideal points of all members so that at least half are on either side of the line, including those members whose ideal points are on the line in both groups.[19]

An alternative is a Condorcet winner in a society if, and only if, it is a "median in all directions."

Earlier, for the MVT, we divided voters into two groups: those whose ideal points were less than or equal to the proposal and those whose ideal points were greater than or equal to the proposal, along the single dimension of political conflict. This statement of the "median in all directions," which turns out to be the generalized median voter theorem, is an exact analogue. The difference is that the condition must hold for lines drawn through the median at any angle.

We cannot draw all possible lines, but the nature of the median in all directions can be illustrated by looking at lines 1 and 2 in panel (b) of Figure 6.8. There are three ideal points on or to the right of line 1 (x_B, x_C and x_D), and three ideal points on or below and to the left (x_A, x_B, and x_D – remember that points actually on the line counts twice!). Similarly, for line 2: There are three ideal points on or above line 2 (x_A,x_B, and x_C), and two ideal points on or below it (x_B, and x_D). Thus, x_B satisfies the definition of a median in all directions: for any line segment through x_B, half or more of the total number of ideal points lie in one-half space, and half or more lie in the other half space.

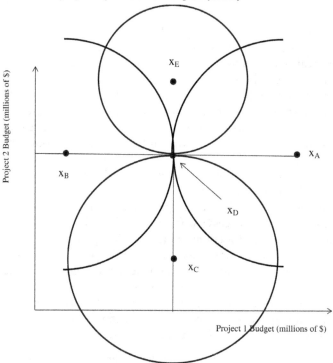

Panel a: Majority rule equilibrium with ideal point symmetry

Project 2 Budget (millions of $)

x_E

x_A

x_B

x_D

x_C

Project 1 Budget (millions of $)

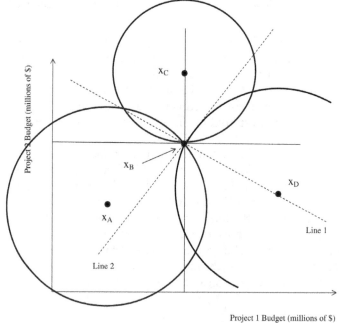

Panel b: Majority rule equilibrium that does not satisfy Plott Conditions

Project 2 Budget (millions of $)

x_C

x_B

x_D

Line 1

x_A

Line 2

Project 1 Budget (millions of $)

FIGURE 6.8. Examples of existence of Condorcet winners, with and without satisfying the "Plott Conditions" (Ideal point symmetry)

MULTIPLE DIMENSIONS: WEIGHTED EUCLIDEAN DISTANCE

We will now refine the material presented so far by introducing matrix notation. Instead of two dimensions, however, we will assume that the policy space has n dimensions, where n is an arbitrary number. Technically, the policy space $\mathcal{P}$ will be defined as the generalized Cartesian product, when n is arbitrarily large but finite:

$$\mathcal{P} = P_1 \times P_2 \times \ldots P_n \qquad (6.3)$$

As before, each dimension measures the budget of one project, and members are assumed to have preferences over all the projects, though of course the salience of some issues is zero for some members.[20] Matrix notation allows clearer, more concise definitions of the ideas of *salience* and *nonseparability* than those we presented graphically earlier.

SED AND WED

The sustained premise of the spatial model is that voters like a proposal less as it is a greater distance from their conception of the best policy. But now we must define "distance," or the difference between proposals, in several dimensions rather than just one. Generally, the simplest measure of distance is *simple Euclidean distance* (SED).

In a single dimension, the SED between two platforms y and z is just the absolute value of the difference. Consider *representative citizen i*, who has an *ideal point* x_i. In Chapter 5, we used the absolute value of the difference between budgets to define preference by voter i as a spatial utility function based on distance:

$$y \succ_i \text{to } z \text{ if and only if } |y - x_i| < |z - x_i|$$

and indifference:

$$y \approx_i z \text{ if and only if } |y - x_i| = |z - x_i|$$

This approach works fine as long as the proposals being compared are on the same side of the ideal point, or if preferences are symmetric.

We can define the points in two-dimensional space, using vectors. An element in our two-dimensional policy space will be represented as a column vector with the Project 1 budget on top and the Project 2 budget below it. For example,

$$y = \begin{bmatrix} y_1 \\ y_2 \end{bmatrix} \qquad z = \begin{bmatrix} z_1 \\ z_2 \end{bmatrix} \qquad (6.4)$$

are two alternatives (y and z) in the policy space. We will often write such expressions this way: $y = [y_1 \ y_2]^T$, where "T" means that the column vectors are transposed so that they can be written in linear fashion.

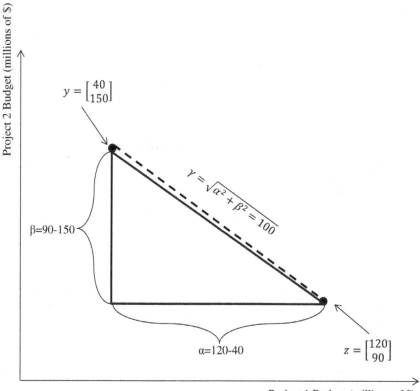

FIGURE 6.9. Computation of simple Euclidean distance in a two-dimensional space

Each member's ideal point is also a vector, with an ideal budget for each project. How are we to represent the distances from ideal points to budgets using vectors? The difference between the vectors is just another vector, giving the difference in the budget *in each project*. However, a vector is not, itself, a distance. To compute distance, we apply the Pythagorean Theorem. Imagine we are given an arbitrary right triangle with sides measuring α and β and hypotenuse measuring γ. The Pythagorean Theorem says that $\gamma^2 = \alpha^2 + \beta^2$. Solving for γ, we get:

$$\gamma = \sqrt{\alpha^2 + \beta^2} \qquad (6.5)$$

The dotted line in Figure 6.9 is the "distance" between proposals y and z, because it is the hypotenuse γ of the triangle.

That means that the formula for SED(y, z) in two-dimensional space is just the Pythagorean Theorem.

$$SED(\mathbf{y}, \mathbf{z}) = \sqrt{(y_1 - z_1)^2 + (y_2 - z_2)^2} \qquad (6.6)$$

More generally, for an arbitrary number of dimensions $n \geq 1$, the distance between two points y and z is:

$$\text{SED}(y, z) = \sqrt{\sum_{j=1}^{n} (y_j - z_j)^2} \tag{6.7}$$

That is, SED is the square root of the sum of the squared differences in each respective dimension. Using matrix notation, we can rewrite (6.4) as:

$$\text{SED}(y, z) = \sqrt{[y - z]^T \ [y - z]} \tag{6.8}$$

Here is an illustration of the advantage of matrix notation: Equation (6.7) would have to be rewritten for any specific n. But n does not appear in (6.8); matrix notation is more general and applies to any number of dimensions without modification.

SED is the simplest way to represent preferences in spatial theory, but not the only way. A trivial generalization of SED is the set of order-preserving "affine" transformations of SED. Order-preserving affine transformations are linear rescalings that keep the same direction of increase from small to large. We say y is an affine transformation of x if

$$y = h + (k \times x) \tag{6.9}$$

where h and k are arbitrary scalars ($k > 0$). If $x_1 > x_2$, then a transformation of x is "order preserving" if $y_1 = h + (k \times x_1)$ and $y_2 = h + (k \times x_2)$ have the same order: $y_1 > y_2$. SED or any affine transformation of SED is equally valid as a representation of preference.

To enable the spatial utility function to represent salience and nonseparability, we will need to define a generalization of SED called "weighted Euclidean distance" (WED). SED requires separability and equal salience; WED relaxes both requirements. The formula for WED, letting the matrix of weights A be voter specific (i.e., subscripted by i, and using i's ideal point x_i as the point from which to measure distance), is:

$$\text{WED}(x_i, z) = \sqrt{[x_i - z]^T \ A_i \ [x_i - z]} \tag{6.10}$$

Compare Equation (6.10) to Equation (6.8): The difference between SED and WED is the matrix of salience and interaction terms A_i. If there are two projects, A_i would look like this:

$$A_i = \begin{bmatrix} a_{11} & a_{12} \\ a_{21} & a_{22} \end{bmatrix} \tag{6.11}$$

We can distinguish two types of terms, salience and interaction terms, in the matrix of preference weights A_i.

- The *main diagonal* elements, a_{11} and a_{22}, are the *salience* terms. Salience terms are defined to be nonnegative, and we will consider only positive salience terms. A salience term equal to zero means the voter does not even consider this project or policy in making decisions.[21]
- The *off-diagonal* elements are interactions, and measure complementarity. As discussed earlier in this chapter, complementarity measures how much the voter's evaluation of proposed *changes* in one project depends on the expected *level* of another project. We will generally assume that $a_{12} = a_{21}$, though there is nothing in the theory itself that requires this restriction.[22]

It is important to remember that, though as a matter of convention it is common to use the square root of the expression, in principle any root is a candidate for a "spatial" utility function. We use the square root most commonly because that is the actual formula for distance, but all that is required for utility to be "spatial" is that it is represented as some order-preserving transformation of distance.

Thus, the more general expression would something like 6.10′.

$$\text{WED}(y,z) = \sqrt[G]{[x_i - z]^T \quad A_i \quad [x_i - z]} \tag{6.10′}$$

The "G" in the expression above is the Gth root of the formula contained under the radical sign.[23] If G=1, then the result is just $[x_i - z]^T \quad A_i \quad [x_i - z]$, which yields the standard quadratic loss function:

$$\text{Utility} = -[x_i - z]^T \quad A_i \quad [x_i - z] \tag{6.12}$$

Then the following utility functions would be equally valid[24], though they have very different properties:

$$\text{Utility} = -\sqrt[2]{[x_i - z]^T \quad A_i \quad [x_i - z]} \text{ (Euclidean distance)}$$

$$\text{Utility} = -\sqrt[3]{[x_i - z]^T \quad A_i \quad [x_i - z]} \text{ (Cube root, decreasing intensity of preference)}$$

$$\text{Utility} = -\sqrt[1/2]{[x_i - z]^T \quad A_i \quad [x_i - z]} \text{ (1/2th root, increasing intensity of preference)}$$

Symmetric preference. If $A_i = I$ (meaning that $a_{11} = a_{22} = 1$, and $a_{12} = a_{21} = 0$), then $\text{SED}(x_i, z) = \text{WED}(x_i, z)$. It is useful to define symmetric preferences for the multidimensional setting. Preferences of voter i are symmetric if and only if the voter likes equally well any two points y and z that (a) lie on a straight line passing through x_i and (b) are equidistant from x_i (in terms of SED).

We can also define the concept of indifference more generally.

Indifference. A voter *i* is indifferent between any two alternatives y and y′ if and only if $\text{WED}(y - x_i) = \text{WED}(y' - x_i)$. In general, we can identify a set of alternatives y among which the voter is indifferent: $\{y \mid \text{WED}(y - x_i) = K\}$. The variable K is a constant whose value can range from zero (at the ideal point) to an arbitrarily large number. The graph of the elements of this set of points among which the voter is indifferent is the indifference curve.

As we saw earlier in this chapter, if salience is the same for all issues, and preferences are separable, then indifference curves are circles. But if salience is different for different issues, indifference curves are ellipses. If preferences are nonseparable, indifference curves are ellipses whose major axis tilts at an angle. But all of these types of indifference curves have the property that $\text{WED}(y - x_i) = K$, where y is the locus of point on the ellipse itself.

Each distinct value of K defines one indifference curve for the voter. Since any particular K defines one indifference curve, it follows that each point in the policy space P is located on exactly one indifference curve. Consequently, there can be no intersection of indifference curves in preferences measured by WED, just as was true for SED. If two indifference curves intersect, that would imply that the individual's preferences are intransitive.

We can now write the three categories of indifference curves in terms of matrix notation.

- If $A_i = k\text{I}$ (k an arbitrary scalar, I an identity matrix of order n), then indifference curves are *circles* with centers at the voter's ideal point, because issues are weighted equally and preferences are separable.
- For any $A_i = s\text{I}$ (where s is a n × n diagonal matrix of salience weights, so that A_i is diagonal), indifference curves are *ellipses* centered at the ideal point, with major axes parallel to the policy dimensions. The reason is that the voter values issues differently, so equal departures from his ideal have different impacts on his utility, depending on the project.
- For any A_i that is not diagonal, preferences are not separable. As we saw earlier, this means that the form of the preference ellipses is complex, with the major axis of the ellipse tilted at an angle rather than parallel to one of the policy dimensions.

AN EXAMPLE USING (SEPARABLE) WED IN
TWO-DIMENSIONAL SPACE

Returning to the preferences of the subcommittee members, consider first B's preference rule. We will say he prefers y to z if and only if y is closer to his ideal point x_B, or

$$\text{WED}_B(y, x_B) < \text{WED}_B(z, x_B)$$

where $y = [40 \ 150]^T$, $z = [80 \ 60]^T$, and $x_B = [50 \ 40]^T$. As Figure 6.10 shows, Mr. B is indifferent among alternatives that lie exactly K units (in WED, not SED) from his ideal point.

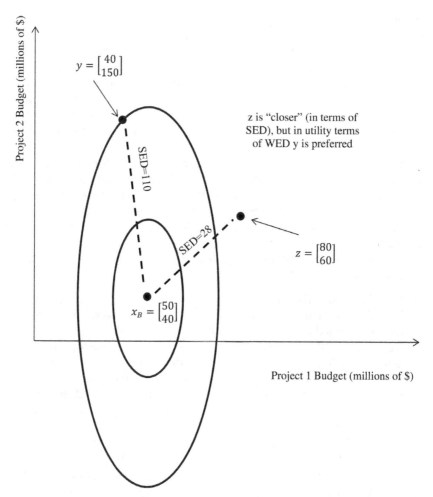

$$y = \begin{bmatrix} 40 \\ 150 \end{bmatrix}$$

z is "closer" (in terms of SED), but in utility terms of WED y is preferred

SED=110

SED=28

$$z = \begin{bmatrix} 80 \\ 60 \end{bmatrix}$$

$$x_B = \begin{bmatrix} 50 \\ 40 \end{bmatrix}$$

Project 1 Budget (millions of $)

Project 2 Budget (millions of $)

FIGURE 6.10. Comparison of WED and SED – Accounting for salience

Assume that the A_B matrix looks like this:

$$A_B = \begin{bmatrix} 15 & 0 \\ 0 & 1 \end{bmatrix} \tag{6.13}$$

Mr. B's preferences for Projects 1 and 2 are separable (you can tell because $a_{12} = a_{21} = 0$). The issue salience values are very different, however: Each dollar difference from his ideal in Project 1 "counts" more because $a_{11} > a_{22}$.

Given the weights in A_B, does B prefer $y = [40, 150]^T$ or $z = [120, 90]^T$, remembering $x_B = [50, 40]^T$? For comparison, first calculate SED(y, x_B) and SED(z, x_B):

$$\text{SED}(y, x_B) = \sqrt{[-10 \quad 110] \begin{bmatrix} -10 \\ 110 \end{bmatrix}}$$

$$= \sqrt{(-10)^2 + 110^2} = 110 \tag{6.14}$$

$$\text{SED}(z, x_B) = \sqrt{[30 \quad 20] \begin{bmatrix} 30 \\ 20 \end{bmatrix}} = \sqrt{30^2 + 20^2} = 36$$

The definition of WED implies that if A_B were an identity matrix (remember, it isn't), WED and SED would be identical. Equations (6.13) and (6.14) would then establish that B prefers z to y, because $\text{SED}(z, x_B) < \text{SED}(y, x_B)$.

For $A_B \neq I$ (as given in Equation (6.11)), however, we must use WED:

$$\text{WED}(y, x_B) = \sqrt{\begin{bmatrix} -10 & 110 \end{bmatrix} \begin{bmatrix} 15 & 0 \\ 0 & 1 \end{bmatrix} \begin{bmatrix} -10 \\ 110 \end{bmatrix}}$$

$$= \sqrt{(-10^2) \times 15 + 110^2} = 117 \tag{6.15}$$

$$\text{WED}(z, x_B) = \sqrt{\begin{bmatrix} 30 & 20 \end{bmatrix} \begin{bmatrix} 15 & 0 \\ 0 & 1 \end{bmatrix} \begin{bmatrix} 30 \\ 20 \end{bmatrix}}$$

$$= \sqrt{(30^2 \times 15) + 20^2} = 118 \tag{6.16}$$

Now, because of the large weight attached to Project 1, B prefers proposal y, because $\text{WED}(z, x_B) < \text{WED}(y, x_B)$. The reason can be seen in Figure 6.10: B cares more about small differences in the Project 1 budget. Consequently, horizontal movements cause a larger decline in utility as distance x_B increases.

WHAT IF PREFERENCES ARE NONSEPARABLE?

In matrix notation, nonseparability in two-space means $a_{i12} \neq 0$. So where salience is determined by the *diagonal* terms in A_i: *nonseparabilities* are captured in the off-diagonal terms of A_i. Larger values of the a_{ij} ($i \neq j$) represent larger complementarities, or interactions, in the member's evaluation of issues.

To see this, let's expand the formula for $\text{WED}(z, x_i)$:

$$\text{WED}(z, x_i) = \sqrt{[x_i - z]^T \quad A_i[x_i - z]}$$

Dropping the i subscript, for simplicity:

$$= \sqrt{[x_1 - z_1 \quad x_2 - z_2] \begin{bmatrix} a_{11} & a_{12} \\ a_{21} & a_{22} \end{bmatrix} \begin{bmatrix} x_1 - z_1 \\ x_2 - z_2 \end{bmatrix}} \tag{6.17}$$

$$= \sqrt{\left[\left((x_1 - z_1)a_{11} + (x_2 - z_2)a_{21} \right) \left((x_1 - z_1)a_{12} + (x_2 - z_2)a_{22} \right) \right] \begin{bmatrix} x_1 - z_1 \\ x_2 - z_2 \end{bmatrix}} \tag{6.18}$$

$$= \sqrt{a_{i11}(z_1 - x_{i1})^2 + \underbrace{[2a_{i12}(z_1 - x_{i1})(z_2 - x_{i2})]}_{\text{Interacton}} + a_{i22}(z_2 - x_{i2})^2} \qquad (6.19)$$

From (6.19), it is clear why WED simplifies to SED if $A_i = I$ ($a_{12} = a_{21} = 0$ and $a_{11} = a_{22} = 1$). The "interaction" term in (6.19) drops out and the salience terms can be ignored, so the expression simplifies to:

$$\text{WED}_j(z, x_i) = \sqrt{(x_1 - z_1)^2 + (x_2 - z_2)^2} \qquad (6.20)$$

In general, the only difference between separable and nonseparable preferences is the interaction term in (6.19). The interaction is the product of the differences between z and x_i on each of the two issue dimensions, multiplied by twice the interaction weight a_{12}. Thus, we can summarize the implications of nonseparability by focusing on a_{12}. Since larger values of WED mean less utility for the voter, we have to be careful to interpret the signs on a_{12} carefully. Again, complementarities have to do with increase or decreases in utility when two policies are considered together. A positive interaction is an increase in WED, *reducing* utility. Thus, $a_{12} < 0$ is a positive complementarity, and $a_{12} > 0$ is a negative complementarity.

Recall that, intuitively, nonseparability requires that the voter consider *all* issue positions before choosing *any*. We can summarize the specific impact of the interaction term in three statements about the voter's conditional preferences:

1. If $a_{12} < 0$ (*negative* interaction, implying *positive complementarity*) and the position on issue j is fixed for some reason at $\tilde{x}_j > x_{ij}$, then the conditional ideal on issue k will be *larger* than x_{ik}. If the position on issue j is fixed at $\tilde{x}_j < x_{ij}$, then the conditional ideal on issue k will be *smaller* than x_{ik}.

2. If $a_{12} > 0$ (*positive* interaction, implying *negative complementarity*) and the position on issue j is fixed at $\tilde{x}_j > x_{ij}$, then the conditional ideal on issue k will be *smaller* than x_{ik}. If the position on issue j is fixed at $\tilde{x}_j < x_{ij}$, then the conditional ideal on issue k will be *larger* than x_{ik}.

3. No matter what the form of the interaction, if $\tilde{x}_j = x_{ij}$ (position on issue j is *fixed at the voter's ideal point*), the interaction term is zero. Non-separability has no impact on choices on issue k: The conditional ideal given z_j is still x_{ik}.

We can derive the conditional preference of the voter (dropping the i subscript for now) for Project 2 by fixing Project 1 at an arbitrary budget we will call $\tilde{x}_1$. (Note: The derivation of the ideal point for Project 1, given a fixed budget for Project 2, is analogous and will not be presented.) The voter's *conditional* preference for Project 2, or x_2^c can be written in terms of the WED between x and the policy vector $[\tilde{x}_1 \ x_2^c]^T$. The value of x_2^c that minimizes WED given $\tilde{x}_1$ is unknown, but we can find it in two steps. First, write out the expression as WED:

$$\mathrm{WED}([\tilde{x}_1 \quad x_2^c]^T, x) = \sqrt{a_{11}(\tilde{x}_1 - x_1)^2 + 2a_{12}(\tilde{x}_1 - x_1)(x_2^c - x_2) + a_{22}(x_2^c + x_2)^2}$$

(6.21)

The second step is to find the value of the Project 2 budget that conditionally minimizes WED, which of course maximizes utility, conditional on $\tilde{x}_1$ being the (fixed) budget for Project 1. Enelow and Hinich (1984b) performed these two steps and solved for x'_2, the value of Project 2 that conditionally maximizes the voter's utility:

$$x'_2 | \tilde{x}_1 = x_2 - \left(\frac{a_{12}}{a_{22}}\right)(\tilde{x}_1 - x_1)$$

(6.22)

As (6.22) demonstrates, $x'_2 \neq x_2$ whenever preferences are nonseparable and $\tilde{x}_1 \neq x_1$.

There is nothing perverse about this preference rule. In fact, as Enelow and Hinich demonstrate, the preferences in (6.22) are symmetric and single-peaked around the conditional ideal point on issue 2, x'_2. But x is still the *package* of proposals the voter most prefers, and it differs from x_2^* on Project 2.

STABILITY OF MAJORITY RULE: THE GENERALIZED MEDIAN
VOTER THEOREM

In the main section of this chapter, we outlined the problems of defining a Condorcet winner in more than one dimension. We argued that the general condition for stability is the existence of a median in all directions. As the reader will recall, an alternative is a median in all directions if every line drawn through it divides the ideal points of all members so that at least half are on either side of the line. It is important to note that points on the line are counted as belonging to each of the two groups, or half spaces.

This definition is designed for a two-dimensional policy space and is suitable for graphical examples on a printed page, which is after all a two-dimensional surface. How are we to generalize to situations where there are more than two dimensions? Many people find it hard to visualize three dimensions, and we certainly cannot represent three-space very well on a flat printed page. Worse, higher dimensions, with eight, 136, or an arbitrary number of policies, defy graphical interpretations. We cannot use "lines" to split groups of ideal points. Mathematicians use a mental construct called a "separating hyperplane" to understand such a splitting of spaces. We will denote the separating hyperplane $\mathcal{H}$. In general, to split a space $\mathcal{H}$ must have *one fewer dimensions* than the space itself.

As we have already seen, in the one-dimensional example $\mathcal{H}$ was of dimension zero (a point). In two-dimensional spaces, $\mathcal{H}$ must be of dimension one (a line). In more complex spaces with arbitrary dimension n, $\mathcal{H}$ must always be of dimension $n-1$. For our purposes, $\mathcal{H}$ must have the same property in a space of any dimension: No matter how $\mathcal{H}$ is tilted or rotated, as long as it passes through the median position, $\mathcal{H}$ must divide all ideal points so that (to use the Schwartz, 1986, definition) no majority of ideal points lies strictly on either side.

Obviously, this condition becomes harder to satisfy in higher dimensions. But the general principle (McKelvey, 1976a, 1976b) is precisely the same in every case: There must be *at least N/2* ideal points on *each side* of the separating hyperplane (including in each case points on $\mathcal{H}$ itself, counting these twice in effect). This principle implies a generalized statement of the MVT, simultaneously accounting for any number of dimensions from one to infinity.[25]

Generalized Median Voter Theorem (GMVT)

Assumptions

(a) Let there be N voters choosing one set of policies in a space X of k policy dimensions.

(b) Let preferences be separable and symmetric around each ideal point x_i, for $i = 1,\ldots, N$.

(c) Define a "separating hyperplane" $\mathcal{H}$ of dimension $k-1$ as a point (when k = 1), line (when $k = 2$), plane (when $k = 3$), or hyperplane (when $k > 3$) that divides the N ideal points into two groups. Each group comprises the ideal points on one side on $\mathcal{H}$, including those ideal points that lie on the surface of $\mathcal{H}$. Then the number of members in each group is N_1 and N_2, respectively.

GMV Theorem. An alternative y is a median position for the society if and only if, for every $\mathcal{H}$ containing y, $N_1 \geq N/2$, and $N_2 \geq N/2$. When (if) this condition is met, the number of votes for y is greater than or equal to the number of votes for any other alternative z.

Interestingly, we have already seen the "proof" of the GMVT.[26] It is the same as that offered in Chapter 5 for the simple MVT in one dimension. The reason is that although the MVT is a special case of the more general theorem, the principle is the same.

The central themes of our presentation of the multidimensional model are:

- A definition of "preference," using distance in space as a metric.
- A discussion of the importance of different priorities, or "salience," of issues in determining preference over two or more issues.

- A discussion of the importance of separability, or the effect of the expected level of one policy on the preferred level of another policy.
- A consideration of the conditions that cause instability of majority rule decision processes when two or more issue are decided at the same time.

The result of this exercise is that we can now give precise definitions for a useful and general form of a "utility function," based on the idea that voters prefer policies that are closer to their ideal. And "closer" can be defined as any order-preserving variation on Euclidean distance, ranging from the commonly used quadratic loss function (so that utility declines with the square of distance) to Euclidean distance itself (so that utility is linear) to other non-linear variants (so that voters only care about differences that are within some range of their ideal points).

The idea of representing preferences with a utility function (in this case, the spatial utility function) puts another important tool in the analytical kit of the political scientist. Rather than being restricted to cumbersome preference orders over alternatives, the spatial utility function allows the analysis of many voters in a shared space of political conflict, with continuous issue dimensions and differences in salience. As we will see in later chapters, this is a powerful tool, and one that analytical political scientists have used very successfully.

TERMS

Chaos
Condorcet winner
Complementarity
Equilibrium
Germaneness
GMVT
Logrolling
Manipulation
Median in All Directions
Multidimensional Amendments
Pareto Set
Plott Conditions
Preference Induced Equilibrium
Salience
Separability
Simple Euclidean Distance
Structure Induced Equilibrium
Vector
Weighted Euclidean Distance
Win Set

EXERCISES

6.1 Suppose that there are three committee members, A, B, and C, with ideal points in a two-dimensional policy space (issues 1 and 2) as follows: $x_A = (4, 16)$, $x_B = (5, 10)$, and $x_C = (6, 4)$. Suppose the status quo policy is $z = (6, 16)$. Draw a graph depicting the decision problem, including circular indifference curves through the status quo point. Is z a Condorcet winner?

6.2 For the same set of members and ideal points as in Exercise 6.1, imagine that the issues are voted one at a time starting with issue 1. What will be the resulting vector of policies?

6.3 Again, for the same set of preferences as in Exercises 6.1 and 6.2, what will be the outcome if two-dimensional alternatives can be proposed? Is there a Condorcet winner? Is there a median in all directions?

6.4 Prove the Kramer-Kadane result, that if preferences are single-peaked and separable, and issues are voted one at a time, the result will be the vector of issue-by-issue medians.

*6.5 Suppose $A = \ell \times I$, where $0 < \ell < 1$. What is the specific relationship between the SED and the WED measures of distance?

*6.6 Suppose committee member i has an ideal point ($x_i = [\,10 \quad 12\,]^T$) on two budget items and that $A_i = \begin{bmatrix} 2 & -3 \\ -3 & 1 \end{bmatrix}$. Imagine that for some reason the budget for Project 1 is set at \$20 and that all members take this as given. Is member i's conditional ideal on Project 2, given $\tilde{x}_1 = 20$, larger or smaller than \$12? What is the exact numeric value of $x_{i2}^*|\tilde{x}_1$?

*6.7 Use the Pythagorean Theorem to prove that the SED between two points z and y in three-dimensional space (dimensions 1, 2, and 3) is:

$$SED(x, y) = \sqrt{(z_1 - y_1)^2 + (z_2 - y_2)^2 + (z_3 - y_3)^2}$$

*6.8 Prove that SED and WED preferences are symmetric, given this definition of symmetry: *Preferences of voter i are symmetric if and only if the voter likes equally well any two points y and z that (a) lie on a straight line passing through x_i and (b) are equidistant from x_i (in terms of SED).*

III

EXTENSIONS: COLLECTIVE CHOICE,
UNCERTAINTY, AND COLLECTIVE ACTION

7

The Social Choice Problem: Impossibility

George: It is unthinkable that [someone] could manipulate the democratic process.
Dotty: Democracy is all in the head...
George: ...Furthermore, I had a vote!
Dotty: It's not the voting that's democracy, it's the counting.

Tom Stoppard, *Jumpers*, Act I, p. 35.

Until now, we have made two simplifying assumptions. First, society makes all of its collective decisions by some variant of majority rule. Second, spatial utility functions can represent preference orderings. However "social choice" theorists work in a much broader context than spatial preferences or majority rule. Their goal is to select the most general possible representation of preferences, and the most encompassing possible conception of institutions. These generalizations require some careful definitions.

SOCIAL CHOICE

Social choice analyzes alternative decision rules, or deciding how to decide. We have discussed in this book a hierarchy of choices, and it is important to understand the differences.[1]

   I. *Deciding how to decide how to decide*: Are we a group? Are we going to kill each other, or cooperate? How will we constitute ourselves?
  II. *Deciding how to decide*: What decision rule will we use, and what are the rules for changing the rules, in our constitution?
 III. *Deciding*: What will be our policies and everyday political decision about speed limits, budgets, and regulation of pollution, in the context of a constituted group with relatively fixed formal decision rules and amendment processes?

In this book, Chapters 1 and 2 were about step I above. Most of the rest of the discussion in Chapters 3–6 skipped to step III, representing preferences and analyzing choices under majority rule In this chapter we turn back to step II, and compare different ways of choosing.

DECIDING HOW TO DECIDE

The group wants to choose one outcome that matches (as closely as possible) the collective "will" of the constituted group. So when the group constitutes itself, it must choose among different ways of deciding. That is the essence of the problem of social choice. Donald Saari (2008: i; emphasis added) sets up the "deciding how to decide" stage succinctly: "We decide by elections, but do we elect who the voters *really want?*" Posing the question this way makes the problem one of epistemology: The voters, as a group, as an organic collective, really do want *something*. The unique best solution exists, but it is hidden. The group should choose the rule that most accurately uncovers the hidden "best" outcome.

This project is venerable, harking back to Rousseau's "General Will." The group is not a "they," but an "it." The group just needs to figure out what it wants, using as data the individual preference orderings reported by each voter. It may be that we cannot say the group has a "preference," but it is true that the members of the group have goals, and that they want something from their membership in the group. Asking if members get "what they want" is quite sensible, and in fact, this view is at the core of social choice. Groups do things; do groups do what the members want?

Social choice specifies criteria on which to evaluate decision procedures, and then formulates and evaluates those procedures.

- Start with the (sincere) preference orderings of each member of a group of people. Since we know that each person may have incentives to manipulate the preference order he or she reports, this is not easy. But those are the data needed to start.
- Imagine that membership in the group is well defined and uncontroversial; no one else can join the group and no members wish to leave. Again, this is not an easy problem to solve, since people may try to leave the group if they disagree with a decision. However, a constituted group is required before we can start work on social choice.
- Define the domain, or feasible set of choices. What are the outcomes or states of the world among which the group can choose? Imagining alternatives that are desirable but not feasible will get in the way of eliminating alternatives that are feasible but not desirable.
- Define evaluative criteria, such as justice, fairness, transactions costs, manipulability, transparency, and so forth, as means of judging decision rules.

TABLE 7.1. *Four Subgroups of a Larger Group*

Number of People in Sub-Group	Sub-Group Preference Profile
Group I:10 persons	A ≻ B ≻ C ≻ D
Group II: 9 persons	A ≻ C ≻ D ≻ B
Group III: 8 persons	D ≻ B ≻ C ≻ A
Group IV: 7 persons	D ≻ C ≻ A ≻ B
Total Members: 34	Overall "Best" Alternative: Undefined

• Specify the set of decision rules available.
• Finally, use the evaluative criteria to compare, and ultimately to select, the decision rule that will be used to map individual preference orderings onto the constituted group ordering.

Consider a simplified example. Table 7.1 lists four subgroups of a larger group, with the number of people in each subgroup and their "preference" profiles (each subgroup is unanimous, in terms of the preference orders of their members)

Since there are four alternatives, there are six possible pairwise comparisons.[2]

A vs. B: A wins, 26–8
A vs. C: A wins, 19–15
A vs. D: A wins, 19–15
B vs. C: B wins, 18–16
B vs. D: D wins, 24–10
C vs. D: C wins 19–15

What does the group "want"? Clearly, A is a Condorcet winner, beating each of the other alternatives. Good voting rules select the Condorcet winner, if one exists.

We have seen situations where the Condorcet winner does not exist, of course. The astute reader will have already noted that in the example above, though A is a Condorcet winner, the group preference over the remaining three alternatives is a cycle (B ≻ C ≻ D ≻ B). So if alternative A is unavailable for some reason there would be a problem, because no Condorcet winner exists among the remaining three feasible alternatives.

Of course, if A were the policy forever, then Sub-Groups III and IV would not be very happy. The fact that there is turnover in alternatives can lead to something like "sharing," over time. If the group disagrees, the cycling "problem" can actually lead to a solution. If A is available forever, then Sub-Groups III and IV would have no alternative but to leave the group, or revolt. As Buchanan (1999) put it:

Aren't 'majority cycles' the most desirable outcome of a democratic process? After all, any attainment of political equilibrium via majority rule would amount to the permanent imposition of the majority's will on the outvoted minority. Would not a guaranteed rotation of outcomes be preferable, enabling the members of the minority in one round of voting to come back in subsequent rounds and ascend to majority membership? My concern, then and later, was the prevention of discrimination against minorities rather than stability of political outcomes. The question, from an economist's perspective, was how to obtain a combination of efficiency and justice under majority rule.

In other words, what the group should want everyone to get a chance to get what he or she wants, at least some of the time. Rather than stability, and always choosing the "General (majority) Will," justice and shared power might be a valid objective of constitutional construction.[3]

One path explored Knut Wicksell, James Buchanan, William Riker, and others, is true consensus, or unanimity. A group that agrees that alternative A is better than B, because literally every member of the groups prefers A to B, is unanimously giving consent to choose A over B. Consent is an ethically powerful conception of the common good. Any other decision rule guarantees that some people will be better off, and others worse, because consent is not unanimous.

Condorcet's concern was different; it is best illustrated with a different example, using spatial preferences instead of preference orders. For simplicity, imagine that voters are distributed uniformly along a left-right continuum ranging from 0 to 100, with a voter located at each integer. That is, there are 101 voters, with one having an ideal point at 0, one at 1, one at 2, and so on, with one at 99 and one at 100. Imagine that there are three candidates, A, B, and C, with platforms as depicted below.

If the election is held in the "plurality rule" fashion, or in what the British call a "first past the post" election, the winner is determined simply by who gets the most votes. There is no necessity of receiving a majority. In our example, it is easy to forecast voting outcomes, because one voter is located at every integer point on the line from 0 to 100, so there are 101 voters each of whom votes for the candidate closest to him or her. (For simplicity, let's assume that if two candidates are equidistant voters choose the candidate to their right).

In Panel (a) of Figure 7.1, we see that candidate B receives all the votes to the left of the midpoint between B's position (30) and A's position (50). Therefore, B receives the votes from the voters at positions 0 through 39. A receives the votes from voters at positions 40 through 52, for a total of 13 votes. C receives all the votes from voters with ideal points greater than the midpoint (52.5) between A's and C's platforms. That means the vote tally is C-47; B-40; A-13.

Let's see if this satisfies Condorcet's condition, by conducting all possible pairwise elections. In Panel B, we see that in the election of A vs. B, A wins easily, 61–40. In Panel C we see that in the election of A vs. C, A wins again, 54–47.

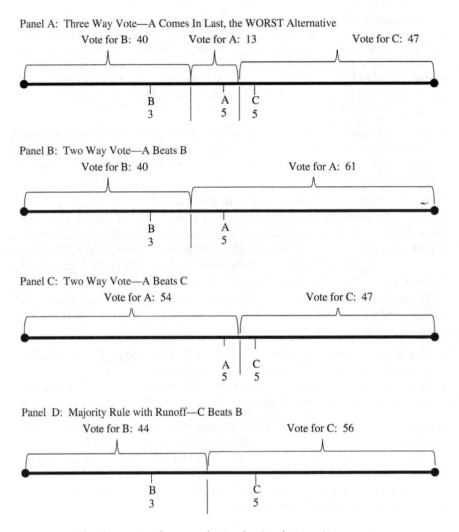

FIGURE 7.1. Plurality voting does not choose the Condorcet winner

Of course, this follows from the MVT, but only for majority rule *pairwise* elections; in other words, we have implicitly been assuming the Condorcet procedure all along, but only for two candidates at a time. The problem is that many elections use the "first past the post" system, and have more than two candidates. In our example, candidate A – the Condorcet winner! – comes in *dead last* in a "first past the post" election.

That is precisely the problem that concerned Condorcet. After going through an example very similar to the one outlined above, Condorcet concluded:

So the candidate who really had plurality support is the very one who by the conventional method received the fewest votes...It is already clear that the conventional election method must be rejected. It can be retained only for cases where we are not obliged to elect someone immediately and where we can decide to consider a candidate elected only when he has obtained more than half the votes. Even then, this method still has the drawback of making us view a candidate who in fact had very great plurality support as unsuccessful.

In general, therefore, we should replace this method with one in which *each voter simultaneously shows his preferences among all the candidates* by placing them in order of merit. (from "Essay on the Application...," 1785, in McLean and Hewitt, 1994; 123; emphasis added)

One might think that Condorcet is mistaken, and that "Majority Rule with Runoff" is a solution. However, Condorcet was right, as Panel D illustrates. Since A is eliminated (A comes in last) in the first round, the runoff is conducted between B and C. C wins the runoff, 57–44; that may be encouraging, since the Majority Rule with Runoff winner is the same as the First Past the Post winner, but as problem 7.3 at the end of this chapter shows, that need not be true.

These two examples of choices – where there is a clear Condorcet winner but some other alternative is selected – illustrate why social choice is such a complex problem.

- The group "wants" to select a voting rule that solves the problem of indeterminacy, *should the problem of cycling arise.*
- The same group "wants" to ensure that the chosen voting rule selects the Condorcet winner, *if one exists.*

The problem is that voting rules that preclude cycles are bad solutions to the "what do voters really want?" problem. And vice versa. It is useful to lay out the menu of alternatives, however, so that we can evaluate different voting rules on these grounds.

Consequently, we turn now to a short review of the general problem of social choice, and Arrow's "Impossibility" Theorem.

GENERAL SOCIAL CHOICE AND IMPOSSIBILITY

Arrow (1963) laid out a set of properties or conditions that (arguably) are desirable features of a social choice mechanism.[4] The impossibility theorem is a deduction that no social choice mechanism can possess all these features. In particular, all voting procedures must violate at least one of the conditions that Arrow demonstrated to be mutually inconsistent. Since Arrow's paradox applies to *any* nondictatorial aggregation mechanism, it encompasses all of what we might consider "democratic" decisions by societies.

Decisions might be made by one person (a dictatorship), by some group of people (an oligarchy, or a majority), or by everyone (unanimity). To make the treatment as general as possible, we will designate the set of citizens able to make a choice is the "decisive set."

Decisive set. A set C of citizens is "decisive" if for two alternatives y and z the fact that all members of C like y better than z is sufficient to ensure that y is selected over z by the society, regardless of the opinions of citizens not members of C. That is, the citizens in the complement of C might agree, or disagree; it does not matter: what C says, goes.

We will call K(C) the "size" of C, or the minimum number of people required to be decisive. We have seen an example of a decisive set under majority rule: C is any group of $(N/2) + 1$ citizens.[5] Thus, there are many different potential Cs, each of which must have K(C) $\geq (N/2) + 1$ citizens.[6]

Both the inclusion of a given person's preferences in a decision (enfranchisement) and the decision to use a particular means of summarizing these preferences (aggregation mechanism) can affect the decision.[7] One way of choosing, in fact, a very common way, is dictatorship or monarchy, but that is not really a social choice. "Social choice" usually requires that the decision is in some way *collective*, or that more than one person will make the choice. Technically, all this means is that C > 1. If collective decisions are made by majority rule, K(C) $\geq (N/2) + 1$. If the rule is unanimity, the only decisive set is the entire group of enfranchised citizens: K(C) = N.

Arrow's interest was in a deep question: Can dictatorship be avoided, if a group wants a decisive, transitive, just ordering for the society? One way of answering the question is stark: No.[8]

Arrow's paradox. The only logically consistent collective choice mechanism that is always transitive and obeys the Pareto criterion, allowing for any possible fixed set of pairwise preferences over alternatives, is dictatorship.

The only transitive collective decision rule that obeys the apparently innocuous technical criteria Arrow sets out is dictatorship, or rule by one. The paradox is that such a decision rule is not "collective," but resolves disagreements by restricting the decisive set to one person. How did Arrow arrive at this conclusion?

THE "IMPOSSIBILITY" RESULT

We will consider only a simplified paraphrasing of Arrow's theorem and will not consider the technical aspects of the proof of the theorem at all. In addition to looking at Arrow (1963), it is useful to review Schwartz (1986), Kelly (1988), Mueller (1989, especially chapters 19–20), and Austen-Smith and Banks (1999).

Here is the outline of the result.

(1) Specify a set of desirable characteristics for an aggregation mechanism, or way of "counting" preferences registered by enfranchised citizens.

(2) Determine the set of collective choice mechanisms that have these desirable characteristics.

(3) Ask how many of these choice rules are not dictatorial. The answer is none. Any social choice mechanism exhibiting all the characteristics Arrow listed as desirable must be dictatorial. The clearest statement may be that of Austen-Smith and Banks (1999, p. 30): "If an aggregation rule is (conditions), then it is dictatorial."

Some scholars have questioned the merit of Arrow's list of "desirable criteria." Others have suggested substitute axioms that are weaker or quite different. Still, Arrow's original set of desirable characteristics is not implausible. To describe the list of desirable characteristics for social choice mechanisms, we will need to define some terms and concepts.[9]

Consider three different states of the world, S_1, S_2, S_3, representing discrepant policy vectors 1, 2, and 3, respectively. (That is, state of the world S_i has policies described by vector $S_i = (x_{i1}, x_{i2}, \ldots x_{in})$ if there are n policy dimensions to be decided.) We can then describe the set of desirable characteristics as follows:

1. *Unanimity* (also, the Pareto criterion)[10]: If all enfranchised citizens j agree (for example) that $S_1 \succ_j S_2$, then S_1 is selected by the collective choice rule to S_2.

2. *Transitivity:* The collective choice mechanism is transitive, so that if S_1 is collectively selected over S_2, and S_2 is collectively preferred to S_3, then S_1 must be collectively preferred over S_3.

3. *Unrestricted domain:* For any individual and for any triple of alternatives S_1, S_2 and S_3, any of the following six preference orderings (from best to worst) is possible:

	1	2	3	4	5	6
Best	S_1	S_1	S_3	S_2	S_2	S_3
Middle	S_2	S_3	S_1	S_1	S_3	S_2
Worst	S_3	S_2	S_2	S_3	S_1	S_1

4. *Independence of irrelevant alternatives* (IIA): The social choice between any two alternatives must depend only on the individual rankings of the alternatives in question in the preference profile of the group. Thus, if S_1 is socially preferred to S_2, then it still will be socially preferred if we rearrange the orderings of the other alternatives while leaving the paired rankings of S_1, and S_2 the same. For example, the following two sets of preference profiles of three citizens must yield the same social ordering for S_1, and S_2, if the social choice rule is IIA:

Preference profile set I (for persons 1, 2, and 3)

	1	2	3
Best	S_1	S_2	S_1
Middle	S_2	S_1	S_3
Worst	S_3	S_3	S_2

Preference profile set II

	1	2	3
Best	S_1	S_3	S_1
Middle	S_3	S_2	S_2
Worst	S_2	S_1	S_3

Notice that the relative rankings of S_1 and S_2 are the same in profile sets I and II. All that is different is the relative position of S_3 in the rankings. For example, in set I, person 1 ranks the alternatives S_1, S_2, S_3. In set II, person 1 ranks them S_1, S_3, S_2. In both cases, $S_1 \succ_1 S_2$. Independence of irrelevant alternatives requires that this pairwise comparison of rankings does not depend on the position of other "irrelevant" alternatives (such as S_3 in our example).

The final "good" characteristic of mechanisms for the democratic aggregation of preferences is probably the most obvious: No one person possesses all power to decide.

5. *Nondictatorship*: There is no dictator. If person 2 (for example) is a dictator, then if for 2 thinks $S_1 \succ_2 S_2$, then "S_1 better than S_2" is the social ranking, regardless of how anyone else, or even everyone else, ranks S_1 compared with S_2. More generally, any set that contains the dictator is decisive, even if the set is a singleton with the dictator as its only member, and everyone else prefers S_2.

With these conditions established, we can state a version of the "impossibility" theorem.

Impossibility theorem. Consider the set of all collective choice rules that satisfy requirements 1–4 (unanimity, transitivity, unrestricted domain, and IIA). Every element of the set of collective choice mechanisms satisfying these requirements violates requirement 5, implying the existence of a dictator.

Therefore, any non-dictatorial mechanism for aggregating individual preferences must lack at least one of the (arguably) desirable properties 1–4. If one is willing to accept dictatorship, of course, one might have the other attractive features.

But if the government is a dictatorship, the other features aren't really all that attractive. With a dictator, all that unanimity implies is that if everyone (including the dictator) agrees, that is the social choice. Of course, if everyone (except the dictator) opposes something, then the dictator still gets his way. It is just that unanimity does not matter in that instance. Therefore, we will consider only *social* choices or choices where there is no dictator.

A similar argument (for restricting the menu of choice for ideal forms of government) applies to the Pareto criterion, though on more practical grounds: It is hard to imagine adopting a rule that would prevent change if literally everyone favored the change. If nothing else, society could get unanimous consent to change the rules.[11]

If we agree that nondictatorship and unanimity are the two non-negotiable elements of our social choice rules, Arrow's theorem leaves us with three options, one of which must be sacrificed if we are to have the others. By relaxing Arrow's conditions, we could pick one of the following:

- rules that allow *intransitivity*
- rules that allow *independent alternatives* to affect pairwise choices of other alternatives
- rules that restrict the set of *preferences* that will be allowed (i.e., violate universal domain)

Interestingly, the set of rules that are possible for these violations of the assumptions of Arrow each have certain advantages, and disadvantages. A complete discussion of the implications of relaxing the postulates of the impossibility theorem is beyond the scope of this book; the interested reader should consult Schwartz (1986), Kelly (1988), or Mueller (1989).[12]

INFORMATION AND VOTING PROCESSES

A recent book by Donald Saari (Saari, 2008), offers a simple, and – if correct – profound explanation of the "negative results" in axiomatic social choice theory.[13] He claims that the negative voting results arise because information we believe the decision rule is using is actually never used, discarded, or at best ignored. He makes a significant claim for this observation: "This ignored information, which by not being used...makes these negative conclusions obvious rather than surprising ..." (p. 21)

Saari focuses on the Independence of Irrelevant Alternatives axiom as "the culprit causing ... this dictatorial problem." (p. 23) He is allowed this conceit, of course, in terms of choosing one axiom as "the culprit," but as a general matter each of the axioms is necessary for the paradox, and is therefore a candidate for "the" culprit. Saari's reason for focusing on IIA becomes clear in his chapter 2, where he compares the situation to dog training. He claims that an owner trying to teach a dog to roll over understands the command. But what information, exactly, is the dog understanding and using? The dog may just slump sadly and hang his tail, uncertain what is being demanded.

What Saari (2008) means is that Arrow's theorem – like most voting "paradoxes," in his view – takes a peculiar and not very useful form. It is true enough that individually transitive preferences, aggregated through any filter or choice mechanism, can yield an intransitive social ordering. But voting mechanisms, or rather most voting mechanisms (including majority rule), don't "know" this. Using pairwise comparisons, for example, in majority rule, produces Condorcet's Paradox because majority rule does not "know" that chains or orders longer than two are transitive, or that chains longer than three are acyclic, for individuals.

Saari's point is that if you took as data individual orders that were intransitive, Arrow's result would be not only still true, but also mind-numbingly trivial. But then aggregation mechanisms that ignore, or do not incorporate, the information of individual transitivity lead to the same result, and for the same reason. The thread that ties together all the impossibility results is willfully ignoring information.

What is necessary is a system that actually uses all the information contained in transitive preference orders, or weak orders, over outcomes for the individual. Saari proposes that we use aggregation mechanisms that reflect not just the binary rankings, but also the *intensity* of preference.

To say this is controversial is an understatement. It harks back to Borda's famous response to Napoleon that "My system is for honest men." Of course, it is perfectly true that many decision rules do not ask that voters register an intensity of preference. Instead, voters are asked for (at most) an ordinal ranking over multiple alternatives. More often, voters are asked only for the single most preferred option (as in plurality voting).

However, the reason is not that such voting rules are deficient. The reason is that, as Napoleon believed, people will manipulate their preference revelation data if those data will affect the outcome.

An important set of results built on the Gibbard- Satterthwaite theorem (Gibbard, 1973; Satterthwaite, 1975) make Napoleon's intuition more formal. Gibbard-Satterthwaite demonstrated that if there are three or more candidates, then one of two conditions must be true for any collective decision rule: the rule is either dictatorial or manipulable. Saari does not ignore the G-S theorem (though he relegates his discussion of the result to a lengthy footnote, p. 60). His answer is that IIA is not really worth defending in the first place, and sacrificing it "costs" less in terms of increased manipulability than one might think.

However, this is a very debatable claim, and clearly worth more than a footnote. Ian McLean famously said, "IIA is there [in the Arrow list] for a good reason, as Satterthwaite indirectly shows. Take out IIA and you have gross manipulability."[14] Mechanisms that fail IIA are susceptible to extravagant, organized campaigns at manipulation in ways that are likely to raise serious questions in voters' minds about the legitimacy of voting as a means of choosing governments, leaders, or policy. It is hard to imagine persuading citizens that the way to discover truth is to lie like crazy.[15]

To sum up, the problems that Arrow and the G-S theorem have raised suggest humility in advocating a particular choice rule. All "responsive" collective choice procedures, meaning voting rules where each voter's view counts toward the aggregate result, have to violate at least one of Arrow's strictures. And all voting rules where three or more candidates can in principle be selected are manipulable, meaning that voters have strong incentives to misrepresent the information they report to the authorities.

This problem famously led Winston Churchill to say:

Many forms of Government have been tried, and will be tried in this world of sin and woe. No one pretends that democracy is perfect or all-wise. Indeed, it has been said that democracy is the worst form of government except all those other forms that have been tried from time to time.

We turn now to some of the many forms of democratic decision rules.

ALTERNATIVE DEMOCRATIC DECISION RULES

Voting rules other than simple majority are common. In fact, the use of pure pairwise majority rule is rare. We have focused on it because pairwise comparisons over alternatives are useful in constructing preference orders. That is not the purpose of most decision rules. The difficulty is that the choice of aggregation mechanism will determine, in part, the nature of the society by advantaging certain alternatives. As we have seen, the decision rule matters in the way the group is constituted. We will consider three major sets of alternatives to simple majority rule: optimal majority rule, the Borda count and approval voting, and proportional representation.

Optimal Majority Rule

The first variation on majority rule is some form of majority rule itself, allowing the size of the required "majority" (i.e., decisive set) for an affirmative decision to be different from the simple majority $K(C) = (N/2) + 1$. After all, what is so special about 50 percent (plus one voter) as the minimum group in favor? In theory, as we have discussed above, the size of the group making a decision can vary from one person to the entire society.

In practice, lots of normal collective business follows majority rule. But even within the context of real-world collective decisions, the size of the proportion of enfranchised voters required to make a decision varies widely. In many legislative assemblies, unanimous consent is required to amend or suspend the rules of procedure. To change the U.S. Constitution, the intersecting consent of two different supermajorities (two-thirds of a national assembly to *propose*, three-quarters of state assemblies to *ratify*) is required.

At the other end of the scale, a variety of choice rules rest on the expressed preference of numbers less than a majority. Under the standard "Robert's

Rules of Order," a motion dies unless it is seconded, meaning that it takes two people to achieve access to the agenda. The U.S. Supreme Court grants access by affirming a writ of *certiorari* based on a vote of four of the nine justices.

What is the "best" decisive set as a proportion of the polity? The answer to almost all important questions, of course, is that "it depends." But what does the answer depend on?

The classic analytical treatment of optimal majority is Buchanan and Tullock's *The Calculus of Consent*. Taking an economic approach, Buchanan and Tullock note that there are *costs* of widely shared decision power as well as *benefits*. The *costs of including* more people in the required majority entail defining and amending the proposal, explaining it to the voters, providing payoffs to solve strategic maneuvering of swing voters, and so on. These "decision costs," falling on those whose preferences count in the decision, are a kind of public good, and may mean that participants spend "too few" resources on making good decisions. High decision costs are a problem for the quality of the decision, for the entire polity.

The cost of excluding members of the constituted group from the required majority is an *externality*. Costs can be imposed on an individual without his consent, and because of the goals and actions of other members. Interestingly, externalities such as pollution are one of the core justifications for government action, even actions that involve coercive force. Buchanan and Tullock point out that being forced to accept a decision you have not consented to, and in fact, oppose, is an externality also.

Of course, the nature of "consent" in markets differs from what goes on in constituted groups. Still, as Buchanan (2007: 211) points out:

there is a categorical separation between the market and the political relationship between and among interacting persons. In the stylized limit, that of fully competitive markets for both, inputs and outputs, the individual faces no costs of exit from any relationship. The individual is maximally free from the power of others. In dramatic contrast, the individual in a political relationship is necessarily subject to the exercise of some power or authority by another. In the stylized limit, this power is absolute: no exit is possible, regardless of cost.

Thus, one might think of being "bound by wills not your own" as a kind of external cost, just as Rousseau (1973) claimed.

We can depict the problem of optimal majority graphically, as in Figure 7.2. Decision costs rise dramatically as we near a rule of unanimity, because each voter becomes a potential swing voter. Anyone can threaten to withhold approval unless certain concessions or payoffs are made. Similarly, external costs fall as we near unanimity, because by definition there is less chance a policy can be enacted without approval of everyone affected.

The optimal majority is K/N, because it minimizes the sum of the costs of inclusion and the costs of exclusion. These costs, though hard to quantify,

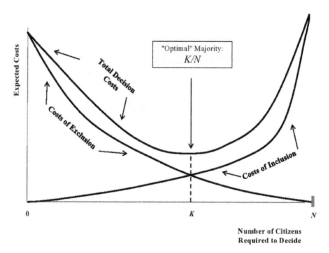

FIGURE 7.2. Buchanan and Tullock's "optimal majority" analysis

clearly figure in how we choose how to choose, as public decisions fall into three categories:

(a) *Access decisions*: $0 < K < (N/2) + 1$. One member of the U.S. House or Senate is required to introduce a bill. If no one introduces the bill, it is completely blocked. At least four members of the U.S. Supreme Court are required to grant a writ of *certiorari*, or petition for a case to be heard. Neither of these decisions by any means ensures success; all that is granted is access.

(b) *Routine decisions*. $K = (N/2) + 1$. The smallest strict majority is a very common value for the decisive set in democracies, from tiny private clubs to the U.S. Congress and Supreme Court. This value for K is the smallest value that ensures no simultaneous passage of two directly contradictory measures. Thus, both inclusion and exclusion costs are moderate. For simple majority rule to have such wide real-world application, it must minimize the (perceived) costs of making routine collective decisions.

(c) *Changing the Rules*: $(N/2) + 1 < K \leq N$. The rules of choice govern the kinds of outcomes that the choices represent. A decision to change the rules has more far-reaching and unpredictable effects than a decision made under a fixed set of rules. Consequently, the cost of excluding enfranchised members is higher for rule change decisions, and the optimal majority for rule changes is more than 50 percent + 1.

There is no single decision rule used for all choices; it depends. Nonetheless, it does appear that we require larger majorities for larger questions. This conclusion is also consistent with the approach advocated by Rousseau, though his justifications are very different from those given by Buchanan and Tullock:

A difference of one vote destroys equality; a single opponent destroys unanimity; but between equality and unanimity, there are several grades of unequal division, at each of which this proportion may be fixed in accordance with the condition and needs of the body politic.

There are two general rules that may serve to regulate this relation. First, the more grave and important the questions discussed, the nearer should the opinion that is to prevail approach unanimity. Secondly, the more the matter in hand calls for speed, the smaller the prescribed difference in the numbers of votes may be allowed to become: where an instant decision has to be reached, a majority of one vote should be enough. (Rousseau, 1973, Book II, chapter 2, p. 278).

Still, there is something interesting and important about 50 percent+ 1 as a decision rule. It is likely that the diagram in Figure 7.2 does not fully capture a key fact: for any decisive set *less than* 50 percent + 1 it is quite possible that both A and (not) A could be passed, exposing almost the entire population to the chance of being excluded from a decision. Requiring a decisive set *larger than* 50 percent + 1, on the other hand, increases the costs of including more people.

There is a discontinuity in the "costs of exclusion" curve, causing a kink in the total decision-making costs curve (Figure 7.3). Majority rule is the least costly solution for many decision problems, because it minimizes decision costs subject to the constraint that two directly contradictory measures cannot both pass.

EQUILIBRIUM FOR LARGER MAJORITIES

It appears that different decisive sets are appropriate for different choice situations. Now we must ask what effects these differences may have on the existence and nature of equilibrium. We will still face the generic failing of majority rule systems, of course: The society may cycle among alternatives within a subset of the overall space of feasible political choices. But given this caveat, is there a generalization of the MVT that applies to optimal majorities K/N, where $K > (N/2)$?

The answer is yes.[16] As in Chapter 5, define N_1 as the number of points on one side of a hyperplane $\mathcal{H}$ (including points on $\mathcal{H}$), and N_2 as the number of points on the other side (again, including points on $\mathcal{H}$). The generalized K-majority voter theorem (KMVT) is then just an obvious generalization of the GMVT.[17]

The KMVT can be stated as follows:

An alternative y is a K-majority equilibrium for the society if and only if $N_1 \geq (N - K + 1)$ and $N_2 \geq (N - K + 1)$ for every $\mathcal{H}$ containing y.

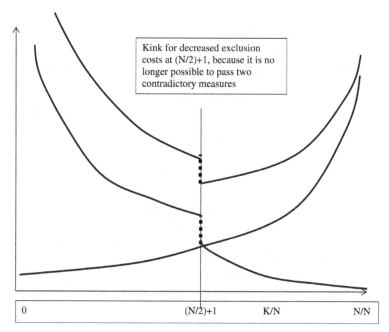

Kink for decreased exclusion costs at (N/2)+1, because it is no longer possible to pass two contradictory measures

0   (N/2)+1   K/N   N/N

FIGURE 7.3. Optimal majority, with kinked decision cost function

It is obvious that the KMVT reduces directly to the MVT for majority rule, since for majority rule $N - K + 1 = N/2$, where $K = N/2 + 1$.

The problem with supermajority rules is the way they privilege the status quo, whatever it happens to be. There are many more equilibria, but they cannot easily be changed, which explains the sharp upturn in the decision costs curve in Figure 7.2 as the size of the K gets larger. As Figure 7.4 shows, supermajority rules ensure stability, but at the expense of flexibility. The status quo is preserved like an insect in amber, even if most citizens support some other alternative.

As the figure shows, larger majorities imply broader equilibrium intervals, illustrating why the KMVT is a generalization of the GMVT. If $K = N$, the set of equilibria is the Pareto set. For $N > K > N/2$, the set of equilibria is an interval. As K shrinks to $N/2$, the set of equilibria is the median ideal point (as in our example), or a median interval connecting two ideal points and containing all the points in between.

BORDA COUNT

Condorcet's criterion for value in elections was that if a majority preferred an alternative, that alternative should be selected. Borda was concerned about an additional factor: intensity of preference. Majorities might pick the wrong

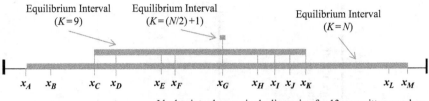

FIGURE 7.4. An example of supermajority rule: many equilibria, little change

alternative, even if Condorcet's criterion was satisfied. The issue for Borda was in elections with several candidates. As he put it in his 1784 paper:

There is a widespread feeling, which I have never heard disputed, that in a ballot vote, the plurality of votes always shows the will of the voters. That is, that the candidate who obtains this plurality is necessarily preferred by the voters to his opponents. But I shall demonstrate that this feeling, while correct when the election is between just two candidates, can lead to error in all other cases. (Borda, 1784 / 1993 MacLean and Urken, p. 83).

Interestingly, Borda wrote in 1784, exactly twenty years *before* Lewis and Clark's Corps of Discovery used plurality, the very decision rule that Borda thought would "lead to error" in deciding where to camp at the mouth of the Columbia.

Borda gave several examples. The simplest (MacLean and Urken, 1993; 84–86) suggested that there are twenty-one voters, who must choose over three alternatives A, B, and C. Imagine that the preference rankings of voters fall into three categories, as in Figure 7.5. If we use plurality rule, only first-place votes count. We do not know the second- and third-place preferences of voters in the first group. All we know for sure is that they like alternative A best, and they are the most numerous (eight first-place votes for A). Since B receives seven votes and C gets only six, A is the chosen policy.

Borda's point was that thirteen voters, a clear majority, might actually like alternative A *least*. The problem with plurality rule, he felt, was that it counted only first-place votes. Borda suggested a number of alternative decision rules, but the one most often associated with him is the "Borda count." Each voter is asked to assign to each alternative a number corresponding to her ranking of that alternative.

Thus, each voter in the middle group in Figure 7.5 gives alternative B a rank of 1, C a rank of 2, and A a rank of 3. (If there were more alternatives, say, q of them, then the ranks would go down to the worst, or qth, alternative on each voter's ballot.) The authority conducting the election then adds up the scores, or "marks," for each alternative, and that alternative with the smallest number (for Borda, the most "merit") wins.

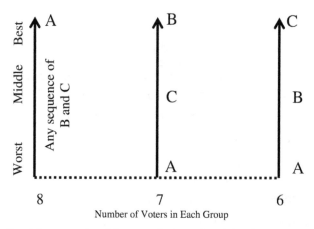

FIGURE 7.5. Borda's example of how majority rule picks the "wrong" alternative: A wins, but either B or C is better. (From Borda, 1781; reprinted in Black, 1958, p. 157, Fig. 156)

Borda left the exact distribution of preferences for C and B in the first group unspecified (again, see Black, 1958; especially 59–66 and 157–159). For the sake of example (just as we did earlier for Lewis and Clark), suppose that four of the eight voters like B better than C, and the others prefer C to B. What would be the result of using the Borda method? Alternative A has eight first-place votes, zero second-place marks, and thirteen third-place marks, for a Borda count of forty-seven. Alternative B has seven first-place votes, ten second-place, and four third-place, for a count of thirty-nine. Alternative C has six first-place marks, eleven second-place, and four third-place, for a count of forty. Using the Borda count, then, B wins over C in a close race, with A well back in the voting.

We might change the preferences of the first group for B over C in the example, but the basic result would be the same: No matter what preference for B over C is used, A always comes in last, rather than first as under majority rule. When the preferences of voters beyond their first place rankings are considered, A is eliminated from serious consideration in this example. What might Lewis and Clark have done if they had read Borda (and ignored Napoleon)?

APPROVAL VOTING

The Borda count has been criticized as requiring both too much character and too much information, because all voters must rank all alternatives. If some do not, the outcome will depend on the way abstention is counted. Further, though Borda noted, "my scheme is intended only for honest men,"[18] the Borda count provides opportunities for voting strategically, misrepresenting one's preference ordering to change the outcome.[19]

An alternative that preserves some of the qualities of the Borda count is *approval voting*: Each voter votes for as many of the candidates as he or she likes, and the candidate with the most votes wins.[20] Another way to think of approval voting is to imagine that each voter makes a list of candidates, ranked from best to worst. The voter then draws a line between the worst acceptable candidate and the best unacceptable candidate. Every candidate the voter approves of gets a vote, but those below the line get nothing.

Returning to the example in Figure 7.5, suppose that voters in the first group think that only **A** is acceptable. Imagine that voters in the middle and last groups consider both **B** and **C** acceptable. What will be the result under approval voting? **A** will receive eight votes, just as under plurality rule. Candidates **B** and **C** will each receive thirteen votes, so that the specific outcome will depend on how we assume ties are broken. The point is that **A** will not have a chance as long as **A** is judged not acceptable by a majority of voters, which is the spirit of Borda's example.[21]

Both the Borda count and approval voting must violate one of Arrow's axioms, but which one? The answer is independence of irrelevant alternatives (IIA). The social choice under the Borda rule or approval voting may depend on the relative positions of two alternatives compared with other (irrelevant) alternatives, which means that voters can manipulate the outcome by moving alternatives strategically down in their reported ranking.

A simple example (adapted from Arrow, 1963, p. 27) illustrates another property of the Borda count: It is *not independent of path*.[22] This is actually a different problem from independence of irrelevant alternatives, since it involves the presence or absence of particular alternatives, not their relative locations in the preference rankings of voters. The interesting thing about Arrow's example is that it reveals an access point for strategy: For the Borda count and related social choice rules, outcomes can be sensitive to the set of alternatives that appear on the ballot, even in a single-stage decision.

Imagine there are three voters (A, B, and C) and four alternatives (x, y, z, and w). Further, suppose that all voters use the Borda count and vote sincerely. Consider two different ballots, one with four alternatives and another with only three, as in Table 7.2.

Clearly, x wins, because it has the smallest Borda count, if there are four alternatives.

Now, however, suppose that one alternative, y, is eliminated from the contest, as in Panel b. The outcome is now different: x and z tie, though nothing about their relative value has changed. All that is different is the decision context: For vote 1, y was on the ballot, and for vote 2, y did not appear. Furthermore, if there is now a run-off between x and z, z actually wins. Consequently, dropping y from consideration changes the outcome.[23] This sensitivity to the inclusion or absence of other alternatives is different

TABLE 7.2. *With Borda Count, Alternatives Matter Too Much*

Panel a: A comparison of x, z, and w with y also considered

Rank of alternative	Voter A	Voter B	Voter C	Borda count
x	1	2	2	5
z	4	1	1	6
w	2	4	4	10
y	3	3	3	9

Panel b: A comparison of x; z, and w, deleting y

Rank of alternative	Voter A	Voter B	Voter C	Borda count
x	1	2	2	5
z	3	1	1	5
w	2	3	3	8

from the relative rankings of irrelevant alternatives, having more to do with how alternatives are retained or dropped in the early stages of elections or amendment procedures. That is the reason the "path" is important in this example.

PROPORTIONAL REPRESENTATION

Various collective decisions, particularly choices of political representatives in national assemblies for geographic districts, are made with proportional representation (PR) rules. There are many PR rules, but they all share the characteristic that each party's share of seats in the assembly is approximately that party's share of votes in the last election. The ideal for a pure PR system, then, would be:

$$\frac{\text{Party's Seats}}{\text{Total Seats}} \approx \frac{\text{Party's Votes}}{\text{Total Votes}}$$

In practice, this ideal is violated in many ways and for very practical reasons. One of the most common modifications made to pure PR systems is the threshold, or minimum vote required for a party to seat members in the assembly (Laver and Shepsle, 1996; Laver and Schofield, 1990). For example, Greece requires that a party receive at least 15 percent of the votes. Israel has an "exclusion threshold" of only 1.5 percent (Sartori, 1994). Such rules have two effects:

- There is a departure from the ideal of pure proportionality, since a party can receive up to the vote threshold, minus one vote, and receive no seats in the legislature.
- Consequently, people may vote strategically, eschewing sincere votes for small parties that have no chance and concentrating on one of the larger parties.

The difference between the proportion of the vote won and the proportion of legislative seats controlled is the "seat bias." Small parties will have less than a proportionate number of seats, and larger parties a more than proportionate number. Still, as Schwingenschlögl and Pukelsheim (2006) show, the size of the seat bias shrinks rapidly as parties grow beyond the threshold to gain seats.[24]

The process of coalition government formation is complex; the interested reader should consult Laver and Schofield (1990) and Laver, et al. (2011). Our point is simply that once a PR election has been held, it is by no means clear that a government has been selected; in fact, the process may have barely begun. Any two of the three parties in our example are capable of joining and forming a government. On the other hand, no one party can govern. Consequently, the nature of the government is very much in doubt. Cycling over coalition partners simply moves the incoherence of the democratic process from voter choice to bargaining among elites.

The problem may be especially acute in bargaining problems, because the structure may be close to "divide the dollar," which in the setting of three or more players has no determinate outcome.[25] However, the real-world problem of choosing a government actually is solved quite quickly, in most cases.[26]

Dennis Mueller gives a summary of the difference between plurality and PR rules:

If the purpose of the election is to select a government, a chief executive, a single party to rule the country, then the plurality rule for electing representatives, or for electing the chief executive, should be employed. This rule will tend to produce two parties or candidates... If the purpose of the election is to select a body of representatives that mirrors as closely as possible the preferences of the citizenry, then PR is the appropriate electoral rule... PR is a system for choosing representatives, not for picking between final packages of outcomes. (1989, pp. 222, 226; emphasis in original)

In some ways, the consideration of whether plurality elections or PR is better mimics our earlier discussion on the optimal size of majorities. If a single decision among several mutually exclusive alternatives is required, then plurality rule, or majority rule with runoff, has clear advantages. The polity may simply need to decide something *right now*, so the costs of delay from deliberation and negotiation in a PR system may not be worth paying.

On the other hand, questions of far-reaching consequence for all citizens may require a representation of many points of view, at least in terms of access. In such decisions, representation may even be an end in itself, since not just the decision but also the legitimacy of the decision is crucial to the survival of the society. For such decisions, voters may want to be sure they have a representative of their own choosing, because having someone in the room gives a sense of access. PR systems are appealing in such circumstances because the deliberative process of the legislative assembly mimics, in proportions of perspectives, the population as a whole.

SUMMARY AND CONCLUSIONS

In this chapter, we have outlined some intuition behind alternative voting institutions. The use of the word "alternative" means "ways of choosing other than simple majority rule," for majority rule holds a privileged status as a benchmark in social choice. Gary Cox (1987), in discussing alternative voting institutions, notes:

Another way to organize the findings herein is along a "degree of centrism" axis. Holding down one end of this axis would be the Condorcet procedures, under which candidates have a dominant strategy of adopt the position of the median voter. Other procedures (such as Borda's method and approval voting) under which the unique convergent Nash equilibrium is the situation in which all candidates adopt the median position would come next, followed by systems (such as negative voting) under which there are multiple convergent equilibria. Finally, holding down the other end of the centrism axis would be procedures such as plurality rule, under which candidates will not converge at any point, instead spreading themselves out more or less evenly along the policy dimension. (p. 99).

Dictatorship, for most of us, is unacceptable as a way of organizing government. In the weighing of order versus liberty on the scales of choosing a "good" society, dictatorship provides only order. But liberty without order may lead to chaos. The signal contribution of social choice theory has been to demonstrate implications of choosing how to choose. Arrow's work, as well as that of the many scholars who followed him, would appear to concede that there might be no perfect alternative to dictatorship, but that at the same time some form of responsive government is tenable and workable.

It is important to note, in closing, that an advocate for state power – even sovereign power employed by a single ruler, a monarch or dictator – is really arguing for the advantages of stability against chaos and anarchy. Thus, dictatorship or the "strong man" that many nations around the world seem to seek out is an antidote to chaotic instability and constant fighting. The most famous statement of this dark alternative was by Thomas Hobbes:

...the nature of War, consisteth not in actual fighting; but in the known disposition thereto, during all the time there is no assurance to the contrary... Whatsoever therefore is consequent to a time of War, where every man is Enemy to every man; the same is consequent to the time, wherein men live without other security, than what their own strength, and their own invention shall furnish them withall. In such condition, there is no place for Industry; because the fruit thereof is uncertain; and consequently no Culture of the Earth; no Navigation, nor use of the commodities that may be imported by Sea; no commodious Buildings; no Instruments of moving, and removing such things as require much force; no Knowledge of the face of the Earth; no account of Time; no Arts; no Letters; no Society; and which is worst of all, continual feare, and danger of violent death; And the life of man, solitary, poore, nasty, brutish, and short. (Chapter 13, p. 186).

Hobbes himself saw that his pessimistic portrayal of the condition of human-kind without a constituted state might not be literally accurate: "It may perad-venture be thought, there was never such a time..." (p. 187). That is not his point. What Hobbes is analyzing are the conditions or conventions that enable a society to avoid the cataclysmic "war of every man against every man." (p. 188).

In Hobbes' view, groups of people can avoid the war of all against all by constituting themselves as groups. They avoid the state of nature by vesting power, and the legitimate ability to focus force, in the person of the sovereign. As democratic theory has progressed, we have adapted and elaborated Hobbes' notion of sovereignty into rule by the will of the people, expressed through some form of voting rule or aggregation mechanism. This is really quite an astonishing intellectual achievement, and we should not take it for granted.

We start with a state of nature, move to the person of the sovereign, who literally embodies the power and legitimacy of the state, and then mentally divide this sovereign person into three parts:

(a) the general will of the people, the public welfare, the abstraction that the state serves
(b) the institutional office of the head of state, with powers and institutions to assist in carrying out the law
(c) the physical person, chosen through some constituted procedure, to use the powers of (b) to carry out (a)

The result is that the person who holds the office is reduced, in theory though often not in practice, far below the status of dictator. The real sovereign is the law, or the will of the public expressed by voting. Given how difficult this problem of "social choice" is, in both technical and practical terms, it is hardly surprising that democracies fail and dictatorships take their place. What is surprising is how well, in most places and at most times, democracies perform in spite of these difficulties.

TERMS

Approval Voting
Arrow's Theorem
Borda Count
Condorcet winner
Cycling

Decisive Set
k-Majority
Impossibility Results
Independence of Path
IIA
Manipulability
Optimal Majority
Plurality Rule
Proportional Representation
Social Choice
Unrestricted Domain

EXERCISES

7.1 Suppose that there are seventeen members of a committee, with ideal points on a policy line that correspond to their identities (Mr. 1 most prefers a policy of 1, Mr. 11 likes a policy of 11, and so on). Suppose that the current policy is 7. According to the KMVT, what is the smallest K that preserves the status quo (7) as an equilibrium?

7.2 Suppose five voters (Messrs. 1–5) have the following preference rankings for three candidates (A, B, and C).

	Voter				
	1	2	3	4	5
Best	A	B	C	B	A
Middle	C	C	A	C	C
Worst	B	A	B	A	B

Which candidate will win under the following decision rule:

a. Majority rule, each voter gets one vote for first preference, with runoff in the event of no majority on first ballot.

b. Borda count, each voter ranks candidates from 1 (best) to 3 (worst). Smallest total "score" wins.

7.3 Assume that there are 101 voters, with ideal points at 0, 1, 2,...100, and assume that there are three candidates. Give an example of locations for the three candidates of an election where the "First Past the Post" and "Majority Rule with Runoff" winners are different.

7.4 *Give a formal proof of the KMVT.
Note: Exercises marked * are advanced material.

8

Uncertainty

"Certainty is the mother of quiet and repose, and uncertainty the cause of variance and contentions." Edward Coke, *Institutes of the Laws of England*, Part I.

"I will tell you the one thing I really believe, out of all the things there are to believe...All people are insane. They will do anything at any time, and God help anybody who looks for reasons." Kurt Vonnegut, p. 116, *Mother Night*.

Downs (1957) is credited with creating the foundations of the classical spatial model assuming full information. However, Downs sought a more comprehensive model, based on information and an economic conception of "rationality." He tried to incorporate more realistic assumptions about human behavior into his discussion of politics. Downs thought that uncertainty was the central problem:

Our reason for stressing uncertainty is that, in our opinion, it is a basic force affecting all human activity ... Coping with uncertainty is a major function of nearly every significant institution in human society ... (p. 13)

As soon as uncertainty appears, the clear path from taste structure to voting decision becomes obscured by lack of knowledge ... [Some voters] are highly uncertain about which party they prefer ... (p. 83)

More than thirty-five years later, Downs wondered why scholars lost sight of the centrality of uncertainty, or "information costs," in his work.

I personally believe that the way information costs are treated [in *An Economic Theory of Democracy*] is perhaps the most important contribution ... It is more important than the spatial analysis of parties, although the latter has become more famous. (Downs, 1993).

The classical spatial model simplifies candidates' promises, their reasons for making those promises, and their competence and sincerity in translating those promises into policy. Therefore, what we perversely called the "Downsian" version of the spatial model assumes the following:

- All participants know – and know that everyone else knows – the distribution of voter ideal points
- Candidates are nothing more than platforms; charisma and valence are ignored
- Candidates' sole motive is election; they are uninterested in policy
- All platforms and promises are implemented, if the candidate is elected

INFORMATION, STRATEGY, AND UNCERTAINTY

These simplifications are crucial to the exposition of the model. Now that the reader has mastered the basics, it is time to incorporate some of Downs' own caution about applying the spatial theory to actual elections where *strategic uncertainty, rational ignorance, plays by nature,* and *the perspective of the observer* are central features. These are different things, and the differences teach us a lot about the way elections and politics are likely to work.

Strategic uncertainty: Person A does not know what Person B knows, or what Person B will do. As a result, Person A has to choose an action or make a decision under uncertainty. Under some circumstances, Person B may be in the same position. Then each is trying to guess what the other person knows, or will do. A's best strategy depends on what B does, and vice versa.

Rational ignorance: Person A, perhaps intentionally, lacks information that would help Person A make a better decision. The decision is technically available, and is objective and factual (unlike in the case of strategic uncertainty). However, the (expected) cost of acquiring the information exceeds the (expected) benefit of using the information in making better decisions.

Plays by nature under risk or uncertainty: Where the rationally ignorant person may know what he does not know, in many situations political actors do not know, and do not know what they do not know. The situation in politics, statecraft, and technology changes in ways that are fundamentally unknowable in advance. Thus, when a candidate makes promises, he may intend to carry them out, but factors beyond his imagination may intervene to prevent him from doing so. Or, he may change his mind about wanting to carry them out. The value to be revealed by nature may be predictable in expectation (risk), or actors may not even know the probability distribution from which future events will be drawn (uncertainty, using the definition by Knight, 1921).

Perspective of the Observer: If we want to know why a person makes a choice, or what she knows, we can ask. We can also watch. This requires that the actor knows why he acted, and that he then tells the truth, and (improbably) that the act of observing has no effect on the behavior being observed. The act of observing is itself a part of the decision context.

It is useful to start with the last of these, the "perspective of the observer." To understand this, we have to consider the perspective of the observer in scientific explanations of human behavior.

UNCERTAINTY AND IGNORANCE: THE PERSPECTIVE OF THE OBSERVER

The "perspective of the observer" problem pops up in different ways in both the physical and social sciences. Heisenberg's "uncertainty principle" claims that the electron cannot simultaneously "know" its location, velocity, and direction.[1] Newton's Laws, on the other hand, require that all these things can be known, at least from the perspective of the electron.[2] In the classical interpretation, the act of measuring affects what is being measured. Thus, there is a limit on what can be known from the perspective of the observer. That means that the observer is fundamentally, and in fact irreducibly, uncertain.[3] But what does the electron know? Is there an objective set of facts about physical variables such as location, velocity, and momentum, which the electron knows but which we observers do not?

The quantum interpretation is that the answer is "no"; the uncertainty is actually an inherent property of the phenomenon itself, and exists separately from the perspective of the observer. It would seem, however, that this problem is peculiar to sub-atomic quantum phenomena, so it would not apply to large bodies. Since humans have relatively large bodies, compared to electrons, it would appear that the observer would not be limited in the same way. Fair enough. However, the social sciences face an analogous problem: Humans are sentient, self-aware, and purposive. Human agents may change their behavior because they are *aware* they are being observed.

This problem sometimes is called the "Hawthorne Effect," after the results obtained in an efficiency study at the Hawthorne Works, a Western Electric facility in Cicero, a suburb of Chicago. The managers of the facility – employing more than 40,000 workers at its height – were interested in learning whether the immediate environment of the workplace had an effect on productivity.[4]

Among other things, they experimented with levels and types of lighting, recording worker productivity under different conditions. Right away, they noticed changes. If the lights were bright, productivity increased. If the lights were dim, productivity increased. In fact, in the short run, any new context that was observed increased productivity, though it also led to increased measures of anxiety for the workers. Over a longer period, regardless of whether the observation was continued or not, productivity reverted to its previous (lower) level. If observation ended, then anxiety also fell.

The problem is clear, with hindsight. Workers worked harder because there were strangers with clipboards monitoring their activities. They were told that conditions, not workers, were being evaluated, but they didn't believe it. The "Hawthorne Effect" is a calculated, rational response to anticipated punishment or reward because of observation. The reward need not be purely monetary, or the chance of being fired. We care what other people think about us, and we may change what we do because someone is watching.[5]

Randomness and the Sources of Uncertainty

The "perspective of the observer" has two implications for studying politics. First, attempts at measurement, or evaluation, may change the underlying behavior, or even motivations, in hard-to-predict ways. If I talk to a person with a clipboard, my "opinion" is likely some combination of my honest opinion and the opinion that I want a stranger with a clipboard to attribute to me.[6]

Second, any attempt to make aggregate statements about a set of people will contain what appears to be a "random" element, even if in fact the actions of each individual agent are internally rational and deterministic.[7] That is, idiosyncrasies in individual motivations, differences in information sets, and differences in the mental models that citizens use to make sense of politics may appear, from the perspective of an observer, to have an unexplained – that is, unpredicted – component.

In what follows, we will use a random error term to capture this uncertainty. In most cases, the use of a random component in the behavioral model itself is a reflection not of the inherent randomness of the decision process of the individual agent – there are no quantum choosers here – but rather residual or unexplained motivations and information not available to the researcher as an outside observer.[8]

WHERE THE VOTERS ARE

In political campaigns, lots of time and money are spent asking voters questions, conducting focus groups, or looking at demographic characteristics of different parts of the electorate. Why would politicians and their staffs do this? Candidates need to know, but do not know, what voters want, what their preferences are. In the parlance of spatial theory, campaigns try to learn the distribution of voter preferences so candidates can appeal to the middle of that distribution.

Knowing that candidates do not know what voters want, can we predict what politicians will do? The outcome might have what appear to be random elements: If voter preferences cannot be directly observed, then different candidates will have access to different sets of information about those preferences.[9] Politicians might just pick a platform based on a guess, or incomplete

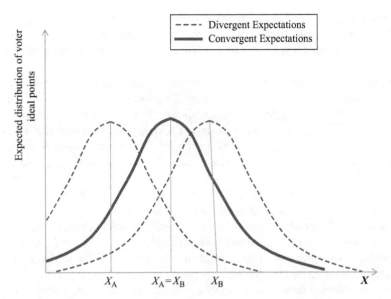

FIGURE 8.1. Probability X is a median position, two candidates A and B

information, or experience with the district. The candidate who turns out to be closer to the center of the (unobservable) distribution of voter ideal points has an advantage. But then, what of the prediction of convergence to the center?

Would candidates still converge toward the center? Suppose candidates pick the platform representing their best guess at the ideal point of the median voter (or the interval of median positions). If the candidates had access to the same information then their "best guesses" about the location of the median voter will also be the same, meaning that the prediction of convergence is preserved. Further, if pollsters' estimates are (on average) correct, then the estimated mean of the distribution of poll results will center on the actual location of the median voter.

To see how this works, consider the distributions of expected median positions in Figure 8.1. The middle distribution (solid line) represents one distribution of the probabilities candidates attach to the event that these are the actual median positions for voters in the upcoming election. Most positions have no probability of being a median position, of course. Positions near the center of the distribution, or the mean, are fairly likely, however, because there is a good chance that the median voter will have one of those ideal points. The solid curve is labeled "convergent expectations," meaning that the two candidates (y and z) have similar data about the voter preference distribution.

If candidates (a) care only about winning and (b) have the same expectations about the location of the median voter, they will choose the same platform.

The optimal platform (assuming the distribution of expected median positions is single-peaked and continuous) is the "mean median," or center of the distribution of medians.[10] Thus, in Figure 8.1, $x_Z = x_Y$ if expectations are convergent.

If expectations about the location of the median voter's ideal point differ, so will candidate locations. If candidate Z chooses a platform based on one set of interviews or advice, and candidate Y uses different information, the two candidates may have different expectations about the location of the median. Consequently, as in Figure 8.1 (dotted curves depicting distributions), the candidates may *initially* choose different platforms $(x_Z \neq x_Y)$.

This "result" means little, for two reasons. First, broadly divergent expectations do not occur in large electorates in campaigns based on polls, unless one of the polling firms is incompetent.[11] Political professionals, faced with similar information, draw similar conclusions. Second, and more important, whatever the initial positions of the candidates, divergence is not an equilibrium, given the logic of political competition. If one candidate takes a position different from the opponent's position, each would immediately notice he could increase his vote share by moving toward the opponent.

It is useful to summarize the discussion above in three theorems, which will be stated without proofs. In addition, it is important to note that the assumptions of the theorems state here are more restrictive than required as necessary conditions, to simplify the intuition.[12]

Theorem 8.1. Suppose exactly one median position is known to exist, but that its location is unknown. If the distribution of possible median positions is unimodal, symmetric, and shared, then candidates will adopt identical positions at the location of the mean of the distribution of medians.

Theorem 8.2. If the distribution of possible median positions is unimodal and symmetric but candidates have different perceptions of this distribution, then candidates will initially adopt divergent positions at the location of the means of the perceived distributions of medians. These divergent positions are not an equilibrium, however. If candidates can move, they will adopt identical positions somewhere between the two divergent perceived means of the distributions of medians.

Theorem 8.3. If candidates are uncertain about the location of voters and candidates seek some mix of policy and reelection, then candidate positions will diverge in equilibrium. In fact, no convergent equilibrium exists under these circumstances. However, the extent of the divergence depends on the extent of uncertainty and the mix of policy-reelection motivations by the candidates. *Only if uncertainty is extreme and reelection motivations are trivial will the degree of divergence be substantively significant.*

The proofs of these theorems are exercises at the end of the chapter.

The key point is that uncertainty about the location of the median is not, by itself, sufficient to reject the convergence prediction. Even if expectations diverge, candidates will adjust toward a convergent equilibrium if they can.[13]

WHERE THE CANDIDATES ARE

The classical model has voters choose based on what candidates say. Real voters may care about what a candidate says, because that may be the only way to tell what the candidate will do. However, as Jeffrey Banks points out:

[The] strong assumption implicit in the [classical] model is that the positions the candidates announce prior to an election will be the positions they subsequently enact once in office. Since voters typically have preferences defined over policy outcomes and not over electoral announcement per se, but their only information at the time of voting consists of these announcements, the equivalence of announced position and policy outcome appears to be one of analytical tractability at the expense of realism. (1990, p. 311)

In this section, we are concerned about the distribution of voter expectations about what candidates will do once in office, *given what the candidates claim they will do*. The classical model depicts candidates deterministically, as *points* in policy space. Allowing voter uncertainty over candidate positions implies a distribution defined over an interval. Within this interval (assuming the set of possible policies is continuous), many different policies have some chance of being implemented after the election. Consequently, there may be some difference in voters' minds between what candidates promise before the election and what happens after the election.[14]

Figure 8.2 shows three very different levels of voter uncertainty about the policy consequences of a candidate's election. Panel (a).depicts a candidate about whom there is no uncertainty: The distribution of expected policy consequences is a point. Panel (b) portrays a candidate whom voters perceive as moderately committed to a particular policy. Voters recognize that this candidate may choose some other policy or for some other reason fail to do as promised. Panel (c) shows a candidate with no credibility at all. As in the first two panels, this candidate's "expected" (that is, mean) policy action is the same as his or her professed platform; but the distribution of actual policies is uniformly distributed over all feasible policies.[15]

If voters have such expectations, we can incorporate the difference between panel (a) in Figure 8.2 (certainty) and the other panels (moderate or complete uncertainty) into our model of voter choice.[16] Suppose candidate Jacob is a committed conservative and has taken one consistent position for twenty years in many different political environments. Jacob's opponent, Edward, is a liberal. Edward has taken a variety of positions on issues. In the campaign, Jacob

a. Candidate policy distribution is a point (perfect commitment/competence)

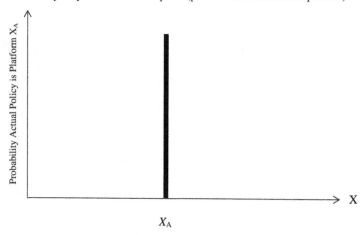

b. Bell-shaped distribution (moderate commitment/competence)

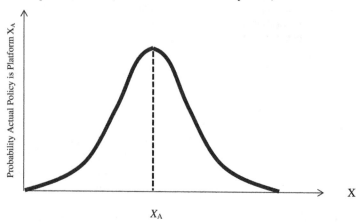

c. Uniform distribution (campaigns are completely uninformative)

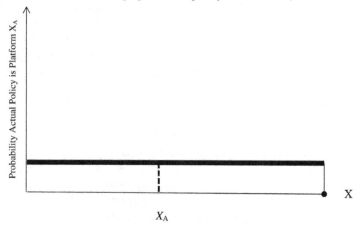

FIGURE 8.2. Voter uncertainty about policy outcomes delivered by candidates, given campaign platform X_A

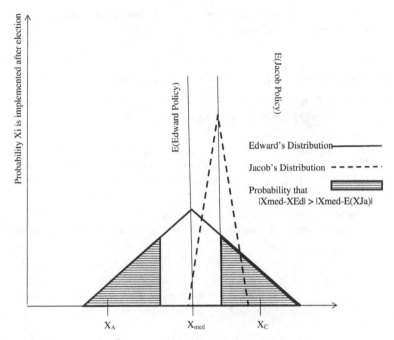

FIGURE 8.3. Voters trade off expected policy against uncertainty

espouses rightist positions; his expected (mean) policy is to the right of the median voter.

Edward, seeing Jacob's "mistake," gleefully proclaims himself the candidate of the people, announces a platform identical to the median voter, and awaits the landslide victory that must be his. (Edward read as far as Chapter 3 of this book and he knows that the MVT is on his side!)

Of course, voters A, B, and C make much more complex and sophisticated choices than Edward's naïve Downsian model allows for. Figure 8.3 depicts the voters' perceptions of the distribution of expected policies from the two candidates. Edward's distribution (solid line) is centered at the median position (x_B), just as he had hoped. But Edward's strategic flip-flopping in the past is also part of voters' decision. The dispersion of Edwards's expected actions once in office is much higher than Jacob's distribution (dotted line).[17]

From the viewpoint of each candidate, there may be nothing random about platform choices. From the perspective of the voters, however, each candidate is seen as a cloud of policies, with a mean and a variance, rather than a point. The choice of the median voter, B, is driven by the crosshatched areas in the left and right tails of the "Edward" distribution. These areas represent the probability that the actual policy carried out by Edward, if he is elected, is worse (further from B's ideal point) than the expected value of a Jacob victory. As the figure shows, the probability that Edward may implement policies far from the median means Jacob may win easily.

The following section gives an overview of the more fully fleshed out model for the reader familiar with basic statistics.

ACCOUNTING FOR UNCERTAINTY AS A CAUSE OF DIVERGENCE

Before presenting the model (adapted from Berger, Munger, and Potthoff, 2000), let's be a little more careful about notation.[18]

x_i Ideal point for voter i, $i \in \{1,...n\}$. Element of unidimensional policy space. where $x \in (-\infty, \infty)$. While the policy space is infinite, however, we will assume that there are finitely many voters, to ensure the existence of a median.

x_Y, x_Z Candidate locations for candidates Y and Z. Elements of the same unidimensional policy space: $x \in (-\infty,\infty)$

Q A specific element of the policy space: the *cut point* for voter preferences.[19]

We will assume that there is a single policy dimension, with voters uniformly distributed along that dimension.[20] We will further assume that voters evaluate candidates Y and Z according to a quadratic loss function, equivalent to comparing the maxima of the following utility functions U (voter ideal, candidate platform):[21]

$$U\,(x_i\,,\,Y) = -(x_Y - x_i)^2 \tag{8.1}$$

$$U\,(x_i\,,\,Z) = -(x_Z - x_i)^2 \tag{8.2}$$

Each voter's utility is maximized – at o – when the candidate's issue position coincides with that voter's ideal point. For convenience, let Z be at least conservative as Y, so that $x_Z \geq x_Y$

Assuming that all citizens (except those who are indifferent) vote, then they will choose according to this rule:

$$\begin{aligned}(x_Y - x_i)^2 &< (x_Z - x_i)^2 \text{ voter } i \text{ casts ballot for Y,}\\ (x_Y - x_i)^2 &> (x_Z - x_i)^2 \text{ voter } i \text{ casts ballot for Z,}\\ (x_Y - x_i)^2 &= (x_Z - x_i)^2 \, i \text{ flips a coin or abstains.}\end{aligned} \tag{8.3}$$

Given the candidates' locations in the policy space, the unidimensionality of the space, and the assumed symmetry of the voter utility functions, the "cut point" Q is the ideal point of the voter who is indifferent between the two candidates. All voters to the left of Q vote for Y, and all to the right vote for Z, the more conservative candidate. Those located exactly at the cut point flip a coin.

If the candidates' deterministic issue positions are not identical, the cut point is the point on the policy dimension halfway between the two candidate positions. If the candidates move closer, the cut point is again at the midpoint of the (now shorter) line segment. If one candidate moves closer to the other candidate, the cut point splits the difference, moves away from the moving candidate, and toward the stationary candidate.

Decision rule 8.3 above implies that the cut point is at the point where a voter would be indifferent between the two candidates. Therefore, we substitute Q for x_j and set the two utility functions equal, cancelling the negative sign at the same time.

$$(x_Y - Q)^2 = (x_Z - Q)^2 \tag{8.4}$$

Expanding, and solving for y:

$$Q = \frac{x_Z^2 - x_Y^2}{2(x_Z - x_Y)} = \frac{x_Y + x_Z}{2} \tag{8.5}$$

Equation 8.5 confirms Black's (1958) median voter theorem, because the cut point splits the difference in candidate positions. If one candidate moves closer, the cut point moves toward the other candidate, so the converging candidate picks up votes at the expense of the stationary candidate. But this means that any arrangement where $x_Y \neq x_Z$ cannot be an equilibrium. The only equilibrium occurs when the platforms converge to the ideal point of the median voter. This is the important point, for our purposes: Any equilibrium must be convergent, *assuming certainty*.

POLITICAL COMPETITION WITH UNCERTAIN VOTERS

Now, suppose voters are uncertain about a candidate's position. Uncertainty may derive from doubts about the candidate's sincerity, or competence, or some other factor, it does not matter for our purposes. Then Candidate *j*'s (where j can be either Y or Z) position in the unidimensional space can be represented as a random variable with mean μ_j, and with an error ε_j with mean $= 0$ and whose variance is fixed but idiosyncratic. This means that different candidates can have different levels of uncertainty associated with their platforms. Consequently:

$$x_j = \mu_j + \varepsilon_j \tag{8.6}$$

$$E(\varepsilon_j) = 0, \quad \text{Var}(\varepsilon_j) = E(\varepsilon_j^2) = \sigma_j^2 \tag{8.7}$$

Following the location convention adopted earlier, we assume that Z is at least as conservative as Y, so that $\mu_Z \geq \mu_Y$. The voter uses the same decision rule as before (equation 3), except that now the comparison is in terms of *expected value* of the utility, which we can obtain by combining the definitions of the utility functions and decision rules with the definition of the candidate locations as random variables, and then rearranging terms.[22] That would imply that the expected value is:

$$E[U(x_i, x_j)] = -(\mu_j - x_i)^2 - \sigma_j^2 \tag{8.8}$$

The voter's decision rule, adapted to account for voter uncertainty, is then:

$(\mu_Y - x_i)^2 + \sigma_Y^2 < (\mu_Z - x_i)^2 + \sigma_Z^2$ i votes for Y,
$(\mu_Y - x_i)^2 + \sigma_Y^2 > (\mu_Z - x_i)^2 + \sigma_Z^2$ i votes for Z,   (8.9)
$(\mu_Y - x_i)^2 + \sigma_Y^2 = (\mu_Z - x_i)^2 + \sigma_Z^2$ i randomizes.

Now, following Berger, Munger, and Potthoff (2000) we can substitute the specific cut point voter position y for the arbitrary ideal point x_i, and solve for y (assuming for the moment that the inequality $\mu_Z > \mu_Y$ is strict). To make comparison easier, we reproduce equation (5), which is the analogous expression under certainty.

$$Q = \frac{x_Z^2 - x_Y^2}{2(x_Z - x_Y)} = \frac{x_Y + x_Z}{2}$$ (8.5)

$$Q = \frac{\mu_Z^2 - \mu_Y^2 + \sigma_Z^2 - \sigma_Y^2}{2(\mu_Z - \mu_Y)} = \frac{\mu_Z + \mu_Y}{2} + \left[\frac{\sigma_Z^2 - \sigma_Y^2}{2(\mu_Z - \mu_Y)}\right]$$ (8.10)

The difference between 8.10 and 8.5 lies in the bracketed expression, involving variances, which cancel if they happen to be equal. If $\sigma_Z^2 \neq \sigma_Y^2$, then the cut point is closer to the position of the candidate with the larger variance. In words, some voters with ideal points closer to the high variance candidate will vote for the more distant but more reliable candidate.

The surprising thing about this result is that it implies a tendency toward divergence: the weaker candidate wants to move *away from*, not *towards*, the lower variance front-runner.[23]

Two Results: No Equilibrium, and a Surprising Cut Point

Berger, Munger, and Potthoff (2000, hereafter BMP) proceed from expression 8.10 to prove two results.[24] For simplicity, we will refer to the candidates as "incumbent" (lower variance) and "challenger" (higher variance). All that really matters is that the variances of the two candidates differ; knife-edge equality is unlikely.

Theorem 8.4. **Nonexistence of equilibrium with uncertainty.** If the policy space is unidimensional, voter utility functions are quadratic, the challenger has greater variance than the incumbent does, and both candidates are free to move their positions, then (i) there is no winning policy position for the challenger *(ii) no equilibrium exists.*

PROOF[25]: Consider the case where $\sigma_Z^2 > \sigma_Y^2$ (the opposite case works precisely the same way). Suppose the two candidates converge to the same position in expectation ($\mu Y = \mu Z$). Then equation 8.10 implies that $E[U(x_i,Y)] > E[U(x_i,Z)]$, *for every voter.* That is, the lower variance candidate not only wins, but wins with 100% of the vote. The high variance candidate will always try to move; the low variance candidate will always try to match. At least one candidate can always improve his/her vote total by moving. Therefore, there is no equilibrium.

All the leader/incumbent has to do is say, "me, too!" and he should win; in fact, the challenger will get zero votes![26] The challenger can continually shift position, and the lower variance incumbent will follow. Therefore, there are no equilibria, under the assumption of free movement, even in one dimension and assuming voter preferences are single-peaked. The advantaged candidate forever shifts with the challenger and always receives all of the votes.[27]

Still, there is something odd here. How can we reconcile the idea of low variance of expected platform, presumably based on some expectation by voters that the candidate will be stable and consistent, with constant wild gyrations in announced platform? Wouldn't voters update their variance estimates, destroying or at least reducing the advantage of the incumbent?[28]

For the second theorem, assume that the incumbent's lower variance is based on an empirical voting record, so that the incumbent is – in spatial terms – immobile.

Theorem 8.5. Assume that the policy space is unidimensional, voter utility functions are quadratic, the incumbent is tied to an established record in policy space, and voter uncertainty is greater for the challenger than for the incumbent. Then the location that maximizes the challenger's vote total:

(a) differs from the incumbent's fixed location (i.e., equilibrium exists but is nonconvergent), and (b) happens to be the location of the cut point.

PROOF[29]: Take the case where $\sigma_Z^2 > \sigma_Y^2$ (the opposite case is symmetric), and $\mu_Z > \mu_Y$. Then as equation 8.10 illustrates, the cut point is closer to the position of Candidate 2 (the challenger, or the candidate with lower variance).

$$Q = \frac{\mu_Z^2 - \mu_Y^2 + \sigma_Z^2 - \sigma_Y^2}{2(\mu_Z - \mu_Y)} = \frac{\mu_Z + \mu_Y}{2} + \left[\frac{\sigma_Z^2 - \sigma_Y^2}{2(\mu_Z - \mu_Y)} \right] \tag{8.10}$$

Take the partial derivative of equation 8.10 with respect to μ_Z, resulting in:

$$\frac{\partial Q}{\partial \mu_Z} = \frac{1}{2} \left[1 - \frac{\sigma_Z^2 - \sigma_Y^2}{(\mu_Z - \mu_Y)^2} \right] \tag{8.11}$$

Take the second partial derivative:

$$\frac{\partial^2 Q}{\partial (\mu_Z)^2} = \frac{\sigma_Z^2 - \sigma_Y^2}{(\mu_Z - \mu_Y)^3} \tag{8.12}$$

8.12 is always positive for $\sigma_Z^2 > \sigma_Y^2$ and $\mu_Z > \mu_Y$. Thus the value of μ_Z that minimizes Q (and maximizes Candidate Z's vote total) is obtained by setting first order condition 8.11 equal to 0 and solving for μ_Z, selecting the optimum that has $\mu_Z > \mu_Y$. The optimum is:

$$\mu_Z^* = \mu_Y + \sqrt{\sigma_Z^2 - \sigma_Y^2} \tag{8.13}$$

This proves Part (a), since Candidate Z's optimal position differs from the incumbent's position whenever the variances differ. Substituting 8.13 into 8.10 and rearranging, we find that:

$$Q = \mu_Y + \sqrt{\sigma_Z^2 - \sigma_Y^2} \tag{8.14}$$

But then $\mu_Z^* = Q$, proving that the cut point is also the vote-maximizing position for the challenger, establishing part (b).

Corollary to Theorem 8.5: If the challenger converges or locates nearer to the incumbent, the cut point is driven outside the interval $[\mu_Z, \mu_Y]$. In fact, as the challenger draws near to the incumbent, the cut point Q is driven arbitrarily far into the tail of the distribution of voters.

Recall again the formula for the cut point, equation 10:

$$Q = \frac{\mu_Z^2 - \mu_Y^2 + \sigma_Z^2 - \sigma_Y^2}{2(\mu_Z - \mu_Y)} = \frac{\mu_Z + \mu_Y}{2} + \left[\frac{\sigma_Z^2 - \sigma_Y^2}{2(\mu_Z - \mu_Y)}\right] \tag{8.10}$$

Consider the *denominator* of the term in brackets. If the incumbent's location is fixed, and the incumbent's variance is less than the challenger's variance, it is obvious that:

$$\lim_{\mu_Z \to \mu_{Y_1}} (y) = \infty$$

If the challenger locates at the same position as the incumbent, the challenger receives zero votes, because the cut point is undefined. But this is the limiting result of convergence: if the challenger's position is different from the incumbent, and the challenger moves closer, the cut point is driven far out on the policy dimension, and the challenger's expected vote shrinks toward zero.

The implications of Theorem 8.5 are profound. Even voters whose ideal points correspond precisely to the higher variance candidate's platform will nonetheless vote for the lower variance candidate. But the higher variance of candidate Z actually works for him out in the tail of the distribution, because voters perceive some chance that Z will actually choose a platform closer to their ideal point than Z promised in his platform. Consequently, extremist voters might well choose based on variance, rather than mean platforms.

CONCLUSIONS

The "Downsian" model, at least the one Downs had in mind, focuses on uncertainty and the inability of voters to figure out what candidates are likely to do once in office. Downs claimed that the nature of campaigns we actually observe, and the focus on ideology instead of issues, is an inevitable byproduct of this uncertainty.

Likewise, candidates cannot be certain where the median preference resides, and substantial resources are spent in politics in ways that are inexplicable unless we account for uncertainty. In this chapter, we have considered some basic models of voter and candidate uncertainty, in effort to bridge the gap between our equations and our understanding of real world politics.

TERMS

Commitment
Convergence
Cut Point
Downsian Model
Existence of Equilibrium
Hawthorne Effect
Perspective of the Observer
Plays by Nature
Randomness
Rational Ignorance
Strategic Uncertainty
Surveys
Uncertainty

EXERCISES

8.1 Suppose that voter i must choose between candidate R, with mean expected policy position x_R, and candidate D, with can expected policy position x_D. The voter has the following information:

$\mu_i = \mu_D = 12$
$\mu_R = 15$
$\sigma_R^2 = 2$
$\sigma_D^2 = 16$

a. Suppose i's choice is described by the utility function Equation 8.8. Who will i vote for?

b. What is the largest variance candidate R can have and still win the election?

8.2 Suppose two candidates, Y and Z, care *equally* about policy and winning. Let the unidimensional policy space be the unit interval $[0,1]$, and let $x_y = 0$ and $x_z = 1$. (Note: These are candidate ideal points!) Assume the candidates have the following

$$U_Y = -.5[(x - xy)2] + .5[WY] \qquad \text{****}$$
$$U_Z = -.5[(x - XZ)2] + .5[WZ]$$

where x is the winning platform (assume platform and actual policy implemented are the same), and W_Y and W_Z each take one of three discrete values: 1 if the candidate wins, 0 if the candidate loses, and 5 if there is a tie.

Finally, assume voter preferences are symmetric, so proximity to x_{med} determines the winner. What platforms maximize each candidate's utility if x_{med} takes the following values?

a. $x_{med} = .95$

b $x_{med} = .10$

c. $x_{med} = .50$

8.3 Consider a two-dimensional policy space, where preferences over both policies. Suppose there are three voters, 1, 2, and 3, with preferences described by the ideal points $x_1 = [8 \ 0]^T$, $x_2 = [0 \ 8]^T$, and $x_3 = [3 \ 6]^T$, and matrices of salience/interaction terms: voters have

$$A_1 = \begin{bmatrix} 4 & 0 \\ 0 & 6 \end{bmatrix} \quad A_2 = \begin{bmatrix} 6 & -2 \\ -2 & 2 \end{bmatrix} \quad A_3 = \begin{bmatrix} 12 & 0 \\ 0 & 3 \end{bmatrix}$$

The two candidates, Y and Z, care only about winning. But they don't know voter preferences, so they aren't sure where to locate. Each candidate hires his own polling firm. Each of the two firms takes a poll, from a slightly different sample and using slightly different -survey questions. The candidates are told to take the following positions: $x_Y = [2 \ 6]^T$, and $x_Z = [5 \ 6]^T$

Which candidate wins the election, and which should hire a better polling firm next time he runs for office? If you could tell the (now) losing candidate where to locate, what would you advise?

8.4 Prove Theorem 8.1

8.5 Prove Theorem 8.2

8.6 Prove Theorem 8.3

9

Voting as a Collective Action Problem

"I would like to see anyone, prophet, king or God, convince a thousand cats to do the same thing at the same time."
— Neil Gaiman, Sandman #18: "A Dream of a Thousand Cats"

What if they had an election and nobody came?

In Newport, England, an election for Police and Crime Commissioner (PCC) had a zero turnout in at least one polling station in Bettws. According to the BBC:

Newport councillor Kevin Whitehead, Independent member for the city's Bettws ward, said it was "staggering" that a polling station had failed to register a single vote. *"It's just apathy. I think apathy rules when it comes to politics in general,"* he said. *"People are more concerned with the bigger picture like the recession."*

Conservative councillor Matthew Evans, who is the leader of the opposition on Newport council, said the fact nobody had voted at a polling station "doesn't show anybody in a particularly good light". However, he said he was not surprised there was a low turnout generally in the elections. "Clearly, *if you've got a polling station where nobody turns up*, it's extremely disappointing," he said. "It's quite frankly a *daft time of the year to have an election – it's cold and miserable.*" "It wasn't a topic that people felt passionately about."

Labour's Newport West MP Paul Flynn, whose constituency includes Bettws, said he believed a lack of enthusiasm for the elections from the Conservative Party which introduced the policy had contributed to the low turnout. But he admitted *another factor was the lack of trust in politics and lack of confidence in politicians generally.* The total turnout for Wales was 14.9%.

BBC News Website, November 16, 2012, "Zero turnout at Newport polling station in PCC election." (Emphases added)

This single example contains what appear to be conflicting explanations for abstention. But they are not mutually exclusive; all are in some sense correct. Consider the explanations highlighted in italics above:

- *Apathy*: (a) My vote doesn't matter. (b) There is no important difference between the parties or candidates on the issues I care about.
- *Bigger Picture*: Local politics are boring and unimportant.
- *Weather*: Like politics, all weather is local. If it is cold and rainy in that place, on that day, fewer people may vote.
- *Lack of trust*: Alienation from the process, the sense that politicians are not talking to "people like me," or working on issues of direct relevance to citizens' lives.

Each of these is an important part of the explanation for why people do not vote. In fact, as we will soon see, the interesting question from an analytical politics perspective is less "Why doesn't *everyone* vote?" than "Why would *anyone* vote?"

VOTING AND COLLECTIVE ACTION

To analyze voting, we have to recognize that the voting decision itself is only the last in a series of decisions, or reactions to costs and constraints, by the citizen. To see this, consider the results of Fort (1995), who elaborates and tests a "sequential barriers" model of turnout suggested by Aldrich (1976), Cox and Munger (1989, 1991), and Ferejohn and Fiorina (1974, 1975). The point is that the "participation rate" of voters in any given election g must be the product of four ratios[1]:

$$\underset{(1)}{\frac{Vote\,in\,Race_g}{Population}} \equiv \underset{(1)}{\frac{Enfranchised}{Population}} \times \underset{(2)}{\frac{Registered}{Enfranchised}} \times \underset{(3)}{\frac{Enter\,Booth}{Registered}} \times \underset{(4)}{\frac{Vote\,in\,Race_g}{Enter\,Booth}}$$

$$(9.1)$$

For a citizen to vote in any given election g, ranging from President to Police and Crime Commissioner in Bettws, England, the citizen must:

(1) be legally enfranchised, or not be legally barred from voting, by the laws and practices of the society
(2) be registered to vote, or have otherwise fulfilled the certification requirements specified by the laws and practices of the society
(3) have made the decision to travel to polling place and enter it
(4) have made the choice, once in the voting booth, to cast a vote in election g and then selected one of the candidates or alternatives actually available, or else write in a choice (if that is allowed)

The "≡" sign means, "equals by definition." We use it here because each of the intervening step (enfranchisement, registration, entering booth) occurs in both the numerator and denominator, so they cancel in the product.

Nonetheless, each step affects the observed turnout rate, and points to a sequence of barriers to cross, or choices to make, before a person has his or her vote counted in election. A serious attempt to analyze turnout empirically in any one election must account for all of these steps. For example, if the political jurisdiction that makes voting rules restricts enfranchisement by race, gender, age, or income, then ratio (1) may be small. If registration is expensive, time-consuming, complicated or intimidating, ratio (2) may be small. The trend in the last two decades towards Election Day registration was designed to bring ratio (2) closer to 1.00, and experienced mixed results.[2]

Finally, there is an important interaction between ratios (3) and (4): The number of registered people who vote may depend on how groups of elections are packaged. If elections are held separately, it may be that few people vote (ratio (3) will be small), but that everyone who enters the booth casts a vote in election g (ratio (4) would be near 1.00).

On the other hand, if there are many elections on the same day, voters are likely to be interested in races at the top of the ticket, because most ballots are organized in decreasing order of scale, at least in federal or mixed systems. National races are at the top, elections to the national legislature come next, then state or provincial races, and then municipal and local elections. A race at the top of the ticket may have high turnout, while races at the bottom of the ticket to have very low turnout, in the "same election." This phenomenon of abstaining from obscure races is "roll-off" (Burnham, 1965).

This raises an important ethical question for what voters should do if they have no idea whom to vote for. Brennan (2012) argues that an ethical person would voluntarily abstain, because a random or confused vote is worse than no vote at all.[3]

How widespread and effective is compulsory voting? Table 9.1 shows the nations with the top thirty turnout rates worldwide, leaving out very small countries or those with few elections. Some of the high turnout nations have compulsory voting. Some nations without compulsory voting have high turnout also. The comparison is sometimes controversial, and the questions Brennan (2012) raised are important: Does the group want uninformed people making choices for the whole group?[4] Wouldn't even the uninformed person prefer not to have to cast an uninformed vote, if it harms everyone?

If our goal is to analyze the *voting decision*, we must restrict our attention to ratios (3) and (4) in equation 9.1, as if this race were the only one on the ballot. The reason is not that most elections actually look like this, but we already know that multiple elections have complicated effects (Cox and Munger, 1989; Fort, 1995; Hamilton and Ladd, 1996; Blais, 2000, Hill, 2006). By considering a single race and a single decision on whether to go to the polls and vote, we isolate the logic of the citizen's choice. In the next section, we discuss the two major reasons the rational choice model gives for abstention: indifference and alienation.

TABLE 9.1. *Top 30 Turnout Rates, 1945–2001 – Compulsory Voting in Italics, Number of Elections in Parentheses**

---

1. *Australia* (22) 94.5
2. *Belgium* (18) 92.5
3. *Austria*† (17) 91.3
4. New Zealand (19) 90.8
5. *Italy*† (15) 89.8
6. *Luxembourg* (12) 89.7
7. Iceland (17) 89.5
8. *Netherlands* (16) 87.5
9. Sweden (17) 87.1
10. Denmark (22) 85.9
11. Germany (14) 85.4
12. *Argentina*† (18) 84.2
13. Czech Republic (4) 82.8
14. *Bolivia*† (11) 82.2
15. *Turkey*† (10) 81.3
16. Philippines (7) 80.9
17. Norway(15) 80.4
18. Israel (15) 80.3
19. *Greece*† (16) 79.9
20. *Chile*† (11) 78.9
21. *Brazil*† (14) 77.8
22. *Costa Rica*† (12) 77.7
23. Portugal (10) 77.0
24. Finland (16) 76.0
25. United Kingdom (16) 75.2
26. *Dominica*† (12) 74.4
27. Sri Lanka (11) 74.3
28. Canada (18) 73.9
29. France (15) 73.8
30. Ireland (16) 73.3

Others of interest:

Japan (22) 69.5
United States of America (17) 66.5
Russia (3**) 58.4
Switzerland (14) 56.5
Guatemala (16) 51.6

---

* Sample: Data adapted from Pintor, et al., 2002. Only includes countries with voting age populations more than 100,000, and which held at least ten elections over the sample period, 1945–2001.
† Compulsory voting is enforced weakly, or sanctions are trivial.
** Not enough elections, included only as an illustration

THE CLASSICAL MODEL: INDIFFERENCE, ALIENATION, AND EXPECTED NET BENEFIT

Within the logic of the classic rational choice model, there are at least three circumstances where enfranchised citizens might not choose to vote in an election.

Indifference: The perception (possibly in expectation, if there is uncertainty) that there are no important differences (in terms of citizens' welfare) among the alternatives presented on the ballot.

Alienation: Voters sense that the issue positions of the candidates are distant from what they care about. One candidate may be closer, but all candidates are outside the range of policy alternatives where the voter has any interest in participating.

Expected Net Benefit: The voter is informed about the election, cares about the outcome, and has a preferred candidate in mind. However, the cost of voting is too high, in terms of opportunity cost of time, or because of bad or dangerous weather, in terms of the expected benefit, which depends on the probability of influencing the election.

The classical spatial model can handle indifference or alienation.[5] To understand the meaning of, and distinction between, the concepts, it is useful to portray indifference and alienation graphically. In Figure 9.1, panel (a) depicts a single voter's ideal point x_i and two sets of positions for candidates A and B. Notice that the voter is *indifferent* between x_A' and x_B'. She is also indifferent between the much more distant x_A'' and x_B'' Of course, if the candidate positions were x_A' and x_B'' the voter would choose candidate A. But paired as the platforms are, she finds herself indifferent in each case, though at two very different levels of utility.

Panel (b) gives the analogous diagram for *alienation*. Riker and Ordeshook first made the argument about alienation – at least in the context of the spatial model (1968; 1973). They claimed: "If one's most preferred candidate supports policies very different from what one would like, then the private incentive to vote diminishes." (Riker and Ordeshook, 1973; p. 324). In other words, the voter is not technically indifferent, because one candidate is preferable. But both candidates are so far away that the issues and rhetoric of the election are likely to seem irrelevant to the concerns of the alienated voter (Hinich and Ordeshook, 1969; Brody and Page, 1973).

If the race is between A and B, both alternatives are so distant that the voter sees no point in participating. It does not matter which is relatively closer; both are too far, in an absolute sense, for the voter to care about the election. More precisely, abstention from alienation requires that beyond the threshold distance δ the voter loses interest in the election. She may perceive herself as lacking efficacy because she is so distant from the campaign she hears about

Panel A: Indifference At Two Levels of Utility

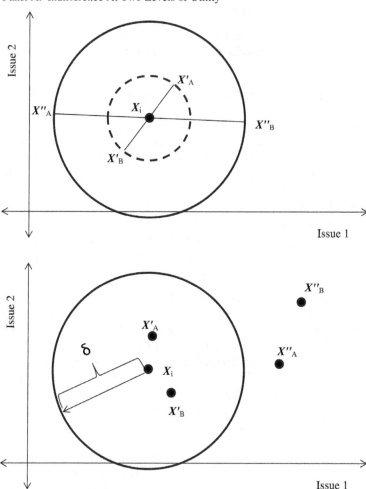

FIGURE 9.1. Indifference and alienation as explanations for abstention

in the media. More formally, the voter is alienated if *no candidate p* has a platform y_p such that $\text{WED}(y_p, x_i) \leq \delta$.

A number of scholars have tested aspects of the alienation/indifference approach to predicting turnout. Some of the earliest were Ordeshook (1969) and Brody and Page (1973). Although their work found some support for the model, the classification of predicted voters was not very accurate (partly for reasons examined in the next section). A review of the work through the 1980's can be found in Aldrich (1993); a more updated review is Geys (2006).

Researchers recently have taken up the alienation/indifference approach. Kees and Wessels (2005), Adams, Dow, and Merrill (2006) and Melton (2009) consider a variety of empirical possibilities, and find that the model, though useful, is at best part of the story. Still, since turnout varies across elections, even in the same electorate, it is important that we can identify variables (such as voter perceptions of candidate locations) that differentiate elections. The problem with the classical model, however, is that it is decision-theoretic and individualistic. This approach cannot allow for the possibility that a voter must consider what *other* voters will do before deciding whether to abstain.[6]

TURNOUT AND STRATEGIC UNCERTAINTY

We can observe the effects of alienation and indifference in real elections in at least two ways. First, polities have widely varying rules governing the number of polling places and their hours of operation. If the polls open late and close early, many "almost indifferent" voters will not make it to the precinct.[7]

Second, the weather on the day of the election may determine turnout. If it rains, the almost indifferent voter stays home – that is to say, precipitation can influence participation.[8] If it snows, many indifferent or almost indifferent voters may stay home. Activists, however, who prefer one candidate to another by a wide margin, are willing to brave storm or snow to cast their ballots. Consequently, the impact of bad weather is not random, because it may drive down turnout from voters in the middle.

Such notions of cost and benefit come together in a particular context. In the previous chapter, we called it "strategic uncertainty." The costs are easy for the individual to calculate, but the benefits of any one vote depend on the decision of other people. To see this, it is useful to recount a (possibly apocryphal) conversation with Gordon Tullock, one of the leading figures in the school of thought called "public choice." Tullock's own work in this area (Tullock, 1976; 1984) was skeptical of the idea that people vote for reasons of self-interest. He was persuaded by the fact (and it is a fact) that viewed from a purely individual, egoistic perspective, one vote stands a negligible chance of influencing an election, even in a small city or county.

So, someone tried the old "fallacy of composition" argument on him: "Professor Tullock, what if *everyone* thought that way? Wouldn't that be bad for democracy?"

Tullock, eyes twinkling behind his black-framed glasses, immediately responded: "Ma'am, if everyone thought that way, then I *would* vote! For myself! I'd be dictator! How's that for 'democracy'?" This "paradox of not voting" shows that it cannot quite be true that it never makes sense to vote, even from a purely egoistic perspective.[9] The apparent paradox is actually easily resolved. However, we first need a model to analyze the problem.

There are two related issues. From a political perspective, voting is fundamentally a *collective action problem*. If one voter believes that everyone on his
side intends to vote, there is no need to vote because the majority is assured. If
that same voter believes that no one on his side intends to vote, there is no point
in voting because the majority is unachievable. In the first case the citizen can
simply "free ride"; in the second instance one vote will not be enough to make
up the deficit caused by all the free riding of others. Not surprisingly, a very
common political tactic by all participants is to portray the race as very, very
close. This encourages partisans of the front-runner to go to the polls, even if
turns out later that their candidate won by a large majority. And a false claim of
closeness encourages partisans of the dark-horse candidate to turn out to vote,
even if turns out later that their candidate never came close to winning. What
this means in practice is that you will never hear either of these statements at a
press conference the night before an election:

- "Look, we got this. Don't bother voting; we're going to win easily."
- "Look, forget it. Don't bother voting; we're going to get smoked."

The second issue is using expectations to solve the problem of *strategic* uncertainty: What is the probability of my vote influencing the outcome? It does not
work to calculate the probability assuming 100 percent turnout, because everyone else is trying to solve the same problem, and may not vote. Thus, each
person's choice is a function of each voter's expectation that other voters will
vote, knowing that others are making the same calculations. This problem has a
solution, in relatively simple game theory, which show that rational choice
theory predicts positive turnout, for the reasons Gordon Tullock recognized.

Collective Action

The conflict between what is good for the individual and what is good for the
group is common in game theory, particularly in non-cooperative game theory.
The particular calculation in electoral turnout is called the "free rider" problem, and is most widely associated with the work of Mancur Olson, particularly
in the *Logic of Collective Action* (1965). Olson claimed that the key to success
in providing collective goods was to induce people to contribute to the creation
of collective benefits.

"Free riders" are people who enjoy collective benefits that someone else's
efforts provide, without contributing any effort or resources themselves. Olson
explicitly recognizes the problem that parties face in turning out their
supporters:

> Though most people feel they would be better off if their party were in power, they
> recognize that if their party is going to win, *it will as likely win without them, and they
> will get the benefits in any case.* … The point is that the average person will not be willing
> to make a significant sacrifice for the party he favors, since a victory for his party
> provides a collective good. (1965, pp. 163–4; emphasis added)

To analyze turnout as a collective action problem, we need to consider the "Downsian" model of voting, from Downs (1957), elaborated by Riker and Ordeshook (1968; 1973).[10] According to this model, an individual will vote if and only if:

$$[P \times NCD] + D \geq C \qquad (9.2)$$

where, for each voter:

P = The probability that this individual's vote will affect the outcome of the majority rule election, either converting a loss into a tie or converting a tie into a victory

NCD = Perceived net benefits – along one policy dimension – of one candidate over another in the eyes of the individual ("net candidate differential" in Downs's parlance). If there are two candidates A and B, then $NCD= |x_i - x_A| - |x_i - x_B|$.

D = The individual's sense of civic duty. This is the utility derived from voting, regardless of the outcome.

C = The costs associated (at the margin) with the act of voting, including the opportunity cost of time spent, chance of inclement weather, and so on.

The logic of this model is cost-benefit: If the (expected) returns exceed the costs, the citizen becomes a voter and casts a vote for the candidate he most prefers. Otherwise, he abstains. Notice how complex the model truly is. A voter decides whether to vote at the same time he or she decides for whom. Imagine that the duty term is negligible ($D \approx 0$). Then the citizen votes if and only if

$$[P \times NCD] > C \qquad (9.3)$$

We know that $C > 0$, because voting entails some identifiable costs, including time spent traveling to the polls and waiting in line, and filling out registration forms. This leads us to predict that $[P \times NCD] >>> C$. is a *necessary condition* for voting.

To put it another way, if either P or NCD is zero, the simple Downsian model predicts certain abstention. If either P or NCD is very small, the Downsian model predicts that abstention is likely.

Duty and Expressive Voting

Suppose that $D > 0$. Though this seems like a simple matter, the D term is actually complicated. As John Aldrich points out:

Adding a D term is the same as subtracting a C term. Thus, C can be thought of as "net costs," that is, as costs of voting, less any positive values, such as doing one's duty. A positive C says that duty only partially outweighs costs of voting... Thus, the D term does not change the fundamental analysis, unless D > C, in which case it is better to vote for [the more preferred candidate] than to abstain in all circumstances. (1993, pp. 251–2).

If D > C the voter always votes, regardless of the locations of the candidates, and even if the voter is indifferent or ignorant of the issues. Whether the motivation is the avoidance of guilt or the enjoyment of the act of voting as an end in itself, the point is the same. Then voting is simply a consumption activity, more like attending a baseball game than an act of rational investment.[11] Some scholars (Barry, 1970; Green and Shapiro, 1994) have argued that this means rational choice models are not useful for explaining levels of turnout, since turnout is simply a matter of taste within the model.

Even worse, as Brennan and Lomasky (1993) argued, there may simply be a disconnection between voting for the best policy for the group and voting as an expressive, essentially selfish, act designed to bring esteem to the person seen by others to be voting. Brennan and Lomasky note that this sort of expressive voting may actually be collectively harmful. Brennan (2012) takes this logic a step further, claiming that voters who are uninformed or distracted by expressive concerns should not, as a matter of ethics, vote at all.

Self-interest and Probability

Suppose that each voter thinks of the electorate as a random sample from the set of eligible citizens. Chamberlain and Rothschild (1981) provide several analytic models that predict the probability of any one person determining the outcome (in the sense listed above for the definition of P). Chamberlain and Rothschild argue that the probability any one voter of influencing the outcome – in an electorate of size 2N+1 – is 1/N. For example, in an electorate of 101, the probability of any one voter determining the outcome is 1/50. They argue (p. 152):

An individual's vote matters if, and only if, the other 2N members of the polity split their votes evenly. The simplest way to calculate the probability of this happening is to suppose that the votes of individual members of society are independent binomial random variables while the probability that any individual votes yes is p. Then the probability that exactly N of the 2N members of society vote yes is

$$\binom{2N}{N} p^{n}(1-p)^{n} \tag{9.3}$$

They note that the probability of a decisive vote implied by this approach is nontrivial, *provided* p≈.50. In an electorate of 100,001, the chance of casting a decisive vote is 0.0025; in an electorate of 1,000,001, the chance of casting a decisive vote is 0.00008, or eight elections in 100,000. Not large, perhaps, but better than a person's chance of winning a lottery, and people often buy lottery tickets.[12]

Of course, this result is highly contingent on the race being "too close to call," so that p≈.50. If the predicted result is not close, the probability of affecting the outcome would be zero, holding constant the turnout decision of other citizens. The problem is that this is not (only) an uncertainty problem, but also a collective action problem for the group predicted by polls to win.

Gelman, Silver, and Edlin (2009: 1–2) use a simulations approach, and make direct empirical estimates of the probability that a single vote "matters" in Electoral College votes in the states. According to Gelman, et al., the states where a single vote was most likely to matter are New Mexico, Virginia, New Hampshire, and Colorado, where a single vote had about a 1 in 10 million chance of deciding the national election outcome. What that means is that a single vote determined the outcome in the home state of the voter, and the difference in the Electoral College vote implied by that state determined the national outcome. On average, according to Gelman, et al., a voter in America had about a 1 in 60 million chance of being decisive in the presidential election.

THE PARADOX OF NOT VOTING

In Downs's model, who would vote if the P term were literally zero? The answer is obvious: no one. And if everyone believed that, everyone would vote. One is reminded of Yogi Berra's famous line about a restaurant in New York: "No one goes there anymore. It's too crowded!" In our case, if no one votes because it will not matter, it will matter. If no one votes, then one vote determines the election. But then P wasn't really zero. In fact, P = 1, because anyone who did vote would have decided the outcome, with certainty.

As before, we are in the infinite regress of "He thinks that I think that he thinks..." Ferejohn and Fiorina (1974) call this the "paradox of not voting": If everyone knows the chances of affecting the outcome are trivial, no one votes. But any one voter's chances of affecting the outcome if he or she had voted are very large. Game theory provides a way out, by allowing us to see if any level of "rational" turnout can be sustained in the face of Ferejohn and Fiorina's paradox. Ledyard (1981, 1984), building on the probabilistic voting model of Hinich, Ledyard, and Ordeshook (1972), demonstrated that such a game among voters has a "mixed strategy" equilibrium.

Mixed strategies require the voter to randomize over pure strategies (in this case voting and not voting). Ledyard showed that each voter might plausibly choose to vote in any given election with only a small probability. Then it will turn out that some voters will actually vote in any given election, and turnout exceeds zero in equilibrium.

This was an important achievement, because the act of turning out was rationalized: Positive levels of political participation were shown to be consistent with purposive, self-interested behavior. Palfrey and Rosenthal (1983, 1985) showed, however, that as the size of the electorate rises, equilibrium turnout shrinks, even in Ledyard's game. In the limit, as the potential electorate goes to infinity, the "rational" level of turnout goes toward zero. Palfrey and Rosenthal show that the maximum level of turnout predicted in equilibrium (for plausibly sized electorates) is about 3–5 percent. But actual rates of turnout in the United States exceed 30 percent, and is usually much higher in U.S. presidential races or in most elections in other countries.

This conflict between theory (no more than 5 percent) and data (more than 30 percent) suggests something else is going on. That "something else" is the attempt by parties and other political elites to persuade voters to vote. Securing the "right" policy from government is a collective good. Somehow, groups of citizens are overcoming the free rider problem, to get what the group wants. More people are participating than a purely self-interested investment strategy would predict. Incorporating groups into an individual decision calculus is difficult, but some progress has been made (Uhlaner, 1989a, 1989b; Aldrich, 1993, 1995; and Lapp 1999).

We have used the model of narrowly self-interested behavior to generate hypotheses about turnout rates. Those hypotheses, that turnout will not exceed 5 percent in any reasonably large electorate, have been disproved. This has led analytical political theorists to seek mechanisms to overcome pure self-interest motives and to solve collective action problems. Further, though the levels of turnout are hard to explain, voters respond to the costs of voting, opportunity costs of time, and other factors as the "rational" model predicts, by being less likely to vote.[13] As we noted earlier, rain or bad weather drives turnout down (Morton, 1991; Knack, 1994; Gomez, Hansford and Krause, 2007) because traveling to the polls is harder. Difficult or time-consuming registration makes people less likely to vote (Kelley, Ayres, and Bowen, 1967; Wolfinger and Rosenstone, 1980; Nagler, 1991; Brians and Grofman, 1999). People with few resources find it hard to take time to vote (Tollison and Willett, 1973; Wolfinger and Rosenstone, 1980; Cho, Gimple and Wu, 2006, provide an interesting counterexample among Arab-Americans after 9/11).

The composition of "voter taste" is at the forefront of research on political participation, and there have been potentially important advances in recent years. Gerber, Green and Larimer (2008) break down the "civic duty" term from the Downsian model and show that a good portion of it can be attributed to the desire to avoid the stigma that goes along with not voting. Fowler (2006) and Rotemberg (2009) explore the positive correlation between altruism and participation – to a moderate extent, people who care more about the way politics can affect others are more likely to vote. Jankowski (2007) uses a Bayesian approach assuming "weak altruism" to generate a prediction of reasonably large-sized turnouts in a plausible electorate. Fowler and Dawes (2008) found a genetic variation that they claim may create a predisposition for political participation. This view was called into question, however, by Charney and English (2012).

CONCLUSIONS

The main causes of voter abstention in the classic rational choice model are indifference, alienation, and costs of vating.

Indifference. If voters perceive little (no) difference between alternatives, they are less likely to vote. This prediction has both *cross-sectional* and *time series* implications: Voters who perceive little distance between alternatives are less likely to vote than other voters who perceive large net candidate differentials. Similarly, any given voter is more likely to vote in an election where the perceived difference is large, compared with other elections where the same voter perceives the difference as small.

Alienation. If both (all) alternatives in the election are far from the voter's ideal point, that voter is less likely to vote. Again, the prediction is made both across voters and over time: The greater the difference between the voter's ideal point and the nearest alternative, the less likely is that voter to turn out, compared with either other voters or other elections where perceptions of the difference are smaller.

Expected Benefits and Costs. Rational voters have two kinds of goals. They want to achieve their goals, but they may be willing to free ride if their chance of changing the outcome is negligible or if they are reasonably certain that other like-minded voters will carry the desired result even if they stay home. But this requires that citizens calculate probabilities in ways that solve the problem of strategic uncertainty.

Ultimately, it may be plausible to conceive voting as primarily an act of consumption, broadly conceived, rather than investment. The prediction of the "investment" model is for positive, but relatively low, turnout in even a moderate-sized electorate. This prediction is not borne out empirically; turnout is "too high."[14] Rational choice has a well-developed theory of consumption, making it possible to specify "determinants" of voting, in terms of costs and benefits at the margin, that affect the satisfaction the voter receives from voting.[15]

The problem is that the point of democratic choice is not participation alone, but also choosing. Three recent books, Caplan (2007), Brennan (2012), and Somin (2013) raise fundamental questions about the capacity of democratic processes to deliver useful democratic results. Caplan claims that voters are fundamentally irrational, and in fact are willfully so. It is not just that voters hold mistaken views – this is pardonable, in a context where information is costly and being informed is a public good. The problem is that voters maintain their biases on ideological, religious, or just idiosyncratic grounds. Rather than updating their beliefs when they are exposed to new and more accurate information (one definition of "rationality," as given by Downs, 1957), voters persist in mistaken beliefs. Voters fail to solve the collective action problem, not because they fail to vote, but because they vote for candidates and alternatives that do not serve either the private interests of voters or the encompassing interests of groups.

Brennan (2012) argues that democracies require that citizens have a universal right to vote. It is a mistake, however, to treat voting as an obligation, as if participation were an end in itself. The problem of choosing in groups is partly aggregating the best information and judgments of those whom the choice will affect. H. L. Mencken, the humorist and social commentator, had his doubts about the ability of voters to perform the function assigned to them:

> It [is impossible] to separate the democratic idea from the theory that there is a mystical merit, an esoteric and ineradicable rectitude, in the man at the bottom of the scale – that inferiority, by some strange magic, becomes superiority – nay, the superiority of superiorities... What baffles statesmen is to be solved by the people, instantly and by a sort of seraphic intuition. (Mencken, 1926, pp. 3–4).

Brennan argues that it is actually morally wrong for the ignorant and uninformed to cast votes, because they are harming themselves and the group by making incorrect choices and misleading signals to political leaders more likely. A darker interpretation might be that the misleading signals actually originate with the political leaders themselves, who come to depend on their ability to mislead voters to remain in power.

Somin argues that the real problem is not a dearth of information, but a lack of interest in the information that is readily available. Voters may very well care deeply about issues, and they may want to make their political world better. Nevertheless, their interest in studying issues and policies in depth is nearly nonexistent. The collective action problem partly explains this lack. But in large measure, this failure is a lack of expertise and familiarity. Somin's proposed solution is to take much of the discretionary power out of the hands of politicians and voters and to empower the judiciary to enforce broad principles of governance.

FINAL WORDS

This final chapter has ended on a pessimistic note. If there are substantial collective action problems in acquiring information and then in acting on that information to go to the polls, it would seem that our ability to choose well in groups is limited. But as with problems of asymmetric information in private markets, public decisions foster institutions that economize on the costs of gathering information. Further, these institutions–parties, candidate reputations, selective incentives to participate in smaller subgroups–mitigate the turnout problem by reducing the costs of organizing in the first place. It would be difficult for a collection of people who don't know each other to organize and influence choices of the government. But the ability to go to the polls and cast an anonymous vote, for all its problems, is one of the most important institutional innovations in human history.

For many human activities there is simply no alternative to some collective choice mechanism, because while individuals have preferences and make choices we act in groups. A healthy skepticism, and perhaps some humility, about what groups can accomplish, while maintaining a core optimism about what is possible for groups that form and act together for their mutual benefit, may be the best we can hope for.

TERMS

Alienation
Collective Action
Downsian Model
Duty
Expected Net Benefit
Expressive Voting
Franchise
Indifference
Mandatory Turnout Laws
Paradox of Not Voting
Registration
Roll-off
Turnout

EXERCISES

9.1 Suppose a state governor, who is concerned that too few people in her state voted in local elections, hires you as a consultant. You ask for more information and find the following facts in a state elections guide:

According to the State Board of Elections, 1,728,693 people voted in local elections last November. Our state has an over-eighteen population of 4,605,000. There were 2,631,978 people in our state registered to vote last year. State election laws restrict eligibility to register to those who are not in jail or mental hospitals, and have not been convicted of a felony, about 96 percent of the adult population. The last statewide election, held at the same time as the local elections and on the same ballot, saw 1,869,351 votes tallied.

The governor wants to know whether the state elections board should try "motor voter" and other registration policies to make it easier to register or "get out the vote" drives and expanded poll hours to get more registered voters to the polls. What would be your advice to the governor?

9.2 Should elections be held online? What are two arguments for, and two arguments against, holding elections using the Internet? Make sure you discuss how to hand fraud, identity theft, and verification in recounts.

9.3* Suppose that a particular citizen 1 has ideal point $x_1, = [9\ -4]^T$, with $A_1, = I$, and $\delta = 10$ (δ is the WED beyond which the voter is alienated). Let one candidate occupy $x_A = [13\ -1]^T$ and the other occupy $x_B, = [-6\ 2]^T$. Does citizen 1 vote? If he votes, which candidate does he prefer?

9.4* Suppose that the two candidates A and B are in the same positions as in Exercise 9.2

($x_A = [9\ -4]^T$, $x_B = [-6\ 2]^T$). Define "indifference" as follows:

The voter is indifferent if $WED(x_A, x_i) - WED(x_B, x_i)\ | \leq 2$

Graph the set of ideal points where voters (if they had those ideal points) would be indifferent.

Note: Exercises marked * are advanced material.

Answers to Selected Exercises

CHAPTER 1:

1. (Subjective/Qualitative)
2. The independent variable is whether someone is an old person, the dependent variable is whether a person votes, and the intervening variable is whether someone has a college degree.
3. Here, as in the Lewis and Clark example, there is an objective "fact of the matter" – one of these options is objectively the best choice, depending on the requirements the three choosers have. If, for example, person 1 wants to stay where they are because he has a broken leg, option B would be tantamount to a death sentence as his companions abandon him to climb a mountain. As we will see, this requires some notion of the intensity of preference, information that simple voting may not be able to elicit.

CHAPTER 2:

1. The set of rules must be agreed upon for it to be a group constitution. The best decision rule for adopting or changing a constitution is ultimately a subjective decision, because there is an inherent trade-off between hold-up costs the closer the rule is to unanimity (the costs that must be paid to convince those most reluctant to agree) and costs of coercion that must be borne by those who are bound by the constitution without consenting. If the size of the group is allowed to vary, so that those who do not consent to a constitution cease to be part of the constituted group, the unanimity rule for adopting the constitution is clearly the best. In addition to "deciding how to decide," a constitution should specify rules that constrain the domain of collective choice and specify the terms under which individuals can exit the group.

2. Any group of people might be said to be choosing among three "strategies" or general approaches to obtaining resources: Raid, Trade, or Defend. If all groups choose to Raid or Defend, then no Trade takes place and there is little prosperity. Roving bandits will find that they have difficulty obtaining enough resources to survive, and groups that try to Defend will lose lots of time and energy that would be better spent trying to grow crops and make items for use. If one group of Raiders decides to occupy a settlement permanently, they can offer specialized Defense services. More importantly, a stationary Raider has reasons to take less than all of the surplus created by the farmers of the settlement.

3. Yes, it matters if the people designing the game are the same people who will be playing it. If they are not, majority rule should work well; if one person can demonstrate superior knowledge of game design, it might also work to make them a leader who is ultimately in charge of making all decisions. If the designers will also be the players, however, a unanimous decision rule for enacting game rules is more appropriate. In this scenario, people know the specific skills that they have to work with when they play the game every day for the next year, and will try to design a game that they will be good at. For example, a person who knows herself to be good at mental math is more likely to support a rule that says the first person to multiply the results of two 20-sided dice gets to go first.

There is, however, an additional problem for people who want to choose in groups: what happens if they are unable to reach an agreement? This "reversion point" is an important part of modeling any bargaining problem.

CHAPTER 3:

1. a. Assuming that people vote sincerely, he should propose Carrots versus Apples first, and then vote the winner against Broccoli.

  b. Again, assuming that people vote sincerely, "foods that can be made into desserts" first (e.g., Apple Pie and Carrot Cake), then "foods that cannot be made into desserts."

2. a. Almost any set of preference orders will work here, but consider for example the case where all 4 people have the same preference order. There cannot be cycles if the electorate is unanimous.

  b. For example:

Chooser	Lyle	Michelle	Nancy	Orville
Best	A	B	C	D
Second	B	C	D	A
Third	C	D	A	B
Worst	D	A	B	C

The key difference is then "disagreement," of a particular kind. In the second example, there is a pairwise election that each option will win and a pairwise election that each option will lose. So, in trying to follow the "will of the majority," we have to decide *which majority*, since they disagree.

3. There is a Condorcet Cycle: A ≻ C ≻ D ≻ A. All 3 choosers prefer A to B, and B can only win a pairwise contest against C. So A≻ B ≻ C, but there is no cycle without D, and B is not involved in set of alternatives over which the cycle occurs.

CHAPTER 4:

1. β is not reflexive or symmetric, and there's not enough information to say if it's transitive.
2. Symmetry: Take x, y ∈ X, where x ≈ y. x ⩾ y and y ⩾ x, so y ≈ x.
   Transitivity: Take x, y, z ∈ X, where x ≈ y and y ≈ z. x ⩾ y and y ⩾ z, so x ⩾ z. z ⩾ y ⩾ x, so z ⩾ x. So x ≈ z.
   Reflexivity: Take x ∈ X, where x ≈ x. x ⩾ x, so x ≈ x.
3. Take x, y ∈ X, where x = y. Either x ⩾ y or y ⩾ x because of completeness; replace y with x, so x ⩾ x. So this binary relation is reflexive.
4. a. *Only if*: Let ≥ be transitive on X. By the definition of transitivity, we know that the asymmetric part of ≥ is transitive (x≻y and y≻z → x≻z), the symmetric part of ≥ is transitive (x≈y and y≈z → x≈z), and any two alternatives in the maximal set are in the same relation to any third alternative (x≈y and y≻z → x≻z, and x≻y and y≈z → x≻z).

   If: Let the three conditions hold. Replacing the given binary relations with their equivalents using ≥ yields:

   (1) (x≥y and ¬y≥x) and (y≥z and ¬z≥y) → (x≥z and ¬z≥x) ⇔ x≥y and y≥z → x≥z
   (2) (x≥y and y≥x) and (y≥z and z≥y) → (x≥z and z≥x) ⇔ x≥y and y≥z → x≥z
   (3) (x≥y and y≥x) and (y≥z and ¬z≥y) → (x≥z and ¬z≥x) ⇔ x≥y and y≥z → x≥z

   This is, by definition, gives transitivity.
   b. Since ≥ is complete, we know that for all x and y, either x≥y or y≥x or both. Splitting ≥ into its symmetric and asymmetric components will create a complete accounting for the various relationships. Proving (3) merely requires tracing all possible combinations of (1) and (2).
5. (Can be solved computationally)
6. We are not aware of the general answer. Readers are welcome to send us one, and we will post it on-line, with attribution!
7. Depends on the weak orders selected. But the choice of agendas will be determined by the expectations of how other members may vote strategically. The result can be indeterminate, and reduces to a bargaining problem.

CHAPTER 5:

1. The median is 6; the mean is 4.8.
2. *y* will win.
3. The medians are now 6 and 7. *y*=8 will win.
4. The median is 6 and the mean is 5.4. Replacing x_3 with x'_3 doesn't change the median, but it changes the mean to 9.
5. It is not; the median is a much better approximation of what Aristotle valued in society. As you can see in the earlier questions in this chapter, the mean position does not need to be occupied by anyone, but Aristotle is placing value on the position of the person or people with moderate views.
6. The Normal or Gaussian distribution, with the familiar bell curve shape, finds the mean, median and mode all located at the same point. Any symmetric distribution will find the median and mean at the same point.
7. Since people cannot have incomes less than zero, but many people have incomes close to zero, we would expect to see that mean income exceeds median income. But this means that there are electoral pressures toward "redistributing" income, because the median voter would prefer to have the average level of income.
8. One simple form of the proof is to use a contradiction. Assume that *N* is odd, but that at least two medians *x* and *y* exist, or that there is an interval bounded by [*x*, *y*]. Suppose for simplicity that *x* < *y*. By the definition of a median position, the number of ideal points n_L to the left of *x* must be the same as the number n_R to the right of *y*. If this is not true, then one or the other point cannot be a median. It is a property of numbers that any integer doubled is even. Since $n_L = n_R$, adding them together is simply doubling an integer. But the total number of ideal points is then $n_L + n_R + 2$ (adding in *x* and *y* as the other two ideal points). Adding 2 to an even number is also an even number, so the total number of ideal points is even. But we required at the outset that *N* be odd. This completes the proof: If *N* is odd, there can be at most one median position (though multiple voters might share that median position).

CHAPTER 6:

1. z is not a Condorcet winner; if you draw the indifference curves that go through z, you can see that any point in the intersection of at least 2 of the indifference curves (for example, (5, 16) or (6,7)) will defeat z in a pairwise election.
2. The median position on issue 1 is 5, and the median position on issue 2 is 10, so (5, 10).
3. It turns out that (5, 10) is in fact a median in all directions – any line through it will have at least half of the ideal points on each side of it.

4. The proof follows directly from the definition of separability, depending on the institutional setting. The simplest case is under the rule "Division of the Question," where the issues are voted separately, and amendments can only involve changes in one dimension. In this case, the MVT simply applies directly. If there is no Division of the Question, then in principle there may be no equilibrium. But the theorem by assumption requires that the issues are voted on separately, ensuring that each dimensional median is selected.

5. The WED is $\sqrt{\varphi}$ times the SED; because φ is defined as between 0 and 1, this means that the WED will be less than the SED.

6. Because the off-diagonal elements of A_i are negative, there is positive complementarity between the issues, and since $\tilde{x}_1 > 10$, member i's conditional ideal is greater than 12. For the exact value, use equation 6.20: $x_{i_2}^* | \tilde{x}_1 = 42$.

7. Beginning in the first two dimensions, we see from equation 6.6 that the two-dimensional distance between y and z is $\sqrt{(x_1 - z_1)^2 + (x_2 - z_2)^2}$. We now use this distance and the distance $(x_3 - z_3)$ as the two legs of a second right triangle, the hypotenuse of which has distance

$$= \sqrt{\sqrt{(x_1 - z_1)^2 + (x_2 - z_2)^2}^2 + (x_3 - z_3)^2}$$

$$= \sqrt{(x_1 - z_1)^2 + (x_2 - z_2)^2 + (x_3 - z_3)^2}.$$

8. The proof follows directly from the algebra of the spatial utility function, provided that $a_{12} = a_{21}$.

CHAPTER 7:

1. K= 11; for K= 10, if someone proposes voting position 7 against position 8, 8 will get 10 votes and 7 will no longer be the status quo.

2. a) A will win in the runoff election between A and B.
   b) A gets 10, B gets 11, and C gets 9, so C wins.

3. Consider candidate A at 25, candidate B at 60 and candidate C at 90. A would win a plurality election, and B would win a majority election in a runoff against A.

4. The proof is analogous to the MVT, except that the definition of the n_L and n_R is now $N-K+1$, not counting the ideal points at the equilibrium. In effect, any group of $N-K$ voters can veto a move away from equilibrium. Depending on the configuration of ideal points, this means that there is generally an interval of equilibria, and that this interval is larger as $N-K$ is smaller.

CHAPTER 8:

1. a) Voter i will vote for R, even though D's platform exactly coincides with i's ideal point. This is because D is less reliable than R, and so the expected policy outcome for R is closer to i's ideal point, overall. This

may seem surprising if you think in deterministic terms, but it means that a resolute and credible extreme candidate might have an advantage against a pragmatist.

b) Voter *i*'s utility function for R is $U=-(12-15)^2-\sigma_R^2$, and for D is $U=-(12-12)^2-\sigma_D^2$. Since the variance for D is 16, $U_D=-16$. Solving for the value of variance for R that makes i indifferent (that is, setting the two utilities equal) gives $16 =-(12-15)^2-\sigma_R^2$. Thus, *i* will vote for D if R's variance is greater than or equal to 7.

2. In every case, they both locate at the median. With perfect information, even candidates who have policy preferences have to obey the dictates of the median voter.

3. Candidate Y wins voters 1 and 3, while Z wins voter 2. Candidate Z could do several things, but the simplest is to closer on issue 1, to $[\ 3\ 6\ ]^T$, picking up Voter 3's vote.

4. Follows directly from the fact that expectations formation are shared. No divergent result could be an equilibrium, and platforms converge in expectation.

5. If expectations are not shared, then the initial platform selection will be divergent (if moves are secret and simultaneous.) But this divergent strategy pair is not an equilibrium, since either candidate could garner more votes by moving toward the other.

6. Depends on the way that "policy preferences" for candidates are modeled. A proof can be found in Calvert (1985).

CHAPTER 9:

1. The ratio of people registered to vote over the population eligible to register is $\frac{2,631,978}{4,605,000*.96} = .55$, while the ratio of voters to registered voters is $\frac{1,728,693}{2,631,978} = .66$. This suggests that "motor voter" and other measures designed to make registration easier are more likely to increase voter turnout.

2. (Subjective/Qualitative)

3. Citizen 1 votes for Candidate A; Candidate B is located so far from his ideal point that Citizen 1 would rather not vote than vote for B.

4. Voters with ideal points with the property that $(12y_2 + 59)/30 \le y_1$ are indifferent.

Notes

1 THE ANALYSIS OF POLITICS

1. That is not to say that human societies are the only ones that exhibit politics, or cooperation. Most primate species, at a minimum, seem to have evolved complex social orders and politics. And naked mole rats have evolved highly cooperative social "norms" and cooperative practices, perhaps as a form of insurance. The difference we are relying on is that such groups are biologically determined by kinship, whereas human political groups are constituted, and rules endogenously chosen and laid on. Thanks to Zach Weiner for pointing to the inaccuracy of earlier versions of this claim. For background, see (just as examples) Jarvis (1981), Maestripieri (2007), Sherman, Jarvis, and Alexander (1991), and Waal (1998, 2007). Interestingly, the naked mole rat is also an existence proof of the power of evolution as a predictive theory (Braude, 1997).

2. Economists tend to think of "division of labor" as an economic phenomenon (Smith, 1776), and it is surely true that markets enable people to take advantage of the gains from voluntary specialization. But many social organizations, including political organizations such as cities and private voluntary groups such as clubs, provide many of the same benefits, and for the same reasons. As Durkheim (1984: 17) argued, "…the economic services that it can render are insignificant compared with the moral effect that it produces, and its true function is to create between two or more people a feeling of solidarity." Later, he credits division of labor with creating the "social consciousness" that weaves the very fabric of society:

   The totality of beliefs and sentiments common to the average members of a society forms a determinate system with a life of its own. It can be termed the collective or common consciousness…. Likewise it does not change with every generation but, on the contrary, links successive generations to one another. Thus it is something totally different from the consciousness of individuals, although it is only realised in individuals." (p. 39)

3. An online source for the journal entries is http://lewisandclarkjournals.unl.edu/.

4. The "hostility" of the Native Americans was both understandable and fully justified, of course, given the later genocides of entire tribes and the violation of treaty promises.

5. There was at first another option: Move west to the mouth of the Columbia, as near as possible to Cape Disappointment to enable them to contact trading ships if any should appear. This would allow the captains to obtain trade goods on the credit of the United States, for which they had a letter of authorization. It would also allow the Corps to ship their journals and scientific cargo back to Washington, D.C., rather than have to carry the precious and fragile material back across the continental divide. But by November 24, when the decision was to be made, this was no longer a live option. The storms on the coast were just too severe, and even if a ship had been sighted there was no way to make contact.

6. It appears there were actually two separate votes, first on whether to explore the southern side, without committing to move there, and a second to choose between options B and C. As we shall see, this sequence of binary votes disguises the potential for complexity in preferences, and so we present the votes here as a composite. For details, see http://stories.washingtonhistory.org/LC-columbia/whyclatsop/station-vote.htm.

7. The Corps had found the Chinooks to be extremely aggressive traders, though this may have meant that the Chinooks failed to give the Corps anything free. The Corps had routinely exploited the Native American custom for giving gifts and given paltry gifts in "exchange."

8. It is remarkable that the members of the Corps would spurn the easy catch from one of the finest fisheries in the world. But fish was not viewed as proper food for gentlemen.

9. At any given time, ten or more of the Corps were likely to be away on hunting, trading, or salt-gathering missions (Clarke, 1970).

10. Clark's journal entry for July 12, 1804 (Clarke 1970, p. 76; the actual language was "*do Sentience* him to receive *One hundred lashes, on his bear back, at four different times in equal proportion.* And Order that punishment Commence this evening at Sunset, and Continue to be inflicted (by the Guard) every evening untill Completed" (emphasis original). Oddly, it appears that Clark later recalled the incident differently, writing in a letter to his brother that the sentence was 70 lashes. A longer discussion of this incident and the question of military discipline on the journey generally can be found in Ambrose (1997: 149–50). Apparently, the discipline, though harsh in our eyes (Willard bore deep scars in his back for the rest of his life, and the whipping on consecutive nights opened the scabs of the previous night's beating), was actually accepted, and perhaps even approved, by the rank-and-file members of the Corps. Willard had fallen asleep while serving as a sentry at night (he said he had lain down but had not fallen asleep). As Ambrose (1997) put it, "One shudders at the thought of Willard's back after the fourth day; one shudders at the thought of what might have happened had a roving band of Sioux come up while Willard was sleeping on guard duty." Falling asleep on guard duty was a capital offense in a military unit in hostile territory. Willard was, if anything, shown mercy and became a useful (though not prominent) member of the Corps. The company, including those being punished, seems to have accepted as just the other whippings, as described by Ambrose.

11. Ambrose gave this description of the vote:

So the captains made up their own minds, but on this occasion they decided to let everyone participate in the decision. They never explained why. Perhaps they felt that, since they were all going to be in this together, they should all have a say; maybe they just wanted to involve everyone so that none would have a right to complain. (p. 316)

12. From Franzen and Pointner (2011):

> For every show the production team records how the audience performed when a candidate asked for its help on a question. Thus, for analyzing how well the audience performs we were able to use this process-generated data. From the 1337 times the audience was asked, the majority vote erred only 147 times. Thus, the majority of the audience provided the correct answer 91% of the time.

13. Ambrose (2002:232; emphasis added) describes the disagreement this way:

> The next day, June 9, Lewis attempted to convince the men of the expedition that the south fork was the Missouri, without success. To a man they were "firm in the belief that the N. Fork was the Missouri and that which we ought to take." Private Cruzatte, "who had been an old Missouri navigator and who from his integrity knowledge and skill as a waterman had acquired the confidence of every individual of the party declared it his opinion that the N. fork was the true genuine Missouri and could be no other."

> Despite Cruzatte's certainty, the captains would not change their minds, and so informed the men. In a magnificent tribute to the captains' leadership qualities, "they said very cheerfully that they were ready to follow us any wher we thought proper to direct but that they still thought that the other was the river."

> *Lewis and Clark were not taking a vote*, but "finding them so determined in this belief, and wishing that if we were in error to be able to detect it and rectify it as soon as possible it was agreed between Capt. C and myself that one of us should set out with a small party by land up the South fork [to]...determine this question pretty accurately."

> The judgment of the Captains was vindicated. The crowd was wrong, and the south fork turned out to be the larger. The Corps headed up the south. The key problem was not so much which fork was the "real" Missouri, as which fork led to the Shoshone (Snake) Tribe, and Sacagawea's people, from whom the Corps hoped to obtain horses for the journey over the mountains.

14. There were actually 32; Lewis and Clark, being officers, did not record votes, because the vote was supposed to be advisory to them.

15. Wap(p)ato is the egg-sized bulb of the arrowhead plant, which tastes and is used much like the potato. This quote from Sakagawea is controversial, though it is usually interpreted as a kind of female deference to male authority. Given Sacagawea's clear intelligence and ability as a leader, however, it is at least possible she was making fun of the ponderous and involved procedure of voting, a process in which she may have had little faith. Her loutish trapper husband Charbonneau apparently abstained, perhaps because he knew his view was not much esteemed. But Sakagawea was actually asked to vote.

16. Moulton, v. 6, pp. 81–84.

17. Gass also wrote, on the night of November 24:

> At night, the party were consulted by the Commanding Officers, as to the place most proper for winter quarters; and the most of them were of opinion, that it would be best, in the first place, to go over to the south side of the river, and ascertain whether good hunting ground could be found there. Should that be the case, it would be a more eligible place than higher up the river, on account of getting salt, as that is a very scarce article with us.

> Thus, the nature of the division among the choices may have been a bit less clear than we are depicting them here. It may be that most of the party favored at least exploring the south side, before making a firm decision.

18. This quote was attributed to Einstein, and then widely repeated. The earliest source Einstein scholars point to is in *Brighter than a Thousand Suns: A Personal History of the Atomic Scientists* by Robert Jungk (1958), p. 249, which says that Einstein made the comment during "a walk with Ernst Straus, a young mathematician acting as his scientific assistant at Princeton."

19. Our preferred definition of "institutions" generally is North's (1990): "The rules of the game in a society or, more formally, the humanly devised constraints that shape human action" (p. 1)

20. This view is characteristic of post-structuralism, developed as a literary theory but applied to notions of scientific paradigms. For example: "Structuralism recognised [that signifieds'] relationship with their signifiers [was] arbitrary. However, once this relationship has been fixed in language, signifier and signified become defined and stable. Poststructuralism denies that stability of this kind is possible." Padley (2001: 181)

21. *Leviathan*, The, Book IV, "Of Speech," Paragraph 22.

22. It is still true, of course, that the use of accumulated wisdom and trusted sources is of considerable value. We are claiming only that a quote or reference to an authority, no matter how trusted, cannot be dispositive by itself. We acknowledge an interesting discussion with Geoffrey Brennan, himself an authority, on this subject.

23. The distinction between "science" and engineering in the study of politics has several sources. The clearest and most direct is Ordeshook (1995), where he summarizes the arguments in favor of engineering.

24. We should emphasize these engineering considerations are about *practical* moral problems. A persuasive argument has been made (e.g., Cohen 2005) that a correspondence between facts and principles is not strictly necessary for moral discourse, and in fact may get in the way.

25. "In every system of morality, which I have hitherto met with, I have always remark'd, that the author proceeds for some time in the ordinary ways of reasoning, and establishes the being of a God, or makes observations concerning human affairs; when of a sudden I am surpriz'd to find, that instead of the usual copulations of propositions, *is*, and *is not*, I meet with no proposition that is not connected with an *ought*, or an *ought not*. This change is imperceptible; but is however, of the last consequence. For as this *ought*, or *ought not*, expresses some new relation or affirmation, 'tis necessary that it shou'd be observ'd and explain'd; and at the same time that a reason should be given; for what seems altogether inconceivable, how this new relation can be a deduction from others, which are entirely different from it."

(David Hume, *Treatise of Human Nature*, Bk III, pt. 1)

26. See Fearon (1995). This explanation is in some ways related to the literature on labor organizations and strikes, but the "our institutions are more just, therefore we are more powerful" explanation is one of the ways nations are different. For a review of the "strikes" literature, see Mauro (1982) and Hayes (1984). Hicks (1963) said: "The majority of actual strikes are doubtless the result of faulty negotiation" (146). And later: "...adequate knowledge will always make a settlement possible" (147). For a discussion of the complexity of this problem, see de Marchi (2005), pp. 90–95.

27. Walzer (1973) calls this the "dirty hands" problem, and problematizes the very notion of right and wrong in statecraft.

28. "Disagreement" within a group may not be a bad thing, of course. A false unanimity, or "group-think," can be much more dangerous. See Whyte (1952) and Janis (1972). On the problem of aggregating judgments, in the context of the "discursive dilemma," and the limits of rationality in group decisions based on reason, see List (2006) and List and Pettit (2012).

29. Whether there is objectively and truly a "fact of the matter" is itself a matter of some debate. Three classic and somewhat different views can be found in Kuhn (1970); Nagel (1996); and Polanyi (1958).

30. Though it is outside the scope of our discussion here, there is a strain of political theory that emphasizes at least the possibility that deliberation and talk can be used to generate a consensus, even on the most difficult issues. See, for example, Habermas (1985, 1989); Bessett (1994); Fishkin and Laslett (2003), and Fishkin (2011).

31. As Monroe (1995) points out, the "collective wisdom" idea is better credited to Aristotle (as demonstrated by the quote earlier in the chapter about "taken all together, be better than the few") though Rousseau develops the idea at greater length. See also Coleman and Ferejohn (1986) and Grofman and Feld (1988).

32. This particular view of Public Choice derives from long hours reading James Buchanan, and arguing with Geoffrey Brennan. While they are cited in much of what follows, no reference could do justice to the debt they are owed, jointly and severally.

33. Attributed to Alistair Cooke, in his BBC-4 program, Letter from America. Quoted from Munger (2014).

34. Nietzsche used the "windows" metaphor in at least three places.
"We are like shop windows in which we are continually arranging, concealing or illuminating the supposed qualities others ascribe to us – in order to deceive ourselves." *Daybreak*, S. 385.
"This same [spirit or will of knowing] has at its service an apparently opposed impulse of the spirit, a suddenly adopted preference of ignorance, of arbitrary shutting out, a closing of windows, an inner denial of this or that, a prohibition to approach, a sort of defensive attitude against much that is knowable, a contentment with obscurity, with the shutting-in horizon, an acceptance and approval of ignorance: as that which is all necessary according to the degree of its appropriating power, its "digestive power"..." *Beyond Good and Evil*, Part III, S. 230.

> Deeply mistrustful of the dogmas of epistemology, I loved to look now out of this window, now out of that; I guarded against settling down with any of these dogmas, considered them harmful–and finally: is it likely that a tool is able to criticize its own fitness? – What I noticed was rather that no epistemological skepticism or dogmatism had ever arisen free from ulterior motives–that it acquires a value of the second rank as soon as one has considered what it was that compelled the adoption of this point of view. (Nietzsche, Section 410, 1901).

2 BECOMING A GROUP: THE CONSTITUTION

1. We would have to add aesthetics and metaphysics to round out the list, but for our purposes, those categories are not as useful, and we will take no note of them.

2. There may be some circumstances where the concept of "group agency" is sensible. But this is rarely true in political settings, at least for large groups. But it is important to note that a group such as a dance troupe, or an athletic team, does in fact try to act as a group. In the limit, the distinction between the group and the individual may be blurred, until only the group matters, as in the case of eusocial insects such as bees or ants. See Bergstrom (2002) and List and Pettit (2011).

3. It is not our intention to debate the merits of methodological individualism, as many others have argued both sides quite effectively. The "pro" side has such diverse advocates as Buchanan and Tullock (1962), Elster (1982), Mises (1949), and Weber (1922). Max Weber offered the earliest clear statement of the theoretical perspective of methodological individualism:

> [It may] be convenient or even indispensable to treat social collectivities, such as states, associations, business corporations, as if they were individual persons. Thus they may be treated as the bearers of rights and duties or as the performers of legally significant actions. But for the subjective understanding of action in sociology these *collectivities must be treated as solely the resultants and context of the particular acts of individual persons, since an individual alone is the subjective bearer of meaningful oriented action.* (Weber, 1922/1968, p. 13; emphasis added).

> Weber's formulation captures the problem faced by any social scientist who wants to study groups of people, but he added a caveat– methodological individualism is not the same as ideological individualism. "It is a tremendous misunderstanding to think that an 'individualistic' *method* should involve what is in any conceivable sense an individualistic system of *values*." Elster (1982) echoes this point.

4. The "individuals want, groups do" distinction is probably simplistic. The problem of "group agency is an important one, but beyond our scope here. For a review and important insights into this debate, see List and Pettit (2011).

5. First Book of Samuel, Chapter 8, from the Jewish Publication Society, *Hebrew Bible in English*, 1917, translated by Bernard Drachman. For a discussion of the background and interpretations of this text, see Abramson (2012), Brennan (2009), and Hillman (2009).

6. The notion of a state of nature was common in Enlightenment thought, and was important for both Rousseau (who distinguished a state of nature and man's "natural state") and Montesquieu. Locke's conception of "natural rights" also relates closely to the unconstituted state.

7. Unanimity may be less restrictive than it seems, for a constitution. Both Rousseau and Rawls likewise require unanimity of constitutional principles.

8. This raises the question of just what "voluntary" means, of course. The issue is discussed at length in Munger (2011) and Guzman and Munger (2013). They argue for a conception of truly voluntary exchange they call "euvoluntary," where parties to exchange are coerced neither by human agency (the usual definition) nor by circumstances (the novel part of the definition).

9. This argument is made at somewhat greater length in Munger (2012).

10. "In order then that the social compact may not be an empty formula, it tacitly includes the undertaking, which alone can give force to the rest, that *whoever refuses to obey the general will shall be compelled to do so by the whole body. This means nothing less than that he will be forced to be free;* for this is the condition which, by giving each citizen to his country, secures him against all personal dependence. In this lies the key to the working of the political machine; this alone legitimises civil undertakings, which, without it, would be absurd, tyrannical, and liable to the most frightful abuses."

Rousseau (1762 / 1913), Book I, Chapter 7; emphasis added.

11. "If then there are opponents when the social compact is made, their opposition does not invalidate the contract, but merely prevents them from being included in it. They are foreigners among citizens. When the State is instituted, residence constitutes consent; to dwell within its territory is to submit to the Sovereign."

Rousseau (1762 / 1913), Book IV, Chapter 2.

12. "When therefore the opinion that is contrary to my own [wins a majority], *this proves neither more nor less than that I was mistaken*, and that what I thought to be the general will was not so. If my particular opinion had carried the day I should have achieved the opposite of what was my will; and it is in that case that I should not have been free."

Rousseau (1762 /1913; Book IV, Chapter 2, emphasis added)

13. Buchanan (2007; p. 211) points out: "...there is a categorical separation between the market and the political relationship between and among interacting persons. In the stylized limit, that of fully competitive markets for both inputs and outputs, the individual faces no costs of exit from any relationship. The individual is maximally free from the power of others. In dramatic contrast, the individual in a political relationship is necessarily subject to the exercise of some power or authority by another. In the stylized limit, this power is absolute: no exit is possible, regardless of cost."

14. Here is Circe's dire warning to Odysseus (Chapman, 2000, Chapter XII, lines 73–89):

> [Order] thy companions
> Beforehand causing to stop every ear
> With sweet soft wax, so close that none may hear
> A note of all their charmings. Yet may you,
> If you affect it, open ear allow
> To try their motion; but presume not so
> To trust your judgment, when your senses go
> So loose about you, but give straight command
> To all your men, to bind you foot and hand
> Sure to the mast, that you may safe approve
> How strong in instigation to their love
> Their rapting tunes are. If so much they move,
> That, spite of all your reason, your will stands
> To be enfranchised both of feet and hands,
> Charge all your men before to slight your charge,
> And rest so far from fearing to enlarge
> That much more sure they bind you.

15. This point is argued at length in Hardin (1989).

16. Some extensions of this argument, and some problems with its logic, are reviewed in Munger (2011, p. 298). The interaction between morals and formal rules is further elaborated in Brennan and Buchanan (1985, p. 6):

> The notion that rules may substitute for morals has been familiar to economists and philosophers at least since Adam Smith. And, of course, the great intellectual discovery of the eighteenth century was the spontaneous order of the market, the discovery that within an appropriate structure of rules ("laws and institutions" in Adam Smith's phraseology), individuals in following their own interests can further the interests of others. The result is the great network of social coordination – refined and extended to the boundaries of the division of labor – that even after centuries defies the imagination when evaluated as a cooperative enterprise. The cooperation of agents in a market, however, requires neither that such agents understand the structure nor that they transcend ordinary precepts of morality in their behavior. What it does require is an appropriate "constitutional context" – a proper structure of rules, along with some arrangements for their enforcement.

17. It is certainly possible to read Buchanan and Tullock (1962) in just this light. More recently, Dougherty (2001), Cooter and Siegel (2010), and Dougherty and Edward

(2011) have presented persuasive evidence, and made theoretical contributions, that considerably extend this view.

18. Some thinkers have been quite scornful of the idea of hypothetical consent. See, for example, Hume (1976), who says of tacit or implicit consent implied by residency:

> Can we seriously say, that a poor peasant or artisan has a free choice to leave his country, when he knows no foreign language or manners, and lives, from day to day, by the small wages which he acquires? We may as well assert that a man, by remaining in a vessel, freely consents to the dominion of the master; though he was carried on board while asleep, and must leap into the ocean and perish, the moment he leaves her.

19. Tomasi (2011), Chapter 5, quoting Hayek: "We should regard as the most desired order of society the one we would choose if we knew that our initial position in it would be determined purely by chance (such as the fact of our being born into a particular family)." Hayek (1940, footnote on p. 132)

20. See Simon (2001) for more about the source and context of Montesquieu's thought in this area. See Liebell (2009) for the connections in Montesquieu between Locke and later thinkers.

21. One institutional arrangement that appears to allow, or at least not prohibit, exit is federalism. See Buchanan (1995) and Epstein (1992). For a review of Buchanan's contributions, see Lynch (2004). More recently, on contract and exit, see North, Wallis, and Weingast (2013).

22. The story of "Caesar's wife" comes from Plutarch's "Parallel Lives," specifically the life of Caesar. The handsome young Clodius, who had tried to visit Caesar's wife Pompeia during the rites of Bona, when only women were allowed in the house, was almost caught. But he escaped. Clodius was charged with sacrilege, for having entered the house, though of course his real crime was in seducing Pompeia. Caesar's reaction was two-fold, reflecting the importance of different levels of "proof:"

> Caesar divorced Pompeia at once, but when he was summoned to testify at the trial, he said he knew nothing about the matters with which Clodius was charged. His statement appeared strange, and the prosecutor therefore asked, "Why, then, didst thou divorce thy wife?" "Because," said Caesar, "I thought my wife ought not even to be under suspicion."

23. This statement will be elaborated later. But the proof is referred to as the Gibbard-Satterthwaite theorem, after Gibbard (1973) and Satterthwaite (1975).

24. Quoted in Black (1958: 182).

25. This problem was recognized long ago, and forms the basis of some useful recent scholarship. Madison was skeptical of what he called "parchment barriers," or written rules that were unlikely to have much effect. And Barry Weingast has repeatedly argued (see Weingast, 2013, for a collection) that constitutions must be "self-enforcing," or that people find it in their objective interests to cooperate after the fundamental transformation, because the fact that "we have an agreement!" is not sufficient to ensure compliance.

26. This particular translation comes from Conaway (1902).

27. This emphasis on explicit barriers to majority action would appear to contradict the claim (North, Wallis, and Weingast, 2009; Weingast, 2013) that constitutions must be self-enforcing. After all, how could an anti-majoritarian rule be self-enforcing in a democracy? Dahl (1963) long ago made this point. But the contradiction is not as stark as it might first appear. A transient majority might

find it in its own interest to forebear the immediate use of power because it values the general protection of minority rights since members of that majority are themselves sometimes members of "the" minority because of cycling majorities and coalitions.

3 CHOOSING IN GROUPS: AN INTUITIVE PRESENTATION

1. As Kreps (2012:22) puts it: "The standard model makes no attempt to answer the question, "Where do preferences come from?' Are they something innate to the individual, given (say) genetically? Or are they a product of experience? And if they are a product of experience, is that experience primarily social in character?" Perhaps the most rationalistic description of "accounting for tastes" is Becker (1998). An interesting summary of the issues of where preferences "come from," at a deep level, is Dietrich and List (2012).

2. This "noninformational" aspect of preferences is described in detail by Dietrich and List (2011). We are assuming that the preference rankings are based on "taste" and are therefore relatively invariant, at least in the period within which a decision must be made. But Dietrich and List's work represents an important advance in our understanding of how preferences might "change," even excluding changes in expressed rankings due to new information under conditions of uncertainty.

3. If the period were a month and the choices were Apples, Broccoli, or Jelly Beans, the relative nutritional value of the foods might become important. Nutrition, unlike taste, is subject to "fact of the matter" considerations. Michael Munger once conducted a class exercise along just these lines at a faculty seminar (with John Aldrich) in Cuba, and the discussion quickly devolved into a discussion of nutrition, rather than taste.

4. Game theorists will recognize this as the "common knowledge" assumption. As experimenters have shown (see, for example, Eckel and Holt, 1989), the condition is important in the sense that the knowledge of participants can dramatically affect the outcome.

5. That raises another question: given that Justin might vote strategically, might Eugene strategically *not* propose his "strategic" agenda? It is indeterminate. But it is interesting to speculate. Suppose that the choosers had read the entire chapter. The person who suggested the tricky agenda to Eugene may have been Willow, because if Eugene proposes that agenda, and Justin votes strategically, Willow gets to eat her first preference, Carrots, for lunch while the two men fuss at each other.

6. As James Buchanan (1954) put it in a review of a book by Kenneth Arrow (1951):

   Social rationality appears to imply that the choice-making processes produce results which are indicated to be "rational" by the ordering relation, that is, the social welfare function. *But why should this sort of social rationality be expected?* ...Rationality or irrationality as an attribute of the social group implies the imputation to that group of an organic existence apart from that of its individual components. (p. 116, emphasis added).

7. A "paradox" is a surprising or unexpected result implied by an innocuous set of assumptions or premises. Perhaps the most famous ancient "paradoxes" were those designed by Zeno of Elea, about 450 BC. They are similar to Zen koans, aids to contemplation or reflection rather than actual results derived from premises. We use "paradox" more in the sense intended by Thomas Schwartz (1986), who notes that

the word derives from the Greek words *para*, meaning "beyond" or "other than," and *doxa*, meaning "belief" or "thought." In this sense, a paradox is a surprising result derived from seemingly innocuous premises. The more surprising the result, or the more innocuous the premises, the more paradoxical the conclusion.

8. McLean and London (1990), page 100.
9. Given the importance of common knowledge in inferring group preference orderings, in real politics, experienced political players will attempt to hide their preferences. Lyndon Johnson as a U.S. Senator was famous (Caro, 2003, Volume II) for two things: First, he had an almost supernatural ability to count votes. Second, he had a fanatical dedication to disguising his own views. Other members, sometimes of opposing views, may have had long conversations with him in which they convinced themselves that he agreed with them but later found it difficult to recall exactly what he said that gave them that impression.

4 THE ANALYTICS OF CHOOSING IN GROUPS

1. The first clear connection between emotions and evolution was Darwin (1872). However, the theory has advanced enormously. For a review of the relation between emotions and "evolved" politics, see Waal (2007). On the way that morals might be "chosen," by an implicit contractual agreement, see Gauthier (1986, 1990).
2. This might not be true for binary relations, and is certainly not a general property. For example, we might be considering (properties, people, and "is owned by") as our ordered triple. The first set might be all the property listings in a town, and the second set might be all the people in the town. In that case, "is owned by" would be work like this: {House at 12 Elm St} is owned by {John Smith}. The S connects properties with people, and properties and people are disjoint sets. Our use of binary relations is thus special, because we are comparing two elements of the same set to each other.
3. Davidson, et al. (1955) famously illustrated that such a preference ordering could not be rational, because it is not biologically adaptive. Substantively, intransitive preferences would allow the money pump paradox: If the chooser were willing to pay (suppose) 5 cents for every improvement implied by his preferences, he would pay 5 cents to get from C to B, then 5 cents to get from B to A, then 5 cents to get from A to C, and so on, forever. The chooser would dissipate all of his wealth in exchanges, each of which make him "better off" but end up with exactly the same alternative he started with. It can't be rational, or so the reasoning goes, to spend all of one's wealth like this and get nothing in return, always making himself slightly better off, until he ran out of money. There are logical problems here. There are some deeper problems, technical issues of social choice, which we are going to pass over, also. The reader would need to understand these issues in some detail before doing work in social choice theory. A very solid introduction can be found in Allan M. Feldman and Robert Serrano (2005), *Welfare Economics and Social Choice Theory*. An immediate concern for the present subject would be the extension of "transitivity" to "quasi-transitivity" or "acyclicity," both of which are defined on p. 15 of Feldman and Serrano (2005). See also Austen-Smith and Banks (1999), p. 4 and p. 30, and Schwartz (1986), p. 48 and following.

4. Completeness sometimes is called "connectedness," for just this reason. It is possible to use a binary relation to connect all elements of the set of alternatives, so that nothing is left out.

5. The combinations calculation uses the standard formula $(N!/[k!(N-k)!])$, where N is the number of alternatives (in this case, 5), and k is the number in each comparison group (in this case, 2). Then we must add the comparison of each alternative with itself, so the correct formula is $(N!/[k!(N-k)!]) + N$.

6. It may be necessary to reverse the order of the alternatives, of course. For example, if D is preferred to C, we might write $D \succeq C$ instead of $\succeq$.

7. It is important to remember that the utility function only represents preferences (weak orders), not actual choice. To model choice in consumer economics one would also information on prices and income. The utility function is just a convenient way of capturing the weak ordering over alternatives, which even for relatively small number of alternatives can be quite complicated.

8. Three useful sources on representation are Rader (1963), Katzner (1970), and Mas-Colell, Whinston, and Green (1995).

9. An interesting paper on the shared features of preference orders that are not representable is Beardon, et al. (2002).

10. Downs (1957) was the first to use "rational ignorance" in this context, with voters having attenuated incentives to learn the information they would need to vote correctly. Other interesting work, taking a variety of perspectives, includes Akerlof and Dickens (1982), Brennan and Lomasky (1993), and Caplan (2007). Others are much more optimistic, including Popkin (1979, 1994), Wittman (1989, 1995), and Lupia and McCubbins (1998).

11. Duncan Black most clearly made this distinction, in his book *The Theory of Committees and Elections* (1958).

12. Criticism of this approach (see, for example, Lewin 1991) has focused on the first assumption, arguing that in fact citizens may well (sometimes) be public interested. However, if we change the first motivational assumption to its most extreme form, "Citizens only want to act in the public interest, though they have private interests as consumers," the cost of information and the value of simple political messages as persuasion are unchanged. What matters is the aggregate *consequence* of individual action. "Public interest" voting cannot be effective if the voters have sharply diminished incentives to acquire accurate information. Very few citizens are aware of even the most basic political facts, and they have only cursory knowledge of how government works (Caplan, 2007). Less than half can name their Representative much less identify her voting record or issue positions. Even fewer can give a coherent attribution of their own political ideology in terms of its specific policy implications (Feldman and Conover, 1986, 1984, 1983, 1982; Caplan, 2007). The rationally ignorant public-interest voter is essentially indistinguishable from the rationally ignorant self-interest voter. Rationality need not imply self-interest, but it clearly does imply, as an empirical matter, that voters have little idea of how policy works and what candidates will do once they are in office.

13. The word "ideological" has many meanings. One view is that ideology is a heuristic, or means of economizing on the costs of gathering information (Down, 1957; Hinich and Munger, 1994; Popkin, 1994). But there are many other meanings (Converse, 1964; Sartori, 1994). One might model such issues as inducing

"lexicographic" preferences in voters, or use some other representation. However, such representations exhibit discontinuities, and are therefore not utility *functions*. The problem of representation is quite general, and if the conditions required to qualify for "representation" are weakened the set of preferences for which a mathematical relation can be substituted is large. For a review, see Herden and Levin (2012).

14. Garrett Hardin wrote his famous essay "The Tragedy of the Commons" about this kind of good with group ownership and no exclusion. Elinor Ostrom (2005, 2009) and others have shown that the special institutions of group choice in common pool resource settings take careful consideration, because they are different from either market settings or standard political settings.

15. See Buchanan (1965) on "club good." Mueller (2003) gives a literature review and context.

16. For a review of the "market failure" literature, beginning with Pigou and Bator, see Munger (2000).

17. It is important to distinguish "group" or social choice from government action. A group action may be chosen by mutual consent, as in the case of a private club with membership dues and provisions for exit. A government is characterized by its use of coercion to enforce agreements, or to force citizens to obey commands.

18. The simplified approach taken here to derive equilibrium conditions is similar to that presented in Mueller (2003), and Hinich and Munger (1994).

19. In other words, the level of consumption may be determined by the weight one receives in the SWF. But at the margin, all that is required is allocative efficiency, not social justice.

20. There are some important qualifications of this pessimistic conclusion. For examples, and a review of the literature, see Epple and Romano (1996a; 1996b; and 2003).

21. Plott (1991), p. 905. To be fair, Plott was conceiving the "fundamental equation" as a description of the set of theories about *economic* behavior, and was describing how experimental methods might serve to distinguish among theories and test their implications. But Plott was one of the founders of spatial theory, and an early president of the Public Choice Society, so requiring that the "fundamental equation" be restricted to academic economics seems unjustified.

22. See for example Dijkstra, Van Assen and Stokman (2008).

5 POLITICS AS SPATIAL COMPETITION

1. For reviews, see Riker (1961), Enelow and Hinich (1990) and Ferejohn(1995). It is common to credit other scholars, especially Hotelling (1926) with the origins of spatial theory, but this is simply incorrect. Hotelling developed (superficially) a notion of spatial competition by firms with linear transportation costs, but he did nothing to represent utility functions of voters as "spatial." In addition, the idea of spatial competition was much better outlined by von Thünen (1966), in 1826. Therefore, either Hotelling did not originate spatial theory, and that credit belongs to Black and Downs, or Hotelling's work is spatial theory, and entirely was anticipated by von Thünen. On the problem of using utilty functions to measure, and compare, desires of citizens in democracies, see List (2004, 2011).

2. William F. Buckley famously described the idea of conservatism, in the U.S. at least, this way: "A conservative is someone who stands athwart history, yelling Stop, at a time when no one is inclined to do so, or to have much patience with those who so urge it." Buckley (1955).

3. Green and Shapiro (1994), among others, have argued that the hybrid nature of some empirical work discredits the spatial model. The problem for such critiques is that it takes a model to beat a model. Using only affect as an explanation for voting behavior simply means that the act (voting for candidate F) is being explained by an answer to a survey question ("I like candidate F"). Not surprisingly, scholars consistently find that voters vote for candidates that those voters say they like. But this correlation is in no way an explanation.

4. See Rabinowitz (1978), MacDonald and Rabinowitz (1987, 1993), Rabinowitz and MacDonald (1989). For some tests of such models see Merrill and Grofman (1999), as well as the work they review.

5. Clearly, there is a large difference between indifference and ignorance. But the difference plays out in the way that new problems become issues. The zero salience weight solution covers both kinds of "nonissues," in static situations.

6. This "nonuniqueness" seems strange, but it is not an uncommon situation in measurement problems. For example, the concept of temperature can be conceived as a large ordered set, whose elements range from very cold to very hot. The specific units we use to "measure" temperature, as well as the zero point in the scale, are arbitrary, however. The exception is the Kelvin scale, which does have a nonarbitrary zero point, corresponding to -273° Celsius, the temperature where Brownian motion ceases completely. But zero degrees Fahrenheit is quite arbitrary as a level of temperature. Zero degrees Celsius corresponds to 32° Fahrenheit; 100° Celsius is the same as 212° Fahrenheit. Consequently, both Celsius and Fahrenheit measure the same phenomenon (ambient heat energy), so clearly neither is unique. Measurement theorists say the two scales "are unique only up to an affine transformation.

7. This process of "constitution" has been discussed at great length earlier, but it is important here also. It is possible, and even likely, that three people with such disparate ideas about the best party budget would not be able to create a binding constitution, and would break up as a group. While this possibility is real, we will not consider it again, taking it for granted that the groups we work with are "constituted" and that agreements are binding.

8. By "unique," we mean that no person has more than one ideal point. Several (or all) members may share a single ideal point, however.

9. The mean may be important if voters try to "balance" in elections, as suggested by Alesina and Rosenthal (1995). The mode is important in a plurality rule system, if alternatives are discrete.

10. "CONVENTION. When n, the number of members, is odd, let us denote $O_{1/2 \cdot (n+1)}$ by O_{med}. When n is even and the chairman's optimum is at $O_{1/2n}$ or lower, let us denote $O_{1/2n}$ by O_{med}; or when n is even and the chairman's optimum is at $O_{1/2 \cdot (n+1)}$ or higher, let us denote $O_{1/2 \cdot (n+1)}$ by O_{med}. Then the results we have arrived at can be summarized as follows:

THEOREM. If the members' curves are single-peaked, O_{med} will be able to get a simple majority over any of the other motions $a_1, a_2, a_3, \ldots a_m$ put forward." (Black, 1958, p. 18).

11. Rasmussen Reports, "Health Care Law: 58% Expect Health Care To Cost More Under Obamacare." www.rasmussenreports.com/public_content/politics/current_events/healthcare/health_care_law

12. This is a common problem in majority rule cycles. There is never a majority clearly in favor of any policy for very long. While the political conflict was much more complex than our depiction here, there is some evidence (see, e.g. Russett and Shye, 1993) that precisely the sorts of preferences that would lead to a cycle in majority rule voting outcomes can be found in public opinion surveys. In the 1960s, Barry Goldwater and his supporters made very explicit arguments that the United States should either fight an all-out war in Vietnam or withdraw all troops immediately. The "middle" course, a limited action where the United States provided a steadily escalating number of advisors and war materiel to the Army of the Republic of Vietnam, was (for the Goldwater faction) the worst alternative. The preferences implied by this perspective are not single-peaked: the outcome implied by a significant faction with non-single-peaked preferences is a majority rule cycle.

13. The best counterargument for Riker's indictment of populism is probably a focus on arriving at judgments rather than choosing based on judgments already made. Coleman and Ferejohn (1986) point out that voting may be the only way of making good judgments. Their defense of "populism" rests on its ability to identify the right thing to do, just as Rousseau argued. "The desirability of a voting rule will then depend on its reliability – the extent to which the collective judgments it generates converge with what is in fact the correct judgment" (Coleman and Ferejohn, 1986, pp. 16–17). This argument is extended and qualified by Ladha (1996) and Ladha and Miller (1996); for substantial extensions see List and Goodin (2001). A key difficulty with the argument is that it requires choices between exactly two mutually exclusive alternatives. If there are three or more alternatives, then voting on judgments is subject to the problem of cycling majorities, as the two examples presented here have shown.

6 TWO DIMENSIONS: ELUSIVE EQUILIBRIUM

1. The more important an issue, the more "salient" for the member's decision about how to vote. But only relative salience matters, if spatial utility functions are ordinal. The reason is that our measures of utility must be scale-invariant, unique only up to an order-preserving transformation. So, for example, if issue 1 has a salience of 2 and issue 2 has a salience weight of 4, then 2 is twice as salient as 1. But if issue 1 had a salience of 63, and issue 2 had a salience weight of 126, exactly the same *relative* salience (2 is twice as salient as 1) would be implied. The absolute scales are irrelevant; only the ratio matters.

2. Why would preferences be nonseparable? Lacy (2001a; 2001b), and Lacy and Niou (2013) give both background and examples. The issues could be linked if the projects affect each other. For example, a voter might favor more spending on flood control levees, but only if an upstream dam is not built. Or members could want a balanced budget, so that increased spending on education is only acceptable if spending can be cut on garbage collection or police protection. That is, the activities or public goods could be "substitutes" (if you have one, you don't need the other) or "complements" (consumed together) in a sense that we have yet to make clear. Finally, as Hinich and Munger (1994) argued, issues can be nonseparable if there is an underlying

left-right "ideological" space that organizes political conflict in the society. Some useful extensions to the "ideology as nonseparability" argument can be found in Asay (2008).

3. More correctly, the Cartesian product is a way of creating a new set by combining several sets, and taking exactly one element of each of the constituent sets to create an element of the new set. So, each element of the set we call "2 dimensional space" is made up of an element from dimension 1 and one element from dimension 2. These could be associated in all sorts of ways, but for spatial models, it is convenient to preserve the ordered and continuous nature of the underlying dimensions.

4. In this case, a "log roll" would involve two members who have a disagreement on policy, and a disagreement on salience. The first might "sell" his vote on the issue he cares least about, in exchange for the other member's vote on the issue she cares least about. If there is some way that the exchange can be monitored and enforced, then both members are better off with the exchange and the strategic vote. The vote-trading idea is developed at much greater length in Buchanan and Tullock, 1962, and the mechanisms for enforcing exchanges over longer periods are discussed in Weingast and Marshall, 1985.

5. This is a point of fundamental importance, both in rational choice theory and political psychology. One important recent development is the measurement of preferences that appear to drift or change depending on context (Zaller, 1992). However, this "framing" effect is precisely observationally equivalent to nonseparability under many circumstances, as Lacy (2001a, 2001b) has argued. See also Braman (2006).

6. A very interesting treatment of the relation between policy choices and institutional choices, using nonseparable preferences, is Finke (2009). Endersby and Galatas (1998) analyze several competing sets of connections, or nonseparable unifying principles, that one might use to understand voter evaluation of party platforms in the 1992 British election.

7. See, for example, Lacy (2001a, 2001b).

8. See also McKelvey (1976a, 1976b), Schwartz (1977), Enelow and Hinich (1984b), and Epple and Kadane (1990).

9. "Germaneness" rules require that amendments can be made only along the dimension(s) proposed in the original legislation. Non-germane amendments are called "riders," and can involve changes in budget or statute language in policies other than that taken up by the original bill. For background on the history of germaneness rules in the U.S. Congress, see Bach (1982). A difficulty with endogenous selection of a germaneness rule is that it may inherit the instability properties (if those exist) of the full multi-dimensional choice problem. See Humes (1993).

10. One other solution concept, the "uncovered set" (Miller, 1980; Feld et al., 1987), is commonly seen in technical articles. The definition of the "uncovered" set is the set of all feasible policy alternatives u such that, for all other feasible points y either (i) u beats y in a majority rule election, or (ii) there exists a feasible alternative $\tilde{y}$ such that u beats $\tilde{y}$ beats y in a majority rule election. The uncovered set can be, at most, the Pareto set, but it can be much smaller. If it is a singleton, the uncovered set is the Condorcet winner. For a review, see Mueller (1989). Considerable background and extensions can be found in Austen-Smith and Banks (2005), and Schofield (2008). There are several other solution concepts, including the yolk, the heart, and the Banks set, that are beyond the scope of this book. For more information, see

McKelvey (1986), Austen-Smith and Banks (1999, 2005), and Schofield (1993, 2008). For reviews of the technical literature, see Miller (1995), Heckelman and Miller, (2014), and Schofield (2006).

11. For details, see Coughlin and Palfrey (1985) and Holcombe (2003).

12. The idea of the win set can be somewhat more complex than the presentation here, especially when applied to a finite set of alternatives using preference orders instead of spatial utility functions. For more precise definitions and some extensions see Feld, et al. (1987) and Feld and Grofman (1991).

13. The most intuitive description of the difference is probably Shepsle and Weingast (1981).

14. The "theorem" is actually a collective effort, produced by Plott (1967), Kramer (1973), McKelvey (1976; 1979; 1986) Schofield (1978; 1980; 1984), McKelvey and Schofield (1986; 1987), Cox (1987), Banks (1995), Saari (1996) and Austen-Smith and Banks (1999; Chapter 5), to name only those from the 20th century. For a more recent review, see Schofield (2006).

15. The clearest statement of the "chaos theorem" comes from Schofield (2006):

> For social choice, the chaos theorem is presented for a voting rule D, with specified voters preferences. If D is collegial, in the sense that there is a collegium, then the core, Core(f), of the social choice rule, f, will generally exist. If D is non-collegial, then there is an integer, w(D), called the "chaos dimension," which characterizes D in the following sense: If the dimension of the space, X, exceeds w(D), then the chaotic domain, Chaos(f), of the social choice rule, f, will be almost the whole of X.

(Schofield, 2006: 5). There is an important sense in which this instability is an example of a more general indeterminacy of outcomes in games where there is disagreement over division of losses and gains. For very general but intuitive treatments of this problem, see Myerson (1991) and Brams and Taylor (2000).

16. A growing experimental literature on the "Pareto set," and the outcomes of voting processes in the laboratory, bears on this question. The original work was Fiorina and Plott (1978). For more recent (1987), Eckel and Holt (1989), McKelvey and Ordeshook (1990), and the papers in Palfrey (1991), especially Plott (1991b). For a very different (but potentially important) approach to mapping out patterns of positions taken by parties, see Kollman, Miller, and Page (1992).

17. A very useful summary of the "chaos" results, as well as an intuitive description of their importance, can be found in Austen-Smith and Banks (1999), Chapter 6.

18. There is some question whether the "distributive" efficiency form of legislative organization implied by the Shepsle-Weingast work actually explains the institutions we observe. For an aggressively opposing view, see Krehbiel (1991). For a more recent review and some extensions, see Alt and Shepsle (1998) and Diermeier and Krehbiel (2002).

19. A median in all directions, if it exists, is the intersection of dimensional medians, (or an element of the closed interval of same), but the reverse is not true. Enelow and Hinich (1983a) sketched the definition given here and McKelvey and Schofield (1987) stated it definitively..

20. In principle, there might be an infinite number of possible "issues." But we have elsewhere defined an issue as having at least one voter have a positive salience (someone has to think it matters). Both the problem of which problems are issues and the problem of adding "new" issues are discussed in Hinich and Munger (1994; 2008).

21. Having a salience term that changes from zero to some positive value is a way of introducing a "new issue." For more involved examples of new issues see Hinich and Munger (2008) or Lacy and Niou (2012).
22. Technically $a_{12} = a_{21}$ means that the **A** matrix is symmetric. Intuitively, it means that the effect of the expected level of one policy on the marginal value of another is the same, regardless of which policy is fixed first. It is worth noting that there is nothing inherent in the model that requires **A** to be symmetric, however, and an interesting area for future research would be to consider the implications if order of consideration determines marginal valuation for this reason. Finally, in order for indifference curves to be ellipses, it must be true that $a_{11} \times a_{22} - a_{12} \times a_{21} > 0$ Since this condition has no obvious intuitive content for political preferences, we will simply mention it in passing.
23. Generally, that means that $\sqrt[n]{x} = x^{1/n}$. So the "1/2th root" of x is x squared, and "cube root" of x is the number r such that $r^3 = x$, and so on.
24. There are important theoretical issues in "representing" preferences in a verisimilous manner, and a number of scholars have raised questions about the quadratic form of utility function. See Eguia (2013) and Bogomolnaia and Laslier (2007) for reviews. See Grynaviski and Corrigan (2006) for an interesting discussion of empirical issues involved in estimating actual spatial preferences.
25. For evolving interpretations of this result, see Davis, DeGroot, and Hinich (1972), Kramer (1973), McKelvey (1976a, 1976b, 1986), Schofield (1978a), Slutsky (1979), Cohen and Matthews (1980), and Enelow and Hinich (1983a, 1984b).
26. Well, sort of. For the real proof, see Davis, DeGroot and Hinich (1972) and McKelvey (1976a, 1976b).

7 THE COLLECTIVE CHOICE PROBLEM: IMPOSSIBILITY

1. It is tempting to think this could be an infinite regress, with a step where people decide how to decide how to decide how to decide. However, the fourth remove is rarely (possibly never) a conscious choice. The kinds of people who encounter each other and might cooperate are the product of culture, history, and a strategically random path-dependent process of aggregation. Migration, language, and culture are all interesting, of course, but they are much closer to emergent processes than "deciding."
2. Technically, this is an irreflexive combinations problem. In principle, for some binary relations it might be necessary to treat A b B and B b A as separate cases, but that is not necessary here. Further, we do not consider A b A because the binary relation $\succ$ is not reflexive; we assume that A≃A so A≻A is not defined.
3. An interesting application of this idea is Durant and Weintraub (2013).
4. The first edition of Arrow's book was published in 1951. But the corrected version of both teh theorem and the proof date to the second edition, 1963.
5. Of course, you would have to round down to the next smallest whole number for odd numbers. That is, if there are 13 citizens, the majority is (13/2) = 6.5, rounded down to 6, plus 1 equals 7.
6. For example, if there are 100 people in the group, and we take any group of 51 as being decisive, there are 9.89×10^{28} different majorities (using the permutations formula of 100 take 51: 100!/49!). And that's only taking exactly 51 as the majority. There is no such thing as "the" majority, in voting.

7. Generally we think of "private" decisions (What will I have for lunch? What shoes will I wear with this outfit?) as very different from "group" decisions (What is the appropriate budget for education? What is the right speed limit on limited access highways?). But distinguishing private and group decisions begs the question. Apparent differences among "kinds" of choices are caused by differences in enfranchisement and aggregation mechanisms, not necessarily by inherent properties of the choices themselves. Lunches and shoes plausibly could be collectively chosen (as in the military or in a school with a dress code). Similarly, levels of spending and speeding might be picked by individuals, at least in principle. Government vouchers could be applied toward the bill at a private school of a family's choice. Drivers might drive as fast as they like on highways, with government road crews occasionally clearing the mangled remains.

8. There are many statements of Arrow's paradox. Ours is closest in spirit to that of Riker (1982, p. 18). An important general discussion, and some extensions, can be found in Sen (1970).

9. The version of these characteristics we will use is adapted from Mueller (1989), itself adapted from Vickrey (1960).

10. The equivalence of Pareto and unanimity is the subject of some debate. See Dougherty and Edward (2011).

11. This statement is too strong. It is quite possible that societies are locked into conventions that nearly everyone knows are not Pareto optimal. See Schelling (1960), Lewis (1969), North (1981, 1990), Arthur (1989), and Denzau and North (1994).

12. More recently Mueller (2003) has again described the implications of the "menu of choice" of violations of the Arrow assumptions. And Saari (2008; 56–59) raises some interesting questions about whether the Arrow definition of "dictator" is useful in the context of the theorem.

13. Portions of this section are adapted from Munger (2010)

14. Cited in Saari (2008), p. 60, from McLean (2003).

15. Munger (2010) notes that Saari repeatedly recognizes what he calls the "curse of dimensionality," but Munger claims that Saari underestimates the power of the strategic proliferation of dimensions, along the lines of Riker's "heresthetics." (Riker, 1982; 1986)

16. It is important to note that rules requiring a fixed $K/N < 50\%$ vote apply only to access, and can allow but two alternatives: Reject the proposal, or pass the proposal along for further consideration. There is no inherent problem with access decisions if multiple alternatives "pass," since all this means is that the alternatives (bills, court cases, etc.) then continue through the process for disposition. The subject of concern in this book is for making a single choice among mutually exclusive alternatives. Consequently, we will restrict our attention to $K/N > 50\%$.

17. The KMVT we present is greatly simplified, compared with the more rigorous treatments in Slutsky (1979). Slutsky's analysis has a different object, however, in that it compares mechanisms for achieving Pareto optimality in public goods provision with endogenous tax shares. The reader interested in the properties of different majorities required for decisiveness should also consult May (1952) and Sen (1970).

18. Quoted in Black (1958, p. 182), quoting from J. Mascart's *La Vie... de Borda* (2000).

19. Strategic voting is generally beyond the scope of this book. See Cox (1997) on the importance and breadth of strategic action in politics.

20. For an in-depth treatment of approval voting, see Brams and Fishburn (1984), and Brains and Nagel (1991). For some interesting background on approval voting, see Cox (1984b).
21. On the other hand, if each group selects only its first alternative as being acceptable, A will win, receiving eight votes compared with seven for B and six for C. Consequently, one might expect the middle and last groups to vote strategically, and include B and C in the acceptable category. This would ensure at worst a second-place rather than worst result for voters in those groups.
22. On "independence of path," see Plott (1973), Parks (1976), and Ferejohn and Grether (1977); on "multi-stage choice processes," see Schwartz (1986). For quite a different interpretation of the problem of social choice in. general, see Nitzan and Paroush (1985).
23. Of course, adding or dropping alternatives could change the outcome for majority rule, or for that matter almost any other decision rule also. Changing the set of alternatives, rather than just their relative rankings, creates a different decision problem altogether.
24. The literature on proportional representation is enormous. For reviews, see Taagapera and Shugart (1989), Gallagher (1992), Laver and Schofield (1990), Laver and Shepsle (1996), Cox (1997), and Colomer (2003).
25. McKelvey and Ordeshook (1980) compare the divide the dollar and the voting majority bargaining games in an experiment. For a review see Diermeier and Morton (2005).
26. For two sides of the "bargaining" problem, see Baron and Ferejohn (1989) versus Laver, et al., (2011). For a broader review, see Laver and Schofield (1990), Laver and Shepsle (1994), and Bassi (2008).

8 UNCERTAINTY

1. The reason to put it this odd way, that the electron doesn't know, rather than that the observer can't know, is that Heisenberg's "effect" should be understood as being present in any interaction between classical and quantum matter; the "observer" is not necessary for the uncertainty to be inherent in "wave-like" systems. This issue is discussed at greater length in Landau and Lifshitz (1981), p. 47–8.
2. As Heisenberg put it:

> It can be expressed in its simplest form as follows: One can never know with perfect accuracy both of those two important factors which determine the movement of one of the smallest particles – its position and its velocity. It is impossible to determine accurately *both* the position and the direction and speed of a particle *at the same instant*. Heisenberg, W., *Die Physik der Atomkerne*, Taylor & Francis, 1952, p. 30.

As written here, the discussion confuses the true Heisenberg principle with a distinct, though related, concept, the observer effect. The quantum interpretation of the problem is more in line with the "many worlds" interpretation: the observation need not have an effect on the system, though it may reveal which of the possible parallel universes the observer finds himself to live in.
3. Again, the more recent interpretations of quantum phenomena and uncertainty do not require the interaction of the observer/measurement act with uncertainty.

The uncertainty is *intrinsic*, and has no outside cause. In simple terms, even the electron does not know for sure. See, for example, Erhart, et al (2012).

4. For more information, see Gillespie (1993; 92).

5. Brennan and Petit (2006) make this argument persuasively, and at length. In particular, they cite the famous peer pressure experiment (Munger and Harris, 1989) where people were much more likely to wash their hands in a public restroom if there was at least one other person in the restroom. Thus, according to Brennan and Petit, the observation effect may be based on what they call "esteem."

6. See for example Davis and Silver (2003), and the work they review.

7. There are at least two views of the difference between "measuring preferences" and "answering survey questions" that would question the value of the survey approach. The first is the "considerations" view (Zaller and Feldman, 1992; Zaller, 1992), where the considerations primed most recently, either in the experience of the respondent or by the previous question in the survey, affect the answer. The other is the "nonseparability" view (Lacy, 2001a, 2001b), which argues that preferences expressed are highly contingent on values that have been established, intentionally or not, on other relevant dimensions of policy.

8. A good review of the issues involved in attributing the source of the uncertainty can be found in Morton (1999; pp. 172–178). There are many broader accounts of the origins and attributes of uncertainty in politics (see, for a review, the essays in Burden, 2003, and especially the paper by Jones, Talbert, and Potosky, 2003).

9. This is much more likely to be true in smaller, local races than in better-funded statewide campaigns. Competent pollsters will largely agree on results.

10. If the object were to be exactly right, of course, the candidates would choose the modal median. However, the object is to be closest, so the mean median is the optimal platform. Nevertheless, there may not be any well-defined middle in a multi-dimensional space of legislator ideal points, as Goff and Grier (1993) point out.

11. Another possibility, beyond the scope of this book, is that the shape of the distribution is sharply bimodal, so that the identity of the median voter is highly discontinuous with respect to small changes in turnout. Further, the issue of how information is obtained is difficult. It is quite possible that campaigns all jealously guard their private knowledge of voter location. For an attempt to model this situation, see Ferejohn and Noll (1978).

12. For early work on the importance of the mean preference under uncertainty, see Davis and Hinich, 1968; for a more detailed discussion and proofs of these results, see Calvert, 1985, Theorems 3–7; and Wittman, 1990. Two recent surveys of this work, with important extensions using different techniques, are Bendor, et al. (2011) and Serraa (2010).

13. As Calvert points out: "Candidates … may choose very different platforms in equilibrium if they have very different ideas about the probabilities of winning. However, this should properly be regarded not as a feature of the electoral institutions themselves, but as a direct result of the candidates' disagreement" (1985, p. 80). To the extent that candidates have a reputation in one particular part of the policy space, of course, an attempt to "move" can achieve a change in expected

platform, but at the cost of a substantial increase in perceived variance (Hinich and Munger, 1994).

14. For significant work on this point, see Ferejohn and Noll (1978), Ferejohn (1986), and Banks (1990, 1991).

15. It is quite possible that the distribution of expected positions is not symmetric, of course. A slightly different modification would allow the mean of the distribution of expected policy to differ from the candidate's announced positions. The latter possibility would require some prior distribution on candidate action, which might or might not be updated in response to new candidate messages. For one, relatively simple updating process using Bayes' rule, see Hinich and Munger (1994).

16. For some alternative ways of inducing voter beliefs over candidates, see Zaller (1992) or Jones (1994). Further, an important contribution to the experimental literature is the demonstration that voters may rely on endorsements or cues rather than direct experience (McKelvey and Ordeshook, 1985; Collier et al., 1987; Williams, 1994). The implication of this work is that elections may look as if all voters had accurate perceptions, even if only some have complete information. More broadly, on the origin of expected platform, see Bernhardt and Ingberman, 1985; Ferejohn, 1986; Banks, 1990; Austen-Smith, 1990; Enelow and Munger, 1993; or Hinich and Munger 1994. A recent paper that tries to take the utility loss problem to voters seriously is Roth (2013).

17. And he is still warm-blooded. For many voters, this is an important consideration. Edward can come across as cold, even if he is all sparkly when he gives speeches outside.

18. The particular formulation here is derived from the approach suggested by Richard Potthoff in extending equations 6.6 and 6.7 in Hinich and Munger (1997), p. 126. In particular, Potthoff is responsible for the explanation of the importance of equation 8.5 later in this text, and for the proofs of the results in this section.

19. The cutpoint is a hyperplane the removal of which causes two half spaces to be disconnected. Since the "space" here is a line, the hyperplane is a point. The political meaning of a cutpoint is that all voters to the left of the cutpoint are predicted to vote for one alternative, and all voters to the right of the cutpoint are predicted to vote for something else. Voters whose preferences fall on the cutpoint either flip a coin or abstain. Since the spatial model is deterministic, then voter choices are predicted as particular votes. In using real data, the prediction would generally be probabilistic.

20. As in the 'ideological' model, there exists a single dimension of political competition (Downs 1957; Poole and Rosenthal 1985b; Hinich and Munger 1994). However, the results do not depend on the dimension being called 'ideology.'

21. The more general form of this utility function would encompass numerous transforms of equations (1), so it might look like this:

$$U(i, j) = K_i - L_i (x_j - v_i)^2$$

Since we are interested in the difference between two candidates, of course, the K_i (constant term) drops out, and the L_i (scale term) is irrelevant to the solution. We have set $K_i = 0$ and $L_i = 1$ for all voters, for the sake of convenience, but any real numbers would serve just as well. The utility function we use is, for convenience, cardinally spatial, in that if $x_j = x_i$ (the candidate is located at the voter ideal point), then $U(\bullet)=0$. If $x_j \neq v_i$, then $U(\bullet)<0$. But the cardinal features of the utility function, reaching a maximum at zero, are an innocuous assumption, and could be dropped

22. We are skipping several steps, which are left as an exercise (8.3). But the steps involve completing the square, taking expectations, and then finishing with two tricks. First, four of the terms are constants, and factor down to $-(\mu_j - x_i)^2$. Second, all that remains is the term $E(\varepsilon^2)$. But this is the same as variance, or $\sigma^2=E[(\varepsilon^2)-E(\varepsilon)^2]$. The reason is that $E(\varepsilon)=0$, by assumption.

23. Several papers by James Adams (Adams, 1999; Adams and Merrill, 2006; Adams et al., 2010) give versions of this intuition with a variety types of uncertainty or probabilistic voting.

24. The intuition contained in the results in this section is clearly present in Bernhardt and Ingberman (1985) and Calvert (1985), and has been developed elsewhere by a number of authors. Perhaps the most interesting general treatment is Groseclose (2001).

25. The original, and more formal, version of this proof was done by Richard Potthoff in BMP. We also acknowledge helpful discussions with Emerson Niou.

26. Clearly, the "zero votes" claim is true only if some arbitrary stopping rule is used where the challenger moves first and the incumbent gets to move last. A more precise way to state the claim is this: the challenger knows that the incumbent's best response to any challenger platform will take all the challenger's votes away, unless the challenger moves again. This is precisely why there is no equilibrium, of course. We thank Tim Groseclose for pointing out that our original statement in this section was inaccurate. Interestingly, this same intuition attends the "follow the trailer" rule in yacht racing, described by Dixit and Nalebuff (1991, p. 10). If one boat has a substantial lead, it should always take the same tack as the trailing boat. That way, if the wind shifts, both boats will be affected in the same way, and there is no way for the trailing boat to catch up. The trailing boat's captain hopes the leading boat's captain will not match, as Dennis Conner failed to match in the America's Cup race in 1983, leading to the victory of the Australia II racing yacht.

27. It obviously makes little sense for the lower variance candidate to have the ability to move literally anywhere, yet keep a fixed variance of voters' perceptions of his or her policy position. Hinich and Munger (1994) present a model of a game in variance, where voters use Bayesian updating in their estimates of variance.

28. This is the argument made in Hinich and Munger (1991; 1994) in favor of a (relatively) fixed, or immobile, incumbent.

29. This version of the proof is due to Richard Potthoff, almost verbatim.

9 VOTING AS A COLLECTIVE ACTION PROBLEM

1. This may not be a true identity without the addition of fifth term, (enter booth/fill out ballot). This is a truly fine distinction, but consider the example brought up by Galatas (2008) of purposively cast blank ballots in Canadian provincial elections.

2. Theoretical and political justifications for Election Day Registration posited that the measure would increase turnout the most among low-income, low-participation groups, and while there was a small across the board increase, the biggest boost, say Brians and Grofman (1999, 2001) came among people with medium levels of income and education.

3. Jakee and Kim (2006) note that compulsory voting is likely to produce more "random" but correlated votes, causing information cascades that make voters much worse off than if they had stayed home. Munger (2013) examines a natural experiment found in a change in Chilean election law, which changed voting procedures in 2011 for "comunas" (municipalities).

4. In Australia, for example, there is a widely held opinion that the political parties depend on ignorant zombies trooping to the polls to vote, without knowledge or thought. This appeared in the Melbourne newspaper: "It is not compulsory in any other Western country – not the U.S. or Canada or Britain or, across the ditch, in New Zealand. Why are adult Australians treated like children?" Derryn Hinch, Broadcaster in Melbourne, Australia, quoted in *Melbourne Sunday Herald Sun*, October 9, 2005. However, this view is not universal, by any means. For background and history, see Birch (2009).

5. Downs (1957) and Riker and Ordeshook (1968) model indifference. Ordeshook (1969), Hinich and Ordeshook (1969, 1970), and Hinich, Ledyard, and Ordeshook (1972) extend the Downsian model to account for alienation.

6. We have also given short shrift to an important empirical perspective on the factors voters use in deciding among candidates: retrospective voting. According to this view (Key, 1966; Fiorina, 1989), voters evaluate the performance of the party or candidate now in office. If the incumbent has performed well (in the voters' judgment), he or she is returned to office. If the incumbent has botched things, voters vote for someone else, punishing poor performance after the fact. Retrospective voting does not completely contradict the classical spatial model, because there is an implicit comparison between the actual performance of incumbents and the expected performance of challengers. Still, the emphasis in the retrospective voting approach is clearly on the evaluation of the effectiveness of incumbents. See also Coate and Conlin (2004).

7. For a review of this literature, see Cox and Munger (1989) and Fraga and Hersh (2011).

8. Knack (1994) considers a variety of explanations for the effect of weather on turnout and outcomes, but finds little effect. Matsusaka and Palda (1999) likewise find few effects of broader measures of temperature and weather patterns. Merrifield (1993) and Schachar and Nalebuff (1999) do find some effects, but their measures are of mean differences in rainfall and simply be correlational rather than causal. The best work seems to be Gomez, Handsford, and Krause (2007), who suggest that deviation from normal precipitation figures causes the effect, rather than absolute levels of rain or snowfall.

9. Ferejohn and Fiorina (1974) and Fedderson (2004).

10. See also Barzel and Silberberg (1973).

11. Hinich (1981) goes further and conceives of voting as if it were an act of contribution. Contributions are usually thought of as monetary, but one can view the time and effort required to vote as a sacrifice by the voter for the sake of the candidate. Fiorina (1976) compares the "expressive" and investment-oriented, or "instrumental," motives for voting.

12. Fiedler and Unkelbach (2011) show that lottery ticket buyers are aware of differences in probabilities, and payoffs, and appear to respond in the direction implied by rationality. But lottery ticket buyers appear systematically to over-estimate their

chances of winning, and respond far more to changes in the value of the possible payoff than to changes in the probability. It is not clear if this difference is borne out in turnout decisions. If it were, the implication would be that voters would respond more to the net candidate differential than to changes in the probability of being decisive.

13. See Tullock (1967), Tollison, Crain, and Paulter (1975), and Silberman and Durden (1975). For a review, see Matsusaka and Palda (1993).

14. For a review of turnout over a longer period, see Aldrich (1976), Aldrich and Simon (1986), and Foster (1984).

15. As Aldrich (1993, p. 261) points out, "Turnout is a decision almost always made 'at the margin.'"

References

Aarts, Kees, and Bernhard Wessels. "Electoral Turnout." In *The European Voter: A Comparative Study of Modern Democracies*, edited by J. Thomassen. Oxford: Oxford University Press, 2005.

Abramson, Paul. *Politics in the Bible*. New Brunswick: Transaction Press, 2012.

Adams, James. "Policy Divergence in Multicandidate Probabilistic Spatial Voting." *Public Choice* 100 (1999): 103–22.

Adams, James, Samuel Merrill and Bernard Grofman. *A Unified Theory of Party Competition: a cross-national analysis integrating spatial and behavioral factors*. New York: Cambridge University Press, 2005.

Adams, James, Jay Dow, and III Samuel Merrill. "The Political Consequences of Alienation-Based and Indifference-Based Voter Abstention: Applications to Presidential Elections." *Political Behavior* 28 (2006): 65–86.

Adams, James, and Samuel Merrill. "Why Small, Centrist Third Parties Motivate Policy Divergence by Major Parties." *American Political Science Review* 100 (2006): 403–417.

Adams, James, Thomas Brunell, Bernard Grofman and Samuel Merrill. "Why Candidate Divergence Should be Expected to be Just as Great (or even Greater) in Competitive Seats as in Non-Competitive Ones." *Public Choice* 145, no. 3–4 (2010): 417–433.

Akerlof, George, and William Dickens. "The Economic Consequences of Cognitive Dissonance." *American Economic Review* (June 1982): 307–19.

Aldrich, John. "Some Problems in Testing Two Rational Models of Participation." *American Political Science Review* 20 (1976): 713–24.

Aldrich, John. *Before the Convention: Strategies and Choices in Presidential Nomination Campaigns*. Chicago: University of Chicago Press, 1980.

Aldrich, John. "A Spatial Model with Party Activists: Implications for Electoral Dynamics." *Public Choice* 41 (1983a): 63–100.

Aldrich, John. "A Downsian Spatial Model with Party Activism." *American Political Science Review* 77 (1983b): 974–90.

Aldrich, John. "Rational Choice and Turnout." *American Journal of Political Science* 37 (1993): 246–78.

Aldrich, John. *Why Parties? The Origin and Transformation of Party Politics in America.* Chicago: University of Chicago Press, 1995.

Aldrich, John, Jacob Montgomery and Wendy Wood. "Turnout as a Habit." *Political Behavior* 33 (2011): 4, 535–563.

Aldrich, John, and Dennis Simon. "Turnout in American National Elections." *Research in Micropolitics* 1 (1986): 271–301. Greenwich, CT: JAI Press.

Alesina, Alberto. "Credibility and Convergence in a Two-Party System with Rational Voters." *American Economic Review* 78 (1988): 796–80

Alesina, Alberto, and Howard Rosenthal. *Partisan Politics, Divided Government, and the Economy.* New York: Cambridge University Press, 1995.

Alt, James, and Kenneth Shepsle. "Rules, Restrictions, Constraints: Structure and Process in the New Institutional Economics." *Journal of Institutional and Theoretical Economics* 154 (1998): 735–44.

Ambrose, Stephen. *Undaunted Courage: Meriwether Lewis, Thomas Jefferson, and the Opening of the American West.* New York: Simon and Schuster, 2002.

Aristophanes. *The Frogs.* Edited and translated by Jeffrey Henderson. Newburyport, MA: Focus Classical Library, 2008.

Aristotle. *Politics and Poetics.* Translated by Jowett and Butcher. Norwalk, CN: Easton Press, 1979.

Arrow, Kenneth J. (1951) 1963. *Social Choice and Individual Values.* New Haven, CT: Yale University Press; 1st edition published by Wiley.

Arthur, W. Brian. "Competing Technologies, Increasing Returns, and Lock-in by Historical Events: *Economic Journal* 99 (1989): 116–31.

Asay, Garrett R. Beeler. "How does ideology matter in the spatial model of voting?" *Public Choice* 135 (2008): 109–123.

Austen-Smith, David. "Information Transmission in Debate." *American Journal of Political Science* 34 (1990): 124–52.

Austen-Smith, David, and Jeffrey Banks. "Information Aggregation, Rationality, and the Condorcet Jury Theorem." *American Political Science Review*, 90 (1996): 34–45.

Austen-Smith, David, and Jeffrey Banks. *Positive Political Theory* I. Ann Arbor: University of Michigan Press, 1999.

Austen-Smith, David, and Jeffrey Banks. *Positive Political Theory* II. Ann Arbor: University of Michigan Press, 2005.

Bach, Stanley. "Germaneness Rules and Bicameral Relations in the U.S. Congress." *Legislative Studies Quarterly* 7, no. 3 (1982): 341–357

Balasko, Yves, and Herve Cres. "The Probability of Condorcet Cycles and Super Majority Rules." *Journal of Economic Theory* 75 (1997): 237–270.

Banks, Jeffrey, and Joel Sobel. "Equilibrium Selection in Signaling Games." *Econometrica* 55 (1987): 647–61.

Banks, Jeffrey. "A Model of Electoral Competition with Incomplete Information." *Journal of Economic Theory* 50 (1990): 309–25.

Banks, Jeffrey. *Signaling Games in Political Science.* Chur, Switzerland; Harwood Academic, 1991.

Banks, Jeffrey. "Singularity Theory and Core Existence in the Spatial Model." *Journal of Mathematic Economics* 24 (1995): 523–536.

Banks, Jeffrey. "Review: Analytical Politics." *Journal of Economic Literature* 36, no. 3 (1998): 1506–1507.

Barker, Graeme. *The Agricultural Revolution in Prehistory: Why did Foragers become Farmers?* Oxford University Press, 2009.

Baron, D., and J. Ferejohn. "Bargaining in legislatures." *American Political Science Review* 83, no. 4 (1989): 1182–1202.

Barr, James L., and Otto A. Davis. "An Elementary Political and Economic Theory of the Expenditures of Local Governments." *Southern Economic Journal* 33 (1966): 149–165.

Barro, Robert. "The Control of Politicians: An Economic Model." *Public Choice* 14 (1973): 19–42.

Barry, Brian. *Sociologists, Economists, and Democracy.* London: Collier-Macmillan, 1970.

Barzel, Yoram, and Eugene Silberberg. "Is the Act of Voting Rational?" *Public Choice* 16 (1973): 61–8.

Bassi, A. *"A Model of Endogenous Government Formation".* Department of Politics, New York University, (2008).

Beardon, Alan F., Juan Candeal, Gerhard Herden, Esteban Indurain, and Ghanshyam Mehta. "The Non-Existence of a Utility Function and the Structure of Non-Representable Preference Relations." *Journal of Mathematical Economics* 37, no. 1 (2002): 17–38.

Becker, Gary. *Accounting for Tastes.* Cambridge, MA: Harvard University Press, 1998.

Beik, William. *Absolutism and Society in Seventeenth-Century France.* Cambridge: Cambridge University Press, 1985.

Bender, Bruce, and John Lott. "Legislator Voting and Shirking: A Critical Review of the Literature." *Public Choice* 87 (1996): 67–100.

Bendor, J. D. Diermeier, D. Siegel, and M. Ting. *A Behavioral Theory of Elections.* Princeton University Press, 2011.

Bental, Benjamin, and Uri Ben-Zion. "Political Contribution and Policy: Some Extensions." *Public Choice* 24 (1975): 1–12.

Berger, Mark M. and Michael C. Munger, and Richard F. Potthoff. "The Downsian Model Predicts Divergence." *Journal of Theoretical Politics* 12 (2000): 228–240.

Bergson, Abram. "A Reformulation of Certain Aspects of Welfare Economics." *The Quarterly Journal of Economics* 52, 2 (1938): 310–334.

Bergstrom, Theodore. "Collective Choice and the Lindahl Allocation Method," in *Economics of Externalities*, S.Y. Lin, Editor. New York: Academic Press, (1973): 111–131.

Bergstrom, Theodore. "Evolution of Social Behavior: Individual and Group Selection." *Journal of Economic Perspectives* 16, 2 (2002): 67–88.

Bergstrom, Theodore, and Robert Goodman. "Private Demands for Public Goods." *The American Economic Review* 63 (1973): 280–296.

Bergstrom, Theodore, and Trout Rader. "An Economic Approach to Social Choice II," *Public Choice*, 33(1978): 17–32.

Bernhardt, M. Daniel, and Daniel E. Ingberman. 1985. "Candidate Reputations and the Incumbency Effect." *Journal of Public Economics* 27 (1985): 47–67.

Bessette, Joseph. *The Mild Voice of Reason: Deliberative Democracy & American National Government.* Chicago: University of Chicago Press, 1994.

Bianco, William. *Trust: Representatives and Constituents.* Ann Arbor: University of Michigan Press, 1994.

Bible: *The New Oxford Annotated Bible: With the Apocryphal/Deuterocanonical Books,* New Revised Standard Version. Edited by Michael D. Coogan. New York: Oxford UP, 2001. Print.

Bierce, Ambrose. (1906) 2011. *The Devil's Dictionary, Tales, and Memoirs.* New York: Library of America, Inc.

Birch, S. *Full Participation: A Comparative Study of Compulsory Voting.* Manchester University Press, 2009.

Black, Duncan. "On the Rationale of Group Decision-making." *Journal of Political Economy* 56 (1948): 23–34

Black, Duncan. (1958) 1987. *The Theory of Committees and Elections.* New York: Cambridge University Press. Reprinted Netherlands: Kluwer Academic.

Black, Duncan, and R. A. Newing. *Committee Decisions with Complementary Valuation.* London: Lowe and Brydon, 1951.

Blais, Andre. *To Vote or Not to Vote? The Merits and Limits of Rational Choice Theory.* University of Pittsburg Press, 2000.

Blin, J.M., and Mark Satterthwaite. "Individual Decisions and Group Decisions." *Journal of Public Economics* 10 (1978): 247–67.

Bogomolnaia, Anna, and Jean-François Laslier. 2007. "Euclidean Preferences." *Journal of Mathematical Economics* 43 (2007): 87–98.

Bonilla, Claudio A. 2004. "A model of political competition in the underlying space of ideology." *Public Choice* 121 (2004): 51–67.

Bonilla, Claudio A., R. Carlyn, G. Love, and E. Silva. "Social or Political Cleavages? A Spatial Analysis of the Party System in Post-Authoritarian Chile." *Public Choice* 146 (2011): 9–21.

Borcherding, Thomas, and Robert Deacon. "The Demand for the Services of Non-Federal Governments." *The American Economic Review* 62 (1972): 891–901.

Brady, Henry. "The Art of Political Science: Spatial Diagrams as Iconic and Revelatory." (APSA Presidential Address). *Perspectives on Politics* 9 (2011): 311–330.

Braidwood, Robert J. "The Agricultural Revolution." *Scientific American* 203 (1960): 130–148.

Braman, Eileen. "Reasoning on the Threshold: Testing the Separability of Preferences in Legal Decision Making." *Journal of Politics* 68 (2006): 308–321.

Brams, Steven. *Mathematics and Democracy: Designing Better Voting and Fair-Division Procedures.* Princeton, NJ: Princeton University Press, 2007.

Brams, Steven, and Peter Fishburn. *Approval Voting.* Boston: Birkhauser, 1984.

Brams, Steven, and J. H. Nagel. "Approval Voting in Practice." *Public Choice* 71 (1991): 1–18.

Brams, Steven, and Alan Taylor. *Fair Division: From Cake-Cutting to Dispute Resolution.* New York: Cambridge University Press, 1996.

Braude, Stanton. "The Predictive Power of Evolutionary Biology and the Discovery of Eusociality in the Naked Mole Rat". *Reports of the NCSE* (National Center for Science Education) 17, no. 4 (1997): 12–15.

Brehm, John. *The Phantom Respondents: Opinion Surveys and Political Representation.* Ann Arbor: University of Michigan Press, 1993.

Brennan, Geoffrey. "The Distributional Implications of Public Goods." *Econometrica* (March 1976): 391–400.

Brennan, Geoffrey. "Collective Coherence?" *International Review of Law and Economics* 21 (2001): 197–211.

Brennan, Geoffrey. "Hobbes's Samuel." *Public Choice* 141, no. 1 (2009): 5–12.
Brennan, Geoffrey, and James Buchanan. *The Reason of Rules: Constitutional Political Economy.* New York: Cambridge University Press, 1985.
Brennan, Geoffrey, and Loren Lomasky. *Democracy and Decision: The Pure Theory of Electoral Politics.* New York: Cambridge University Press, 1993.
Brennan, Geoffrey, and Nicole Mitchell. "The Logic of Spatial Politics: The 1998 Queensland Election." *Australian Journal of Political Science* 34, no. 3 (1999): 379–390.
Brennan, Geoffrey, and Philip Pettit. *The Economy of Esteem: An Essay on Civil and Political Society.* Oxford University Press, 2006.
Brennan, Geoffrey, and Cliff Walsh. "A Monopoly Model of Public Goods Provision: The Uniform Pricing Case." *American Economic Review* 71 (1981): 196–206.
Brennan, Jason. *The Ethics of Voting.* Princeton University Press, 2011.
Brians, Craig Leonard, and Bernard Grofman. "When registration barriers fall, who votes?: An empirical test of a rational choice model." *Public Choice* 99 (1999): 161–176.
Brians, Craig Leonard and Grofman, B. "Election day registration's effect on US voter turnout." *Social Science Quarterly* 82, no. 1 (2001): 170–183.
Brody, Richard A., and Benjamin I. Page. "Indifference, Alienation and Rational Decisions: The Effects of Candidate Evaluation on Turnout and the Vote." *Public Choice* 15 (1973): 1–18.
Buchanan, James. "Social Choice, Democracy, and Free Markets." *Journal of Political Economy* 62 (1954): 114–23.
Buchanan, James. "An Economic Theory of Clubs." *Economica* 32, no. 125 (1965): 1–14.
Buchanan, James. *The Limits of Liberty: Between Anarchy and Leviathan.* Chicago: University of Chicago Press, 1975.
Buchanan, James. "Politics Without Romance: A Sketch of the Positive Public Choice Theory and Its Implications." Inaugural Lecture, Institute for Advanced Studies. Vienna, 1979. In *The Logical Foundations of Constitutional Liberty*, 1999. vol. 1 of *The Collected Works of James Buchanan*, 45–59. Indianapolis, Indiana: Liberty Fund.
Buchanan, James. "Federalism as an Ideal Political Order and an Objective for Constitutional Reform." *Publius* 25, no. 2 (1995): 19–27.
Buchanan, James. *Economics from the Outside In.* College Station, Tex: Texas A&M University Press, 2007
Buchanan, James, and Robert Tollison. *Theory of Public Choice II.* Ann Arbor: University of Michigan Press, 1984.
Buchanan, James, and Gordon Tullock. *The Calculus of Consent.* Ann Arbor: University of Michigan Press, 1962.
Buckley, William F. "Our Mission Statement." *National Review* (19 November 1955).
Burden, Barry. ed. *Uncertainty in American Politics.* New York: Cambridge University Press, 2003.
Burke, Edmund. (1970) 1999. "Reflections on the Revolution in France." In *Select Works of Edmund Burke.* A New Imprint of the Payne Edition. Foreword and Biographical Note by Francis Canavan. Indianapolis: Liberty Fund.
Burnham, Walter D. "The Changing Shape of the American Political University." *American Political Science Review* 59 (1965): 7–28.
Burnham, Walter D. *Critical Elections and the Mainsprings of American Politics.* New York: Norton, 1970.

Calvert, Randall. "Robustness of the Multidimensional Voting Model: Candidate Motivations, Uncertainty, and Convergence." *American Journal of Political Science* 29 (1985): 69–95.

Caplan, Bryan. *The Myth of the Rational Voter: Why Democracies Choose Bad Policies.* New York: Princeton University Press, 2007.

Caro, Robert. *The Years of Lyndon Johnson:* Volumes I–III. Vintage Books, 2003.

Chamberlain, Gary, and Michael Rothschild. "A Note on the Probability of Casting a Decisive Vote." *Journal of Economic Theory* 25 (1981): 152–62.

Charney, Evan, and William English. "Candidate Genes and Political Behavior." *American Political Science Review* 106, no. 1 (2012): 1–34.

Cho, W. K. T., J. G. Gimpel, and T. Wu. "Clarifying the Role of SES in Political Participation: Policy Threat and Arab American Mobilization." *The Journal of Politics* 68 (2006): 977–991.

Clark, William. *Dear Brother: letters of William Clark to Jonathan Clark.* Edited by James J. Holmberg. Yale University Press, 2003.

Clarke, Charles. *Men of the Lewis and Clark Expedition.* Lincoln: University of Nebraska Press, 1973.

Coase, Ronald H. "The Problem of Social Cost." *Journal of Law and Economics* 3 (1960): 1–44.

Coate, Stephen, and Michael Conlin. "A Group Rule: Utilitarian Approach to Voter Turnout Theory and Evidence." *American Economic Review* 94, no. 5 (2004): 1476–1504.

Coates, Dennis, and Michael Munger. "Legislative Voting and the Economic Theory of Politics." *Southern Economic Journal* 61 (1995): 861–73.

Cohen, Gerald. "Facts and Principles." *Philosophy & Public Affairs* 31, no. 3 (2005): 211–245.

Cohen, Linda, and Steven Matthews. "Constrained Plott Equilibria, Directional Equilibria, and Global Cycling Sets." *Review of Economic Studies* 47 (1980): 975–86.

Coleman, James, and John Ferejohn. "Democracy and Social Choice." *Ethics* 97 (1986): 26–38.

Collier, Kenneth, Richard McKelvey, Peter Ordeshook, and Kenneth Williams. "Retrospective Voting: An Experimental Study." *Public Choice* 53 (1987): 101–30.

Colomer, Josep M. *Political Institutions.* Oxford University Press, 2003.

Conaway, Horace Mann. *The First French Republic, a Study of the Origin and the Contents of the Declaration of the Rights of Man, of the Constitution, and of the Adoption of the Republican Form of Government in 1792.* New York: Columbia University, 1902.

Condorcet (M.J.A.N. de Caritat, Marquis de). 1785. "An Essay on the Applications of Analysis to the Probability of Decisions Rendered by a Plurality of Votes." Reprinted in Iain McLean and Arnold Urken (1995; editors and translators), *Classics of Social Choice,* Ann Arbor: University of Michigan Press, pp. 81–90.

Condorcet (M.J.A.N. de Caritat, Marquis de). 1788. "On the Constitution and Functions of Provincial Assemblies." Reprinted in Iain McLean and Arnold Urken (1995; eds and translators), *Classics of Social Choice,* Ann Arbor: University of Michigan Press, pp. 113–143.

Conover, Pamela Johnston, and Stanley Feldman. "Projection and the Perception of Candidates." *Western Political Quarterly* 35 (1982): 228–44.

Conover, Pamela Johnston, and Stanley Feldman. "How People Organize the Political World: A Schematic Model." *American Journal of Political Science* 28 (1984): 95–126.

Conover, Pamela Johnston, and Stanley Feldman. "Emotional Reactions to the Economy: I'm Mad as Hell and I'm not Going to Take It Anymore." *American Journal of Political Science* 30 (1986): 50–78.

Converse, Phillip. "The Nature of Belief Systems in Mass Publics." In *Ideology and Discontent*, edited by David Apter, 219–41. New York: Free Press, 1964.

Cooter, Robert, and Neil Siegel. "Collective Action Federalism: A General Theory of Article I, Section 8." *Stanford Law Review* 63 (2010): 115.

Coughlin, Peter. *Probabilistic Voting Theory*. New York: Cambridge University Press, 1992.

Coughlin, Peter, and Melvin Hinich. "Necessary and Sufficient Conditions for Single Peakedness in Public Economic Models." *Journal of Public Economics* 25 (1984): 323–41.

Coughlin, Peter, and Thomas Palfrey. "Pareto Optimality in Spatial Voting Models." *Public Choice* 1, no. 4: 307–319.

Cox, Gary. "An Expected Utility Model of Electoral Competition." *Quality and Quantity* 18 (1984a): 337–49.

Cox, Gary. "Strategic Electoral Choice in Multi-Member Districts: Approval Voting in Practice?" *American Journal of Political Science* 28 (1984b): 722–38.

Cox, Gary. "Electoral Equilibrium under Alternative Voting Institutions." *American Journal of Political Science* 34 (1987): 903–35.

Cox, Gary. "Centripetal and Centrifugal Incentives in Electoral Systems." *American Journal of Political Science* 34 (1990): 903–35.

Cox, Gary. *Making Votes count: Strategic Coordination in the World's Electoral Systems*. New York: Cambridge University Press, 1997.

Cox, Gary, and Michael Munger. "Contributions, Expenditure, Turnout: The 1982 U.S. House Elections." *American Political Science Review* 83 (1989): 217–31.

Cox, Gary, and Michael Munger. *"Putting Last Things Last: A Sequential Barriers Model of Turnout and Voter Roll-off."* Typescript, University of North Carolina-Chapel Hill, Department of Political Science, 1991.

Dahl, Robert. *A Preface to Democratic Theory*. Chicago: University of Chicago Press, 1963.

Darwin, Charles. (1972) 2007. *The expression of the emotions in man and animals*. New York: Filiquarian.

Davidson, Donald, McKinsey, J. and Patrick Suppes. "Outlines of a Formal Theory of Value," *Philosophy of Science* 22 (1955): 140–60.

Davis, Darren W., and Brian D. Silver. "Stereotype Threat and Race of Interviewer Effects in a Survey on Political Knowledge." *American Journal of Political Science* 47, no. 1 (2003): 33–45.

Davis, Otto, Morris DeGroot, and Melvin Hinich. "Social Preference Orderings and Majority Rule." *Econometrica* 40 (1972): 147–57.

Davis, Otto, and Melvin Hinich. "A Mathematical Model of Policy Formation in a Democratic Society." In *Mathematical Applications in Political Science*, edited by Joseph Bernd, vol. 2, 175–208. Dallas: Southern Methodist University Press, 1966.

Davis, Otto, and Melvin Hinich. "On the Power and Importance of the Mean Preference in a Mathematical Model of Democratic Choice." *Public Choice* 5 (1968): 59–72.

Davis, Otto, Melvin Hinich, and Peter Ordeshook. "An Expository Development of a Mathematical Model of the Electoral Process." *American Political Science Review* 64 (1970): 426–48.

Deemen, Adrian Van. "The Probability of the paradox of voting for weak preference orderings." *Social Choice and Welfare* 16, no. 2 (1999): 171–182.

De Marchi, Scott. *Computational and Mathematical Modeling in the Social Sciences.* New York: Cambridge University Press, 2005.

Denzau, Arthur, and Douglass North. "Shared Mental Models: Ideologies and Institutions." *Kyklos* 47 (1994): 3–32.

Denzau, Arthur, and Robert Parks. "The Continuity of Majority Rule Equilibrium." *Econometrica* 43 (1975): 853–866.

Denzau, Arthur and Robert Parks. "A problem with public sector preferences." *Journal of Economic Theory* 14 (1977): 454–457.

Denzau, Arthur, and Robert Parks. "Deriving public sector preferences." *Journal of Public Economics* 11 (1979): 335–352.

Denzau, Arthur, and Robert Parks. "Existence of voting-market equilibria." *Journal of Economic Theory* 30 (1981): 243–265.

Descartes, Rene. *Discourse on Method.* Hackett Pub Co Inc., 1980.

Diamond, Jared. *The World Until Yesterday: What Can We Learn from Traditional Societies?* New York: Penguin, 2013.

Diba, Behzad and Allan Feldman. "Utility Functions for Public Outputs and Majority Voting." *Journal of Public Economics* 25 (1984): 235–243.

Diermeier, Daniel and Keith Krehbiel. "Institutionalism as a Methodology." *Journal of Theoretical Politics* 15, no. 2 (2003): 123–144.

Diermeier, Daniel, and Rebecca Morton. *Social Choice and Strategic Decisions.* Springer: Berlin, 2005.

Dietrich, Franz, and Christian List. "A Model of Non-informational Preference Change," *Journal of Theoretical Politics* 23 no. 2 (2011): 145–164.

Dietrich, Franz, and Christian List. "Where do preferences come from?" *International Journal of Game Theory* 4, no. 23 (2013): 613–637.

Dijkstra, Jacob and Michael A.L.M. Van Assen, and Frans N. Stokman. "Outcomes of Collective Decisions with Externalities Predicted." *Journal of Theoretical Politics* 20 (2008): 415–441.

Dougan, William and Michael Munger. "The Rationality of Ideology." *Journal of Law and Economics* 32 (1989): 119–42.

Dougherty, K.L. *Collective Action Under the Articles of Confederation.* New York: Cambridge University Press, 2001.

Dougherty, K.L., and J. Edward. "The Pareto efficiency and expected costs of k-majority rules." *Politics, Philosophy & Economics* (2004).

Dougherty, K.L., and J. Edward. "Voting For Pareto Optimality: A Multidimensional Analysis." *Public Choice* (2011).

Dougherty, K.L., and J. Edward. *The Calculus of Consent and Constitutional Design.* New York: Springer, 2011.

Dow, Jay K. "A Spatial Analysis of Candidate Competition in Dual Member Districts: The 1989 Chilean Senatorial Elections." *Public Choice* 97, no. 3 (1998): 451–474.

Downs, Anthony. *An Economic Theory of Democracy.* New York: Harper and Row, 1957.

Downs, Anthony. "The Origins of an Economic Theory of Democracy." In *Information, Participation, and Choice*, edited by B. Grofman, 198–201. Ann Arbor: University of Michigan Press, 1993.

Ducheneaut, Nicholas and Nicholas Yee. "Collective Solitude and Social Networks in World of Warcraft." In *Social Networking Communities and E-Dating Services: Concepts and Implications*, edited by C. Romm-Livermore and K. Setzekorn, 78–100. Hershey, PA: Information Science Reference/IGI Global, 2009.

Dummett, Michael. *Truth and Other Enigmas*, Cambridge, MA: Harvard University Press, 1978.

Dunbar, R.I.M. "Neocortex size as a constraint on group size in primates." *Journal of Human Evolution* 22, no. 6 (1992): 469–493.

Dunbar, R.I.M. "Coevolution of neocortical size, group size and language in humans." *Behavioral and Brain Sciences* 16, no. 4 (1993): 681–735.

Durant, T. Clark, and Michael Weintraub. "An institutional remedy for ethnic patronage politics." *Journal of Theoretical Politics*, 2013 (Forthcoming).

Duverger, Maurice. *Political Parties: Their Organization and Activity in the Modern Sate*. London: Methuen, 1951.

Eckel, C, and C. Holt. "Strategic Voting in Agenda-Controlled Committee Experiments." *American Economic Review* 79 (1989): 763–73.

Economist, 2012. "Russian politics–Not such a strongman: The hidden weaknesses of Putin's Russia." http://www.economist.com/node/21556543. (June 9, 2012) Accessed December 23, 2013.

Edlin, A., A. Gelman, and N. Kaplan. "Voting as a Rational Choice: Why and How People Vote to Improve the Well-Being of Others." *Rationality and Society* 19 (2007): 293–314.

Eguia, Jon. "On the spatial representation of preference profiles." *Economic Theory* 52, no. 1 (2013): 103–128.

Elster, Jon. "The Case for Methodological Individualism." *Theory and Society* 11 (1982): 453–482.

Endersby, James and Steven Galatas. "British parties and spatial competition: Dimensions of party evaluation in the 1992 election." *Public Choice* 97 (1998): 363–382.

Enelow, James. "Saving Amendments, Killer Amendments, and an Expected Utility Theory of Sophisticated Voting." *Journal of Politics* 43 (1981): 1062–89.

Enelow, James. "An Expanded Approach to Analyzing Policy-Minded Candidates." *Public Choice* 74 (1992): 425–45.

Enelow, James, and Melvin Hinich. "Nonspatial Candidate Characteristics and Electoral Competition." *Journal of Politics* 44 (1982a): 115–30.

Enelow, James, and Melvin Hinich. "Ideology, Issues, and the Spatial Theory of Elections." *American Political Science Review* 76 (1982b): 493–501.

Enelow, James, and Melvin Hinich. "On Plott's Pairwise Symmetry Condition for Majority Rule Equilibrium." *Public Choice* 40 (1983a): 317–21.

Enelow, James, and Melvin Hinich. "Voting One Issue at a Time: The Question of Voter Forecasts." *American Political Science Review* 77 (1983b): 435–45.

Enelow, James, and Melvin Hinich. "Voter Expectations in Multi-State Voting Systems: An Equilibrium Result." *American Journal of Political Science* 27 (1983c): 820–27.

Enelow, James, and Melvin Hinich. "Probabilistic Voting and the Importance of Centrist Ideologies in Democratic Elections." *Journal of Politics* 46 (1984a). 459–78.

Enelow, James, and Melvin Hinich. *The Spatial Theory of Voting: An—*, James, and Melvin Hinich—. "The Location of American Presidential Candidates: An Empirical Test of a New Spatial Model of Elections." *Mathematical and Computer Modeling* 12 (1989): 461–70.

Enelow, James, and Melvin Hinich. "A Test of the Predictive Dimensions Model in Spatial Voting Theory." *Public Choice* 78 (1994): 155–69.

Enelow, James, and Michael Munger. "The Elements of Candidate Reputation: The Effect of Record and Credibility on Optimal Spatial Location." *Public Choice* 77 (1993): 757–72.

Engelen, B. "Why Compulsory Voting Can Enhance Democracy." *Acta Politica* 42 (2007): 23–39.

Ensley, M.J., S. De Marchi, and M.C. Munger. "Candidate uncertainty, mental models, and complexity: Some experimental results." *Public Choice* 132 (2007): 231–246.

Epple, Dennis and Joseph Kadane. "Sequential Voting With Endogenous Voter Forecasts." *American Political Science Review* 84, no. 1 (1990): 165–175.

Epple, Dennis, and R. Romano. "Ends Against the Middle: Determining Public Provision when there are Private Alternatives." *Journal of Public Economics* (October 1996a).

Epple, Dennis, and R. Romano. "Public Provision of Private Goods" *Journal of Political Economy* (February 1996b).

Epple, Dennis, and R. Romano. "Collective and Voluntary Provision of Public Goods." *International Economic Review* (March 2003).

Epstein, Richard A. "Exit Rights Under Federalism." *Law and Contemporary Problems* 55 (1992): 147–165.

Erhart, Jacqueline, Stephan Sponar, Georg Sulyok, Gerald Badurek, Masanao Ozawa, and Yuji Hasegawa. "Experimental demonstration of a universally valid error–disturbance uncertainty relation in spin measurements." *Nature Physics* 8 (2012): 185–189.

Erikson, Robert. "Why Do People Vote? Because They are Registered." *American Politics Quarterly* 9 (1981): 259–76.

Eguia, Jon X. "Foundations of Spatial Preferences." *Journal of Mathematical Economics*, 47, 2(2011): 200–205

Eguia, Jon X. "On the spatial representation of preference profiles." *Economic Theory*. 52, 1(2013): 103–128.

Farquharson, Robin. *Theory of Voting*. New Haven, CT: Yale University Press, 1969.

Fearon, James. "Rationalist Explanations for War." *International Organization* 49 (1995): 379–414.

Fedderson, Tim. "Rational Choice Theory and the Paradox of Not Voting." *Journal of Economic Perspectives* 18, no. 1 (2004): 99–112.

Fedderson, Tim, and Wolfgang Pesendorfer. "The Swing Voter's Curse." *American Economic Review* 86 (1996): 408–24.

Fedderson, Tim, and Alvaro Sandroni. "A Theory of Participation in Elections." *American Economic Review* 96, no. 4 (2006): 1271–1282.

Fedderson, Tim, and Alvaro Sandroni. "The Calculus of Ethical Voting." *International Journal of Game Theory* 35, no. 1 (2006): 1–25.

Fedderson, Tim, and Alvaro Sandroni. "Ethical Voters and Costly Information Acquisition." *Quarterly Journal of Political Science* 1, no. 3 (2006): 287–311.

Feld, Scott and Bernard Grofman. "The half-win set and the geometry of spatial voting games." *Public Choice* 70, no. 2 (1991): 245–250.

Feld, Scott, Richard Hartly, Marc Kilgour, and Nicholas Miller. "The Uncovered Set in Spatial Voting Games." *Theory and Decision* 23, no. 2 (1987): 129–155.

Feldman, Allan M. and Robert Serrano. *Welfare Economics and Social Choice Theory*, (2005).

Feldman, Allan M., and Robert Serrano. *Welfare Economics and Social Choice Theory*. New York: Springer Science and Business Media, 2006.

Feldman, Stanley and Pamela Johnston Conover. "Candidates, Issues and Voters: The Role of Inference in Political Perception." *Journal of Politics* 45 (1983): 810–839.

Ferejohn, John. "Incumbent Performance and Electoral Control." *Public Choice* 50 (1986): 5–25.

Ferejohn, John. "The Spatial Model and Elections." In *Information, Participation, and Choice*, edited by B. Grofman, 107–24. Ann Arbor: University of Michigan Press, 1993.

Ferejohn, John, and Morris Fiorina. "The Paradox of Not Voting: A Decision Theoretic Analysis." *American Political Science Review* 68 (1974): 525–36.

Ferejohn, John, and Morris Fiorina. "Closeness Counts Only in Horseshoes and Dancing." *American Political Science Review* 69 (1975): 920–26.

Ferejohn, John, and David Grether. "Weak Path Independence." *Journal of Economic Theory* 14 (1977): 19–31.

Ferejohn, John, and Roger Noll. "Uncertainty and the Formal Theory of Campaigns." *American Political Science Review* 72 (1978): 492–505.

Fiedler, K. and C. Unkelbach. "Lottery attractiveness and presentation mode of probability and value information." *Journal of Behavioral Decision Making* 24 (2011): 99–115.

Finke, Daniel. "Estimating the effects of nonseperable preferences in EU treaty negotiations." *Journal of Theoretical Politics* 21 (2009): 543–569.

Finke, Daniel, and Andreas Fleig. "The Merits of Adding Complexity: Non-separable Preferences in Spatial Models of European Union Politics." *Journal of Theoretical Politics* (2013).

Fiorina, Morris P. "The Voting Decision: Instrumental and Expressive Aspects." *Journal of Politics* 38 (1976): 390–415.

Fiorina, Morris P., *Retrospective voting in American national elections* (3rd ed.) New Haven, CT: Yale University Press, 1989.

Fiorina, Morris P. "Divided Government in the American States: A Byproduct of Legislative Professionalism?" *American Political Science Review* 88 (1994): 304–17.

Fiorina, Morris P., and Charles R. Plott. "Committee Decisions under Majority Rule: An Experimental Study." *American Political Science Review* 72 (1978): 575–98.

Fishkin, James. *Democracy and Deliberation*. New Haven, CT: Yale University Press, 1991.

Fishkin, James. *When the People Speak*. New York: Oxford University Press, 2011.

Fishkin, James, and Peter Laslett, eds. *Debating Deliberative Democracy*. New York: Wiley-Blackwell, 2003.

Fort, Rodney. "A Recursive Treatment of the Hurdles to Voting." *Public Choice* 85 (1995): 45–69.

Foster, Carroll B. "The Performance of Rational Voter Models in Recent Presidential Elections." *American Political Science Review* 78 (1984): 678–90.

Fowler, James H. "Altruism and Turnout." *The Journal of Politics* 68 (2006): 674–683.

Fowler, James H., and Christopher T. Dawes. "Two Genes Predict Voter Turnout." *The Journal of Politics* 70 (2008): 579–594.

Fraga, Bernard and Eitan Hersh. "Voting Costs and Voter Turnout in Competitive Elections." *Quarterly Journal of Political Science* 5, no. 4 (2011): 339–356.

Franzen, A. and Pointner, S. "Calling social capital: An analysis of the determinants of success on the TV quiz show "Who Wants to Be a Millionaire?" *Social Networks* 33, no. 1 (2011): 79–87.

Friedman, David. *Law's Order*. Princeton, NJ: Princeton University Press, 2000.

Friedman, Milton. "*The Methodology of Positive Economics.*" *Essays in Positive Economics*. University of Chicago Press, 1953.

Frohlich, Norman and Joe Oppenheimer. *Political Leadership and Collective Goods*. Princeton, NJ: Princeton University Press, 1971.

Fry, Douglas P. and Patrik Söderberg. "Lethal Aggression in Mobile Forager Bands and Implications for the Origins of War." *Science* 341, no. 6143 (2013): 270–273.

Gaertner, Wulf. *Domain Conditions in Social Sciences*. New York: Cambridge University Press, 2001.

Galatas, S. "None of the Above? Casting Blank Ballots in Ontario Provincial Elections." *Politics & Policy* 36 (2008): 448–473.

Gallagher, Michael. "Comparing Proportional Representation Electoral Systems: Quotas, Thresholds, Paradoxes and Majorities." *British Journal of Political Science* 22, no 4 (1992): 469–496.

Galton, Francis. "Vox Populi." *Nature* 75 1949 (1907): 450–451.

Gauthier, David. *Morals by Agreement*. Oxford: Oxford University Press, 1986.

Gauthier, David. *Moral Dealing: Contract, Ethics, and Reason*. Ithaca: Cornell University Press, 1990.

Gelman, Andrew, Nate Silver, and Aaron Edlin. "What is the probability your vote will make a difference?" *Economic Inquiry* 1–6 (2010).

Gerber, Alan S., and Donald P. Green and Christopher W. Larimer. "Social Pressure and Voter Turnout: Evidence from a Large-Scale Field Experiment." *American Political Science Review* 102 (2008): 33–48.

Geys, Benny. "Rational' Theories of Voter Turnout: A Review." *Political Studies Review* 4 (2006): 16–3.

Gibbard, Allan. "Manipulation of Voting Schemes: A General Result." *Econometrica* 41 (1973): 587–602.

Gillespie, Richard. *Manufacturing Knowledge: A History of the Hawthorne Experiments*. Cambridge University Press, 1993.

Gladwell, Malcolm. *The Tipping Point: How Little Things Can Make a Big Difference*. Little, Brown, and Co, 2000.

Goff, Brian and Kevin Grier. "On the (mis) Measurement of Legislator Ideology and Shirking." *Public Choice* 76 (1993): 5–20.

Gomez, B. T., Hansford, T. G., and Krause, G. A. "The Republicans Should Pray for Rain: Weather, Turnout, and Voting in U.S. Presidential Elections." *The Journal of Politics* 69 (2007): 649–663.

Goncalves B, Perra N, Vespignani A. "Modeling Users' Activity on Twitter Networks: Validation of Dunbar's Number." *PLoS ONE* 6, no. 8 (2011): e22656.

Goodin, Robert E., and Christian List. "A Conditional Defense of Plurality Rule: generalizing May's Theorem in a restricted information environment." *American Journal of Political Science* 50 (2006): 940–949.

Granger, Clive William John. *Empirical Modeling in Economics: Specification and Evaluation.* New York: Cambridge University Press, 1999.

Green, Donald, and Ian Shapiro. *Pathologies of Rational Choice Theory: A Critique of Applications in Political Science.* New Haven, CT: Yale University Press, 1994.

Grofman, Bernard. "The Neglected Role of the Status Quo in Models of Issue Voting." *Journal of Politics* 47 (1985): 230–7.

Grofman, Bernard, and Scott Feld. "Rousseau's General Will: A Condorcetian Perspective." *American Political Science Review* 82 (1988): 567–76.

Grofman, Bernard, and Arend Lijphart, eds. *Electoral Laws and Their Political Consequences.* New York: Agathon, 1986.

Grofman, Bernard, and Arend Lijphart, eds. *Parliamentary versus Presidential Government.* Oxford University Press, 1992.

Groseclose, Tim. "A Model of Candidate Location When One Candidate has a Valence Advantage." *American Journal of Political Science* 45 (2001): 862–886.

Grynaviski, Jeffrey D. and Bryce E. Corrigan. "Specification Issues in Proximity Models of Candidate Evaluation (with Issue Importance)." *Political Analysis* 14 (2006): 393–420.

Guinier, Lani. *The Tyranny of the Majority: Fundamental Fairness in Representative Democracy.* The Free Press, 1994.

Guinier, Lani, and Gerald Torres. *The Miner's Canary: Enlisting Race, Resisting Power, Transforming Democracy.* Harvard University Press, 2002.

Guizot, Francois. *Democracy in France.* New York: Howard Fertig, 1974.

Guzman, Ricardo, and Michael Munger. "Freedom of Contract and the Morality of Exchange: Examples From Locke's Venditio." *Public Choice* (2013).

Habermas, Jürgen. *The Theory of Communicative Action, Volume 1: Reason and the Rationalization of Society,* translated by Thomas McCarthy. Boston, MA: Beacon Press, 1985.

Habermas, Jürgen. *The Theory of Communicative Action, Volume 2: Lifeworld and System: A Critique of Functionalist Reason,* translated by Thomas McCarthy. Boston, MA: Beacon Press, 1989.

Hafer, Catherine and Dimitri Landa. "Majoritarian Debate." *NYU Political Science Working Paper,* January 16, 2008.

Hamilton, James, and Helen Ladd. "Biased Ballots? The Impact of Ballot Structure on North Carolina Elections in 1992." *Public Choice* 87 (1996): 259–80.

Hardin, Garrett. "The Tragedy of the Commons." *Science* 162 (1968): 1243–1248.

Hardin, Russell. "Rationally Justifying Political Coercion," *Journal of Philosophical Research,* vol. 15 (1989–90), pp. 79–91, 1990.

Harsanyi, John. "Cardinal welfare, individualistic ethics, and interpersonal comparisons of utility." *Journal of Political Economy* 63 (1955): 309–321.

Harsanyi, John. *Rational Behavior and Bargaining Equilibrium in Games and Social Situations.* Cambridge University Press, 1977.

Harsanyi, John. "Rule Utilitarianism, Rights, Obligations, and the Theory of Rational Behavior." *Theory and Decision* 12, no. 2 (1980): 115–133.

Hayek, Friedrich A. *The Constitution of Liberty*. Chicago: University of Chicago Press, 1960.

Hayek, Friedrich A. *Law, Legislation and Liberty*. Three volumes. Chicago: University of Chicago Press, 1979.

Hayes, Beth. "Unions and Strikes with Asymmetric Information." *Journal of Labor Economics* 2 (January 1984): 57–83.

Heckelman, Jac and Nicholas Miller. *Handbook of Social Choice and Voting*. London: Edward Elgar Publishers, 2014.

Herden, Gerhard and Vladimir L. Levin. "Utility representation theorems for Debreu separable preorders." *Journal of Mathematical Economics* 48, no. 3 (2012): 148–154.

Hicks, John. "The Foundations of Welfare Economics." *Economic Journal* (1939).

Hicks, John. (1939) 1946. *Value and Capital*. Oxford: Clarendon.

Hicks, J.R. *The Theory of Wages*. New York, 1963.

Higgs, Robert. *Crisis and Leviathan: Critical Episodes in the Growth of American Government*. New York: Oxford University Press, 1987.

Hill, Lisa. "Low Voter Turnout in the United States." *Journal of Theoretical Politics* 18 (2006): 207–232.

Hillman, Arye. "Hobbes and the prophet Samuel on leviathan government." *Public Choice* 141, no. 1 (2009): 1–4.

Hillygus, D. Sunshine and Todd G. Shields. *The Persuadable Voter: Wedge Issues in Presidential Campaigns*. Princeton: Princeton University Press, 2009.

Hinich, Melvin. "The Median Voter Result Is an Artifact." *Journal of Economic Theory* 16 (1977): 208–19.

Hinich, Melvin. "Voting as an Act of Contribution." *Public Choice* 36 (1981): 135–40.

Hinich, Melvin. "Discussion of the 'Positive Theory of Legislative Institutions." *Public Choice* 50 (1986), 179–83.

Hinich, Melvin, John Ledyard, and Peter Ordeshook. "Nonvoting and Existence of Equilibrium under Majority Rule." *Journal of Economic Theory* 4 (1972): 144–53.

Hinich, Melvin, and Michael Munger. "A Spatial Theory of Ideology." *Journal of Theoretical Politics* 4 (1992): 5–30.

Hinich, Melvin, and Michael Munger. *Ideology and the Theory of Political Choice*. Ann Arbor: University of Michigan Press, 1994.

Hinich, Melvin, and Michael Munger. *Analytical Politics*. 1st Edition. New York: Cambridge University Press, 1997.

Hinich, Melvin, and Michael Munger. "The Dynamics of Issue Introduction: A Model Based on the Politics of Ideology." *Mathematical and Computer Modeling* 48, no. 9–10 (2008): 1510–1518.

Hinich, Melvin, and Peter Ordeshook. "Abstentions and Equilibrium in the Electoral Process." *Public Choice* 7 (1969): 81–106.

Hinich, Melvin and Peter Ordeshook. "Plurality Maximization vs. Vote Maximization: A Spatial Analysis with Variable Participation." *American Political Science Review* 64 (1970): 772–91.

Hinich, Melvin, and Walker Pollard. "A New Approach to the Spatial Theory of Electoral Competition." *American Journal of Political Science* 25 (1981): 323–41.

Hirschman, Albert O. *Exit, Voice, and Loyalty: Responses to Decline in Firms, Organizations, and States*. Cambridge, MA: Harvard University Press, 1970.

Hobbes, Thomas. (1651) 1990. *Leviathan*. Hackett Publishers.

Holcombe, Randall G. "The size and significance of the Pareto set in spatial voting models." *Public Choice* 116 (2003): 19–29.

Hotelling, Harold. "Stability in Competition." *Economic Journal* 39 (1929): 41–57.

Humes, Brian. "Majority Rule Outcomes and the Choice of Germaneness Rules." *Public Choice* 75, no. 4 (1993): 301–316

International Institute for Democracy and Electoral Assistance, www.idea.int.

Jakee, K. and G.Z. Sun. "Is compulsory voting more democratic?" *Public Choice* 129, no. 1–2 (2006): 61–75.

Janis, Irving. *Victims of groupthink: A psychological study of foreign-policy decisions and fiascoes*. Boston: Houghton, Mifflin, 1972.

Jankowski, Richard. "Altruism and the Decision to Vote: Explaining and Testing High Voter Turnout." *Rationality and Society* 19, no. 1 (2007): 5–34.

Jarvis, Jennifer. "Eusociality in a Mammal: Cooperative Breeding in Naked Mole-Rat Colonies." *Science* 212 (May 1981): 571–573.

Jones, Bryan. *Reconceiving Decision-Making in Democratic Politics*. Chicago: University of Chicago Press, 1994.

Jones, Bryan, Jeffrey Talbert, and Matthew Potosky. "Uncertainty and Political Debate." In *Uncertainty in American Politics*, edited by Burden, 118–136. New York: Cambridge University Press, 2003.

Kadane. J. B. "On Division of the Question." *Public Choice* 13 (1972): 47–54.

Kalt, Joseph and Mark Zupan. "Capture and Ideology in the Economic Theory of Politics." *American Economic Review* 74 (1984): 279–300.

Kalt, Joseph, and Mark Zupan. "The Apparent Ideological Behavior of Legislators: Testing for Principal-Agent Slack in Political Institutions." *Journal of Law and Economics* 33 (1990): 103–31.

Katzner, Donald. *Static Demand Theory*. New York: Macmillan, 1970.

Kau, James and Paul Rubin. *Congressman, Constituents, and Contributors*. Boston: Martinus Nijhoff, 1981.

Kau, James, and Paul Rubin. "Economic and Ideological Factors in Congressional Voting." *Public Choice* 44 (1984): 385–8.

Keeley, Lawrence. *War Before Civilization: The Myth of the Peaceful Savage*. London: Oxford University Press, 1996.

Kelly, Jerry S. *Social Choice Theory: An Introduction*. Berlin: Springer Verlag, 1988.

Kelley, S., R. Ayres, and W. Bowen. "Registration and Voting: Putting First Things First." *American Political Science Review* 61 (1967): 359–79.

Key, V. O. *The Responsible Electorate*. Cambridge: Harvard University Press, 1966.

Kliemt, H. "The Reason of Rules and the Rule of Reason." *Critica* XIX, no. 57 (1987): 43–86.

Kliemt, H. "Constitutional Commitments." In *Neue politische Ökonomie von Normen und Institutionen*, 145–173. Tübigen: Mohr, 1993.

Knack, Steve. "Does Rain Help the Republicans? Theory and Evidence on Turnout and the Vote." *Public Choice* 79 (1994): 187–209.

Knight, Frank. *Risk, Uncertainty, and Profit*. Houghton-Mifflin, 1921.

Kollman, Ken, John Miller, and Scott Page. "Adaptive Parties in Spatial Elections." *American Political Science Review* 86 (1992): 929–38.

Konrad, Kai. "Investing in regimes with stationary or roving bandits." In *Guns and Butter: The Economic Causes and Consequences of Conflict*, edited by D. Hess, 99–121. MIT Press, 2009. 99–121.

Kontorovich, Eugene. "The Median Voter Theorem in Ancient Athens." Unpublished Manuscript, Northwestern University Law School, 2003.

Kramer, Gerald. "Sophisticated Voting over Multidimensional Choice Spaces." *Journal of Mathematical Sociology* 2 (1972): 165–80.

Kramer, Gerald. "On a Class of Equilibrium Conditions for Majority Rule." *Econometrica* 41 (1973): 285–97.

Kramer, Gerald. "A Dynamical Model of Political Equilibrium." *Journal of Economic Theory* 16 (1977): 310–34.

Krehbiel, Keith. *Information and Legislative Organization.* Ann Arbor: University of Michigan Press, 1991.

Kreps, David. *Microeconomic Foundations I: Choice and Competitive Markets.* Princeton University Press, 2012.

Kuhn, Thomas (1962) 1970 *The Structure of Scientific Revolutions,* 2nd/ed. Chicago, IL: University of Chicago Press.

Kurrild-Klitgaard, Peter and Gert Tinggaard Svendsen. "Rational Bandits: Plunder, Public Goods and the Vikings." *Public Choice* 117 (2003): 255–272.

Lacy, Dean. "A theory of nonseperable preferences in survey responses." *American Journal of Political Science* 45 (2001a): 239–258.

Lacy, Dean. "Nonseparable Preferences, Measurement Error, and Unstable Survey Responses." *Political Analysis* 9, no. 2 (2001b): 1–21.

Lacy, Dean, and Emerson Niou. "Nonseparable Preferences and Issue Packaging in Elections." In *Advances in Political Economy: Institutions, Modeling, and Empirical Analysis,* edited by N. Schofield, G. Caballero, and D. Kselman, 203–215. New York: Springer Verlag, 2013.

Lacy, Dean, and Philip Paolino. "Testing Proximity Versus Directional Voting Using Experiments." *Electoral Studies* 29 (2010): 460–471.

Landau, L.D. and L.M. Lifshitz. *Quantum Mechanics Non-Relativistic Theory,* Third Edition: Volume 3. Burlington, MA: Elsevier Butterworth-Heinemann, 1981.

Ladha, Krishna. "The Condorcet Jury Theorem, Free Speech, and Correlated Votes." *American Journal of Political Science* 36 (1992): 61.7–34.

Ladha, Krishna. "Hypothesis Testing and the Jury Theorem." In *Collective Decision Making: Social Choice and Political Economy,* edited by N. Schofield, 385–92. Boston: Kluwer Academic, 1996.

Ladha, Krishna, and Gary Miller. "Political Discourse, Factions, and the General Will: Correlated Voting and Condorcet's Jury Theorem." In *Collective Decision Making: Social Choice and Political Economy,* edited by N. Schofield, 393–410. Boston: Kluwer Academic, 1996.

Lapp, Miriam. "Incorporating groups into rational choice explanations of turnout: An empirical test." *Public Choice* 98 (1999): 171–185.

Laver, Michael. *Private Desires, Political Action.* London: Sage Publications, 1997.

Laver, Michael, Scott de Marchi, and Hande Mutlu. "Negotiation in legislatures over government formation." *Public Choice* 147, no. 3–4 (2011): 285–304.

Laver, Michael, and Norman Schofield. *Multiparty Government: The Politics of Coalition in Europe.* New York: Oxford University Press, 1990.

Laver, Michael, and K.A. Shepsle. *Cabinet ministers and parliamentary government, Political economy of institutions and decisions.* Cambridge: Cambridge University Press, 1994.

Laver, Michael, and K.A. Shepsle. *Making and Breaking Governments: Government Formation in Parliamentary Democracies*. New York: Cambridge University Press, 1996.

Ledyard, John O. "The Paradox of Voting and Candidate Competition: A General Equilibrium Analysis." In *Essays in Contemporary Fields of Economics*, edited by G. Horwich and J. Quirk, 54–80. West Lafayette, IN: Purdue University Press, 1981.

Ledyard, John O. "The Pure Theory of Large Two Candidate Elections." *Public Choice* 44 (1984): 7–41.

Lerner, A.P. and H.W. Singer. "Some Notes on Duopoly and Spatial Competition." *Journal of Political Economy* 45, no. 2 (1937): 145–186.

Lewin, Leif. *Self-Interest and Public Interest in Western Politics*. New York: Oxford University Press, 1991.

Lewis, David. *Convention: A Philosophical Study*. Cambridge, MA: Harvard University Press, 1969.

Liebell, Susan. "Lockean Switching: Imagination and the Production of Principles of Toleration." *Perspectives on Politics* 7, no. 4 (2009): 823–836.

Lindahl, Erik. (1939) 1970. *Studies in the Theory of Money and Capital*. A. M. Kelley.

Lindahl, Erik. "Just Taxation – A Positive Solution." original in German, 1919. Translated by R. Musgrave and A. Peacock, editors, *Classics in the Theory of Public Finance*. London: Macmillan. 168–176, (1958).

List, Christian. "Multidimensional Welfare Aggregation *Public Choice*, 119: 2004: 119–142.

List, Christian. "The Discursive Dilemma and Public Reason." Ethics, 2006 116: 362–402.

List, Christian. "The Logical Space of Democracy." Philosophy and Public Affairs, 39 2011 262–297.

List, Christian, and R. E. Goodin, "Epistemic Democracy: Generalizing the Condorcet Jury Theorem." *Journal of Political Philosophy*, 9: 2001 277–306.

List, Christian and P. Pettit, "Aggregating Sets of Judgments: An Impossibility Result." Economics and Philosophy, 18(1): 2002 89–110.

List, Christian and P. Pettit, Group Agency: The Possibility, Design, and Status of Corporate Agents. Oxford University Press, 2011

Londregan, John. *Legislative Institutions and Ideology in Chile*. New York: Cambridge University Press, 2000.

Lott, John. "Political Cheating." *Public Choice* 52 (1987): 169–87.

Lott, John, and Michael Davis. "A Critical Review and Extension of the Political Shirking Literature." *Public Choice* 74 (1992): 461–84.

Lott, John, and Robert Reed. "Shirking and Sorting in a Model of Finite Lived Politicians." *Public Choice* 61 (1989): 75–96.

Lupia, Arthur. "Shortcuts versus Encyclopedias: Information and Voting Behavior in California' Insurance Reform Elections." *American Political Science Review* 88 (1994): 63–76.

Lupia, Arthur, and Mathew D. McCubbins. *The Democratic Dilemma: Can Citizens Learn What They Need to Know?* New York: Cambridge University Press, 1998.

Lynch, G. Patrick. "Protecting Individual Rights through a Federal System: James Buchanan's View of Federalism." *Publius* 34, no. 4 (2004): 153–167.

Macartan, Humphreys and Michael Laver. Spatial Models, Cognitive Metrics, and Majority Rule Equilibria. *British Journal of Political Science* 40 (2010): 11–30

Machiavelli, Nicolo. *The Prince.* Translated by Luigi Ricci. New York: Oxford University Press, 1952.

Mackie, Gerald. *Democracy Defended.* New York: Cambridge University Press, 2004.

Maestripieri, Dario. *Machiavellian Intelligence: How Rhesus Macaques and Humans Have Conquered the World.* Chicago: University of Chicago Press, 2007.

Marcus, George E. "The Structure of Emotional Response: 1984 Presidential Candidates." *American Political Science Review* 82 (1988): 737–762.

Martin, Lanny and Georg Vanberg. *Parliaments and Coalitions: The Role of Legislatures in Multiparty Governance.* Oxford: Oxford University Press, 2011.

Mascart, Jean, *La vie et les travaux du chevalier Jean-Charles de Borda (1733–1799): Épisodes de la vie scientifique au XVIIIe siècle, Bibliothèque de la revue d'histoire maritime* (in French) (2nd ed.), Presses de l'Université de Paris-Sorbonne, 2000.

Mas-Collel, Andreu, Michael Dennis Whinston, and Jerry R. Green. *Microeconomic Theory* Oxford University Press, 1995.

Matsusaka, John and Filip Palda. "The Downsian Voter Meets the Ecological Fallacy." *Public Choice* 77 (1993): 855–78.

Matsusaka, John, and Filip Palda. "Voter Turnout: How Much Can We Explain?" *Public Choice* 98, no. 3 (1999): 431–446.

Mauro, Martin J. "Strikes as a Result of Imperfect Information." *Industrial and Labor Relations Review* 35 (July 1982): 522–538.

May, K. O. "A Set of Independent, Necessary, and Sufficient Conditions for Simple Majority Decision." *Econometrica* 20 (1952): 680–4.

McCubbins, Mathew and Thomas Schwartz. "Police Patrols and Fire Alarms." *American Journal of Political Science* 28 (1984): 165–79.

McKelvey, Richard. "General Conditions for Global Intransitivities in Formal Voting Models." *Econometrica* 47 (1976a): 1085–111.

McKelvey, Richard. "Intransitivities in Multidimensional Voting Bodies and Some Implications for Agenda Control." *Journal of Economic Theory* 30 (1976b): 283–314.

McKelvey, Richard. "Covering, Dominance, and Institution-Free Properties of Social Choice." *American Political Science Review* 30 (1986): 283–414.

McKelvey, Richard, and Peter C. Ordshook. "Vote trading: An experimental study." *Public Choice* 35 (1980): 151–184.

McKelvey, Richard, and Peter C. Ordshook. "Sequential Elections with Limited Information." *American Journal of Political Science* 29 (1985): 480–512.

McKelvey, Richard, and Norman Schofield. "Structural Instability of the Core." *Journal of Mathematical Economics* 15 (1986): 179–98.

McKelvey, Richard, and Norman Schofield. "Generalized Symmetry Conditions at a Core Point" *Econometrica* 55 (July 1987): 923–933. Reprinted in *Positive Changes in Political Science: The Legacy of Richard D.McKelvey's Writings,* edited by J.Alt, J.Aldrich and A.Lupia, 281–293. University of Michigan Press, September, 2007.

McLean, Iain. "The first golden age of social choice 1784 – 1803." In *Social choice, welfare, and ethics: proceedings of the 8th International Symposium in Economic Theory and Econometrics,* edited by W. Barnett, H. Moulin, M. Salles, and N. Schofield, 13–33. Cambridge: Cambridge University Press, 1995.

McLean, Iain. "The Reasonableness of Independence." Oxford: Nuffeld College Politics Working Paper, # 2003 W6 (2003).

McLean, Iain, and F. Hewitt. *Condorcet: foundations of social choice and political theory*, edited, translated, and intro by Edward Elgar, 1994.

McLean, Iain, and J. London. "The Borda and Condorcet Principles: Three Medieval Applications." *Social Choice and Welfare* 7 (1990): 99–108.

McLean, Iain, and J. London. "Ramon Lull and the theory of voting." *Studia Lulliana* 32, no. 1 (1992): 21–37.

McLean, Iain, and Arnold Urken. "Did Jefferson or Madison understand Condorcet's theory of social choice?" *Public Choice* 73 (1992): 445–57.

McLean, Iain, and Arnold Urken, eds and translators. *Classics of Social Choice*. Ann Arbor: University of Michigan Press, 1995. 113–143.

Meirowitz, Adam. "Informational Party Primaries and Strategic Ambiguity." *Journal of Theoretical Politics* 17 (2005): 107–136.

Melton, James. *Do Parties' Ideological Positions Matter? The Effects of Alienation and Indifference on Individuals' Turnout Decisions*. PhD Thesis, Department of Political Science, University of Illinois, 2009.

Mencken, Henry Louis. *A Little Book in C Major*. New York: John Lane Company, 1916.

Mencken, Henry Louis. *Notes on Democracy*. New York: Alfred Knopf, 1926.

Merolla, Jennifer, Michael Munger, and Michael Tofias. "In Play: A Commentary on the Strategies in the 2004 U.S. Presidential Election." *Public Choice* 123 (2005): 19–37.

Merrifield, J. "The Institutional and Political Factors that Influence Voter Turnout." *Public Choice* 77, no. 3 (1993): 657–667.

Merrill, Samuel III and Bernard Grofman. *A Unified Theory of Voting: Directional and Proximity Spatial Models*. New York: Cambridge University Press, 1999.

Miller, Nicholas. "A New Solution Set for Tournaments and Majority Voting: Further Graph Theoretical Approaches to the Theory of Voting." *American Journal of Political Science* 24 (1980): 68–96.

Miller, Nicholas. *Committees, Agendas, and Voting*. Chur, Switzerland, 1980.

Miller, Warren E. and Donald F. Stokes. "Constituency Influence in Congress." *American Political Science Review* 57 (1963): 45–56.

Mises, Ludwig (von). *Human Action: A Treatise on Economics*. New Haven: Yale University Press, 1949.

Monroe, Burt L. "Fully Proportional Representation." *American Political Science Review* 89 (1995): 925–40.

Montesquieu, Charles de Secondat Baron de. *The Spirit of the Laws*. Translated by Anne M. Cohler, Basia Carolyn Miller, and Harold Samuel Stone. Cambridge University Press, 1989.

Moore, G.E. *Principia Ethica*. Cambridge University Press, 1903

Morton, Rebecca. "Groups in Rational Turnout Models." *American Journal of Political Science* 35 (1991): 758–76.

Morton, Rebecca. *Methods and Models: A Guide to the Empirical Analysis of Formal Models in Political Science*. New York: Cambridge University Press, 1999.

Moulton, Gary E. Editor. The Definitive Journals of Lewis and Clark. *Volume 8: Down the Columbia to Fort Clatsop. Volume 6.* Lincoln, NE: Bison Books, 1990

Mueller, Dennis. *Public Choice II*. New York: Cambridge University Press, 1989.

240 *References*

Mueller, Dennis. *Constitutional Democracy*. London: Oxford University Press, 2000.
Mueller, Dennis. *Public Choice III*. New York: Cambridge University Press, 2003.
Munger, K. and S.J. Harris. "Effects of an observer on handwashing in a public restroom." *Perceptual and Motor Skills* 69 (1989): 733–4.
Munger, K. and S.J. Harris. *The Effects of Compulsory Voting: A Natural Experiment in Chile*. Working Paper, New York University, Department of Political Science, 2013.
Munger, Michael. *Analyzing Policy: Choices, Conflict and Practice*. New York: W. W. Norton & Company, 2000.
Munger, Michael. "Euvoluntary or Not, Exchange is Just." *Social Philosophy and Policy* 28, no. 2 (2011): 192–211.
Munger, Michael. "Coercion, the State, and the Obligations of Citizenship." *Public Choice* 152 (2012): 415–421.
Munger, Michael. *Public Choice*. International Encyclopedia of the Social and Behavioral Sciences. Elsevier Publishing, 2014.
Muravyov, S.V., and I.A. Marinushkina. "Intransitivity in multiple solutions of Kemeny Ranking Problem." *Journal of Physics: Conference Series* 459 (2013), doi:10.1088/1742-6596/459/1/012006.
Myerson, Roger. *Game Theory: Analysis of Conflict*. Cambridge, MA: Harvard University Press, 1991.
Nagel, Thomas. *The Last Word*. Oxford: Oxford University Press, 1996.
Nagler, Jonathan. "The Effect of Registration Laws and Education on U.S. Voter Turnout." *American Political Science Review* 85 (1991): 1393–1406.
Nash, John. "Equilibrium Points in N-Person Games." *Proceedings of the National Academy of Sciences* 36 (1950): 48–9.
Nelson, Douglas and Eugene Silberberg. "Ideology and Legislator Shirking." *Economic Inquiry* 25 (1987): 15–25.
Nietzsche, Friedrich. *The Will to Power: An Attempt at the Revaluation of All Values*. Peter Gast, et al., eds. Berlin: C. G. Naumann, 1901.
Niou, Emerson. "Strategic Voting under Plurality and Runoff Rules," *Journal of Theoretical Politics* 13, no. 2 (2001): 209–227.
Niou, Emerson, and Dan Kselman. "Protest Voting: A Theory of Voter Signaling," *Public Choice* 148, no. 3–4 (June 2010): 395–418.
Niou, Emerson, and Peter Ordeshook. "Universalism in Congress." *American Journal of Political Science* 29 (1985): 246–58.
Nitzan, Shmuel. *Collective Preference and Choice*. New York: Cambridge University Press, 2010.
Nitzan, Shmuel, and Jacob Paroush. *Collective Decision Making: An Economic Outlook*. New York: Cambridge University Press, 1985.
North, Douglass. *Structure and Change in Economic History*. New York: Norton, 1981.
North, Douglass. *Institutions, Institutional Change, and Economic Performance*. New York: Cambridge University Press, 1990.
North, Douglass, John Joseph Wallis and Barry Weingast. *Violence and Social Orders: A Conceptual Framework for Interpreting Recorded Human History*. New York: Cambridge University Press, 2009.
Olson, Mancur. *The Logic of Collective Action*. Cambridge, MA: Harvard University Press, 1965.

Olson, Mancur. *The Rise and Decline of Nations: Economic Growth, Stagflation, and Social Rigidities.* Yale University Press, 1982.

Olson, Mancur. "Dictatorship, Democracy, and Development." *American Political Science Review* 87, no. 3 (1993): 567–576.

Olson, Mancur. *Power and Prosperity: Outgrowing Communist and Capitalist Dictatorships.* London: Oxford University Press, 2000.

Olson, Mancur, and Martin McGuire "The Economics of Autocracy and Majority Rule: The Invisible Hand and the Use of Force." *The Journal of Economic Literature* 34, no. 1 (1996): 72–96.

Ordeshook, Peter. *Theory of the Electoral Process.* Ph.D. dissertation, Department of Political Science, University of Rochester, Rochester, NY, 1969.

Ordeshook, Peter. *Game Theory and Political Theory.* New York: Cambridge University Press, 1989.

Ordeshook, Peter. "Engineering or Science: What Is the Study of Politics?" *Critical Review* 9, no. 1–2 (1995): 175–188.

Osborne, Martin J., and Ariel Rubinstein. *A Course in Game Theory.* Cambridge, MA: MIT Press, 1994.

Ostrom, E. *Understanding institutional diversity.* Princeton: Princeton University Press, 2005.

Ostrom, E. "Building trust to solve commons dilemmas: taking small steps to test an evolving theory." In *Games, groups, and the global good,* edited by S.A. Levi, 207–228. New York: Springer, 2009.

Padley, Steve. *Key Concepts in Contemporary Literature.* Palgrave MacMillan, 2001.

Palfrey, Thomas, and Howard Rosenthal. "A Strategic Calculus of Voting." *Public Choice* 41 (1983): 7–53.

Palfrey, Thomas, and Howard Rosenthal. "Voter Participation and Strategic Uncertainty." *American Political Science Review* 79 (1985): 62–78.

Parker, Glenn. *Institutional Change, Discretion, and the Making of Modern Congress.* Ann Arbor: University of Michigan Press, 1992.

Parker, Glenn. *Self-Policing in Politics: The Political Economy of Reputational Controls on Politicians.* Princeton University Press, 2004.

Parks, Robert. "Further Results on Path Independence: Quasi-Transitivity and Social Choice." *Public Choice* 26 (1976): 75–87.

Patty, John W. "Incommensurability and Issue Voting." *Journal of Theoretical Politics* 19 (2007): 115–131.

Patty, John W. "Arguments-Based Collective Choice." *Journal of Theoretical Politics* 20 (2008): 379–414.

Peltzman, Sam. "An Economic Interpretation of the History of Congressional Voting in the Twentieth Century." *American Economic Review* 75, no. 4 (1985): 656–675.

Pintor, Rafael Lopez, Maria Gratschew, and Kate Sullivan. "Voter Turnout Rates from a Comparative Perspective." In *Turnout Rates: A Global Perspective.* International Institute for Democracy and Electoral Assistance, 2002.

Plato. "The Republic." In *Great Dialogues of Plato,* translated by W H. D. Rouse edited by E, H. Warmington and P G. Rouse. New York: New English Library (Mentor), 1956.

Plott, Charles. "A Notion of Equilibrium and Its Possibility under Majority Rule." *American Economic Review* 57 (1967): 787–806.

Plott, Charles. "Ethics, Social Choice Theory, and the Theory of Economic Policy." *Journal of Mathematical Sociology* 2 (1972): 181–208.

Plott, Charles. "Path Independence, Rationality, and Social Choice." *Econometrica* 41 (1973): 1075–91.

Plott, Charles. "Axiomatic Social Choice Theory: An Overview and Interpretation." *American Journal of Political Science* 20 (1976): 511–96.

Plott, Charles. "Will Economics become an Experimental Science?" *Southern Economic Journal* 57 (1991): 901–20.

Plott, Charles, and M. Levine. "A Model of Agenda Influence on Committee Decisions." *American Economic Review* 68 (1978): 146–60.

Plutarch. *Parallel Lives of the Nobel Greeks and Romans*, edited or translated by AH Clough, J. Dryden, and James Atlas. Cambridge University Press, 2001.

Polanyi, Michael. *Personal Knowledge*. London: Routledge, 1958.

Poole, Keith, and Howard Rosenthal. "The Polarization of American Politics." *Journal of Politics* 46 (1984): 1061–79.

Poole, Keith, and Howard Rosenthal. "Patterns of Congressional Voting." *American Journal of Political Science* 35 (1991): 228–78.

Popkin, Samuel. *The Rational Peasant: The Political Economy of Rural Society in Vietnam*. Berkeley: University of California Press, 1979.

Popkin, Samuel. *The Reasoning Voter: Communication and Persuasion in Presidential Campaigns* (2nd ed.). Chicago: University of Chicago Press, 1994.

Pzeworksi, Adam. *States and Markets: A Primer in Political Economy*. London: Cambridge University Press, 2003.

Rabinowitz, George. "On the Nature of Political Issues: Insights from a Spatial Analysis." *American Journal of Political Science* 22 (1978): 793–817.

Rabinowitz, George, and Stuart Macdonald. "A Directional Theory of Issue Voting." *American Political Science Review* 83 (1989): 93–121.

Rader, Trout. "The Existence of a Utility Function to Represent Preferences." *Review of Economic Studies* (1963).

Rawls, John. *A Theory of Justice*. Cambridge, MA: Harvard University Press, 1971.

Riker, William. "Voting and the Summation of Preferences: An Interpretative Bibliographical Review of Selected Developments during the Last Decade." *American Political Science Review* 55 (1961): 900–911.

Riker, William . *The Theory of Political Coalitions*. New Haven, CT: Yale University, 1963.

Riker, William. "Implications from the Disequilibrium of Majority Rule for the Study of Institutions." *American Political Science Review* 74 (1980): 432–46.

Riker, William. *Liberalism Against Populism: A Confrontation Between the Theory of Democracy and the Theory of Social Choice*. San Francisco, CA: W.H. Freeman and Company, 1982.

Riker, William. *The Art of Political Manipulation*. New Haven, CT: Yale University Press, 1986.

Riker, William. "Heresthletic and Rhetoric in the Spatial Model." In *Advances in the Spatial Theory of Voting*, edited by James M. Enelow and Melvin Hinich, 46–65. New York: Cambridge University Press, 1990.

Riker, William, and Peter Ordeshook. "A Theory of the Calculus of Voting." *American Political Science Review* 62 (1968): 25–42.

Riker, William, and Peter Ordeshook. *Introduction to Positive Political Theory.* Englewood Cliffs, N.J.: Prentice-Hall, 1973.

Rosenstone, Steven, and Raymond Wolfinger. "The Effect of Registration Laws on Voter Turnout." *American Political Science Review* 72 (1978): 22–45.

Rotemberg, Julio J. "Attitude-dependent altruism, turnout and voting." *Public Choice* 140 (2009): 223–244.

Roth, M. Garrett. *Moving Against the Median Voter: The Effect of Representational Risk in a Two-Party Spatial Model.* Duke Political Science Working Paper, July 15 2013.

Rousseau, Jean Jacques. (1762) 1973. *The Social Contract,* translated by G. D. H. Cole. London: Dent.

Runciman, W. G., and Amartya K. Sen. "Games, justice and the general will." *Mind* 74, no. 296 (1965): 554–562.

Russett, Bruce, and Samuel Shye. "Aggressiveness, Involvement, and Commitment in Foreign Policy Attitudes." In *Diplomacy, Force, and Leadership,* edited by D. Caldwell and T. McKeown, 41–60. Boulder, CO: Westview, 1993.

Ryan, John. *The Agricultural Economy of Manitoba Hutterite Colonies.* Montreal: McGill-Queens University Press, 1977.

Saari, Donald. "Disposing dictators, demystifying voting paradoxes." *Mathematical and Computer Modeling* 48 (2008): 1671–1673.

Samuelson, Paul. (1954) 1977. "The Pure Theory of Public Expenditure." *Review of Economics and Statistics* 36, no. 4: 387–389.

Sartori, Giovanni. *Comparative Constitutional Engineering: An Inquiry into Structures, Incentives, and Outcomes.* New York: New York University Press, 1994.

Satterthwaite, Mark. "Strategy-Proofness and Arrow's Conditions: Existence and Correspondence Theorems for Voting Procedures and Social Welfare Functions." *Journal of Economic Theory* 10 (1975): 187–218.

Schama, Simon. *Citizens: A Chronicle of the French Revolution.* New York: Knopf, 1989.

Schofield, Norman. "Instability of Simple Dynamic Games." *Review of Economic Studies* 45 (1978a): 575–94.

Schofield, Norman. "The Theory of Dynamic Games." In *Game Theory and Political Science,* edited by P. Ordeshook, 119–64. New York: New York University Press, 1978b.

Schofield, Norman. "Social Equilibrium and Cycles on Compact Sets." *Journal of Economic Theory* 33 (1984): 59–71.

Schofield, Norman. *Social Choice and Democracy.* Heidelberg: Springer Verlag, 1985.

Schofield, Norman. "Party Competition in a Spatial Model of Coalition Formation." In *Political Economy: Institutions, Competition, and Representation,* edited by W. Barnett, M. Hinich, and N. Schofield, 135–74. New York: Cambridge University Press, 1993.

Schofield, Norman. "The Heart of a Polity." In *Collective Decision- Making: Social Choice and Political Economy,* Norman Schofield, ed. Kluwer Academic Publishers, 1996.

Schofield, Norman. *Architects of Political Change: Constitutional Quandaries and Social Choice Theory.* New York: Cambridge University Press, 2006.

Schofield, Norman. *The Spatial Model of Politics.* Routledge, 2008.

Schwartz, Thomas. "Collective Choice, Separation of Issues and Vote Trading." *American Political Science Review* 71 (1977): 999–1010.

244   *References*

Schwartz, Thomas. "No Minimally Reasonable Collective Choice Process Can Be Strategy-Proof." *Mathematical Social Sciences* 3 (1982): 57–72.

Schwartz, Thomas. *The Logic of Collective Choice.* New York: Columbia University Press, 1986.

Schwingenschlögl, Udo, and Friedrich Pukelsheim. "Seat Biases in Proportional Representation Systems with Thresholds." *Social Choice and Welfare* 27, no. 1 (2006): 189–193.

Sen, Amartya K. *Collective Choice and Social Welfare.* London: Holden-Day, 1970.

Serraa, Giles. "Polarization of What? A Model of Elections with Endogenous Valence." *Journal of Politics* 72, no. 2 (2010): 426–437.

Shachar, R., and B. Nalebuff. "Follow the Leader: Theory and Evidence on Political Participation." *American Economic Review* 89, no. 3 (1999): 525–547.

Shepsle, Kenneth. "Institutional Arrangements and Equilibrium in Multidimensional Voting Models." *American Journal of Political Science* 23 (1979): 27–60.

Shepsle, Kenneth. *Cabinet Ministers and Parliamentary Government.* New York: Cambridge University Press, 1994.

Shepsle, Kenneth, and Barry Weingast. "Structure Induced Equilibrium and Legislative Choice." *Public Choice* 37 (1981): 503–19.

Shepsle, Kenneth, and Barry Weingast. "Uncovered Sets and Sophisticated Voting Outcomes with Implications for Agenda Institutions." *American Journal of Political Science* 29 (1984): 49–74.

Shepsle, Kenneth, and Barry Weingast. "The Institutional Foundations of Committee Power." *American Political Science Review* 81 (1987): 85–104.

Shepsle, Kenneth, and Barry Weingast. "Why So Much Stability?: Majority Voting, Legislative Institutions, and Gordon Tullock." *Public Choice* (2012).

Sherman, Paul W., Jennifer Jarvis, and Richard Alexander. *The Biology of the naked mole-rat.* Princeton, N.J.: Princeton University Press, 1991.

Silberman, Jonathan, and Garey Durden. "The Rational Behavior Theory of Voter Participation: The Evidence from Congressional Elections." *Public Choice* 23 (1975): 101–8.

Simon, Julia. *Beyond contractual morality: ethics, law, and literature in eighteenth century France.* Rochester: University of Rochester Press, 2001.

Skaperdas, S. "Cooperation, conflict, and power in the absence of property rights." *American Economic Review* 82 (1992): 720–39.

Skaperdas, S. "The political economy of organized crime: providing protection when the state does not." *Economics of Governance* 2, no. 3 (2001): 173–202.

Slutsky, Steven. "A Characterization of Societies with Consistent Majority Decision." *Review of Economic Studies* 44, no. 2 (1977): 211–25.

Slutsky, Steven. "Equilibrium Under a-Majority Voting." *Econometrica* 47 (1979): 113–25.

Smithies, A. "Optimum Location in Spatial Competition." *Journal of Political Economy* 49 (1941): 423–39.

Somin, Ilya. *Democracy and Political Ignorance: Why Smaller Government is Smarter.* Palo Alto: Stanford University Press, 2013.

Stokes, Donald. "Spatial Models of Party Competition." *American Political Science Review* 57 (1963): 368–77.

Stokes, Donald, and Warren Miller. "Party Government and the Salience of Congress." *Public Opinion Quarterly* 26 (1962): 531–546.

Surowiecki, James. The Wisdom of Crowds, San Francisco: Anchor Publishing, 2004

Taagepera, Rein, and Matthew Shugart. *Seats and Votes: The Effects and Determinants of Electoral Systems.* New Haven, CT: Yale University Press, 1989.

Taylor, Alan. *Social Choice and the Mathematics of Manipulation.* New York: Cambridge University Press, 2005.

Thünen, Johann Heinrich von, Isolated state *The Isolated State;* an English edition of *Der isolierte Staat,* translated by Carla M. Wartenberg, edited by Peter Hall. New York, Pergamon Press, 1966.

Thurner, Paul W., and Angelika Eymann. "Policy-Specific Alienation and Indifference in the Calculus of Voting: A Simultaneous Model of Party Choice and Abstention." *Public Choice* 102 (2000): 49–75.

Tocqueville, Alexis de. *Democracy in America,* edited by J. P. Mayer, translated by G. Lawrence. Garden City, NY: Anchor, 1969.

Tollison, Robert, W. Mark Cain, and Paul Pauler. "Information and Voting: An Empirical Note." *Public Choice* 24 (1975): 39–43.

Tollison, Robert, and Thomas D. Willett. "Some Simple Economics of Voting and Not Voting." *Public Choice* 16 (1973): 59–71.

Tomasi, John. Free Market Fairness. Princeton, NJ: Princeton University Press, 2012

Tridimas, George. "The economics and politics of the structure of public expenditure." *Public Choice* 106 (2001): 299–316.

Tullock, Gordon. *Toward a Mathematics of Politics.* Ann Arbor: University of Michigan Press, 1967.

Tullock, Gordon. *Private Wants, Public Means: An Economic Analysis of the Desirable Scope of Government.* New York: Basic, 1970.

Tullock, Gordon. *The Vote Motive.* Institute of Economic Affairs, 1976.

Tullock, Gordon. "Why So Much Stability?" *Public Choice* 37 (1981): 189–202.

Tullock, Gordon. "A (partial) rehabilitation of the public interest theory." *Public Choice* 42 (1983): 89–99.

Uhlaner, Carole. "Rational Turnout: The Neglected Role of Groups." *American Journal of Political Science* 33 (1989a): 390–422.

Uhlaner, Carole. "Relational Goods and Participation: Incorporating Sociability into a Theory of Rational Action." *Public Choice* 62 (1989b): 253–85.

Uslaner, Eric. *The Movers and Shirkers: Representatives and Ideologues in the Senate,* University of Michigan Press, 1999.

Vickrey, W. "Utility, Strategy, and Social Decision Rules." *Quarterly Journal of Economics* 74 (1960): 507–35.

Waal, Franz de. *Chimpanzee Politics: Power and Sex Among Apes* (25th Anniversary ed.). Baltimore, MD: JHU Press, 2007.

Walzer, Michael. "Political Action: The Problem of Dirty Hands." *Philosophy & Public Affairs* 2 (1973): 160–80.

Weber, Max. "Politics as a Vocation." 'Politik als Beruf,' *Gesammelte Politische Schriften* (Muenchen) (1921): 396–450.

Weber, Max. (1922) 1968. *Economy and Society,* edited by Guenther Roth and Claus Wittich. Berkeley: University of California Press.

Weingast, Barry R. *Self-Enforcing Institutions.* Cambridge University Press, 2013.

Weingast, Barry R., and William Marshall. "The Industrial Organization of Congress; or why Legislatures, Like Firms, are not Organized as Markets." *Journal of Political Economy* 96 (1988): 132–63.

Whyte, William. *Is Anybody Listening?: How and why US Business Fumbles when it Talks with Human Beings.* New York: Simon and Schuster, 1952.

Wicksell, Knut. *Finanztheoretische Untersuchungen* (Jena: Gustav Fischer Verlag, 1896). Partially reprinted as Wicksell, Knut. 1958 "A New Principle of Just Taxation." In *Classics in the Theory of Public Finance*, edited by Richard A. Musgrave and Alan T. Peacock, London, 72–118. Macmillan.

Williams, Kenneth. "Spatial Elections with Endorsements and Uninformed Voters: Some Laboratory Experiments." *Public Choice* 80 (1994): 1–8.

Williamson, Oliver E. "Transaction-Cost Economics: The Governance of Contractual Relations." *Journal of Law and Economics* 22, no. 2 (1979): 233–61.

Wittman, Donald. "Why Democracies Produce Efficient Results." *Journal of Political Economy* (December 1989): 1395–1424.

Wittman, Donald. "Spatial Strategies when Candidates Have Policy Preferences." In *Advances in the Spatial Theory of Voting*, edited by James M. Enelow and Melvin Hinich, 66–98. New York: Cambridge University Press, 1990.

Wittman, Donald. *The Myth of Democratic Failure: Why Political Institutions are Efficient.* Chicago: University of Chicago Press, 1995.

Wolfinger, Raymond, and Steven Rosenstone. *Who Votes?* New Haven, CT: Yale University Press, 1980.

Zaller, John. *The Nature and Origins of Public Opinion.* New York: Cambridge University Press, 1992.

Zaller, John, and Stanley Feldman. "A Simple Theory of the Survey Response: Answering Questions versus Revealing Preferences." *American Journal of Political Science* 36, no. 3 (1992): 579–616.

Index